The English

It is rare for an historian to be ab.
century. In this provocative and care.
does just that, offering a complete rei.   ...n
from 400 to 500 AD when the Saxons ₊   .. events
and came to dominate both the langua₊   ...t of Britain,
lowland heartland.   ...ial culture of its

The writings of Gildas, who wrote the only near contemporary and
extended description of the 'English Settlement', are central to the story.
Higham offers fundamentally new insights into Gildas's purposes and the
social, political and chronological context in which he worked. He shows
how Gildas wrote around the years 479 to 485 in the context of Saxon
domination south of the Mersey, and how he wrote in order to find a way
to reverse the conquest, using metaphor and imagery as his literary
weapons.

The first volume of a major three-part analysis of the origins of England,
The English Conquest shows how history can still contribute to our
understanding of the 'Dark Ages', and challenges the interpretations now
being offered by many archaeologists researching pagan England.

To Naomi

The English conquest

Gildas and Britain in the fifth century

N. J. HIGHAM

Manchester University Press

Manchester and New York

Distributed exclusively in the USA and Canada by St. Martin's Press

Copyright © N. J. Higham 1994

Published by Manchester University Press
Oxford Road, Manchester M13 9NR, UK
and Room 400, 175 Fifth Avenue, New York, NY 10010, USA

Distributed exclusively in the USA and Canada
by St. Martin's Press, Inc., 175 Fifth Avenue, New York,
NY 10010, USA

British Library Cataloguing-in-Publication Data
A catalogue record for this book is available from the British Library

Library of Congress Cataloging-in-Publication Data
Higham, N. J.
    The English conquest: Gildas and Britain in the fifth century /
N. J. Higham.
        p.   cm.
    ISBN 0-7190-4079-5 (hardback). — ISBN 0-7190-4080-9 (paperback)
    1. Gildas, 516?–570? Liber querulus de excidio Britanniac.
2. Great Britain—History—Anglo-Saxon period, 449-1066—
Historiography. 3. Great Britain—History—Anglo-Saxon period.
449-1066. 4. Anglo-Saxons—Historiography. 5. Britons—
Historiography. I. Title.
DA150.G483H54   1994
942.01'4—dc20   93-45583

ISBN 0 7190 4079 5 *hardback*
      0 7190 4080 9 *paperback*

Typeset in Hong Kong by Best-set Typesetter Ltd.

Printed in Great Britain by Bell & Bain Ltd., Glasgow

Contents

Figures   vi

Abbreviations   vii

Acknowledgements   viii

Introduction   1

1   The rationale of Gildas's *De Excidio Britanniae*   7

2   Gildas and the Saxons   35

3   Gildas and Jeremiah   67

4   The locality of the *De Excidio Britanniae*   90

5   The chronology of the *De Excidio Britanniae*   118

6   Gildas and his contemporaries   146

7   Postscript: Gildas and the 'Age of Arthur'   203

Index   213

Figures

1 The geographical introduction of the *De Excidio Britanniae*   100
2 Central southern Britain   105
3 The British tyrants   109
4 Britannia Prima   112
5 Gildas's Britain   192

Abbreviations

AC: *Annales Cambriae* or 'The Welsh Annals', in *Nennius: British History and the Welsh Annals*, Chichester, 1980, ed. and trans. J. Morris, pp. 85–91.

DEB: *De Excidio Britanniae*, or 'The ruin of Britain', in *Gildas: the Ruin of Britain and Other Documents*, ed. and trans. M. Winterbottom, Chichester, 1978, pp. 87–142.

HB: *Historia Brittonum* or the 'British History', in *Nennius: British History and The Welsh Annals*, ed. J. Morris, Chichester, 1980, pp. 50–84.

HE: *Historia Ecclesiastica* or 'The ecclesiastical history of the English People', in *Bede: Ecclesiastical History of the English People*, ed. and trans. B. Colgrave and R. A. B. Mynors, Oxford, 1969.

Orosius, *Histories*: Paulus Orosius, *Seven Histories against the Pagans*, ed. and French trans. M.-P. Arnoud-Lindet, Paris, 1991 in 3 vols.

Acknowledgements

I would like to express my gratitude to Professor Nicholas Brooks and Professor Patrick Sims-Williams for their encouragement and good will. My work would have been impossible without the computing skills of Mrs Sarah Davnall, which she yet again placed at my disposal. I am eternally grateful. This volume owes much, in addition, to Richard Purslow of MUP, who has responded to its changing shape with unfailing good humour. My thinking on this period has benefited enormously from an entire generation of extra-mural students and several groups of third-year undergraduates, yet the ideas offered herein are my own, as too are any errors. I am grateful in addition to the University of Manchester for a sabbatical term in the summer of 1993, during which the bulk of this text was written. My greatest debt, as ever, is to my family, who have treated my increasing abstraction with a tolerance that I did not deserve. This book is for them.

Introduction

The origins of England have been wrapped in controversy for centuries. We might do worse, in illustration, than quote an American scholar's frustration at the contradictory hypotheses to which he found himself subjected, just over a century ago:[1]

> the Saxon conquest is, in Mr Coode's conception, very little more than the comfortable absorption and education of barbarians by a resident mass of civilized people; to Dr Guest and Dr Freeman it is a grim and thorough slaughter for more than a hundred years; to Mr Green it is a slow beating back, with a few of the vanquished left within the victor's lines until the Severn valley was gained; to Archdeacon Jones it is the winning of the low ground only, the Celt remaining in the uplands even today; to Mr Wright it is in the west, a comparatively harmless overrunning of a region already devastated by the Celts of Brittany; while Mr Pearson makes it partly a matter of bargain or compromise, partly a championship of the cities against the unruly country people. In so long a contest there must have been instances of almost everything. An adequate understanding of it would include the above and much more.

Modern scholarship has come a long way since this was written, yet the characteristics of this 'Saxon conquest' are no less controversial today: within archaeological works published over the last two decades, it is possible to find the earliest Saxon incomers described variously as 'a substantial immigration';[2] as late fourth-century *foederati* (federate troops) in Roman pay;[3] as migrant peasant farmers entering an apparently empty land,[4] as refugees from flood damage in Germany, who remained in Britain after their attack thereon in 410,[5] or as a comparatively small, immigrant warrior elite, whose culture the indigenes adopted[6] – all

1

beside the otherwise near-ubiquitous theory of a massed, tribal migration.[7]

Although several of these works have conscientiously taken account of written sources, each of these syntheses is based primarily on archaeological data. Some can be disproved,[8] but most cannot within the context of this data base. Indeed, it is fast becoming apparent that archaeologists are capable of producing an almost endless array of models of infinite variety through which to explain the emergence of England, each of which is (more or less) equally incapable of either proof or refutation.

The intractability of these hypotheses derives in part from the nature of archaeological data. This consists primarily of artefacts of various kinds – including pottery, metalwork, textiles, glass and buildings – and the spatial relations existing between those artefacts when found. Archaeology offers fundamental insights into a wide variety of cultural activities – such as burial practices, exchange, technology, architecture and the use of space within a settlement – but it provides only a very distant reflection of the social conditions, the political system, the language, religion and ideology then prevalent within a community. We cannot be sure what language – or languages – were spoken by the inhabitants of a pagan English settlement, nor even (in most instances) the name by which they identified that site. Nor is it an easy matter to establish the social and economic status of its occupants. Once the archaeologist departs from interpretation which is site-specific and seeks to make general comments concerning the entirety of society, his problems multiply: he is confronted primarily by the imponderable question: 'How representative of the total population is the site, or small group of sites, which has been investigated?' Those who prefer a migrationist view of the period assume (generally without discussion) that excavated sites and cemeteries reflect the culture – and so the ethnicity – of the majority, or even the totality, of society, while those who prefer 'elite dominance theory' assume the presence of a large but archaeologically in-visible underclass of indigenes.

The very nomenclature in use reflects these different perspectives and, at one and the same time, conditions the way we view the past: a 'migration' conjures up a specific group of images; so too does a 'settlement'; so too does a 'conquest' – which is a term which is now rarely used of the period, yet has a pedigree as good as any other.[9] A more neutral term is 'the arrival of the English', often still offered in the Latin as *adventus Saxonum*, which derives ultimately from Bede's interjection into his otherwise Gildas-derived account of the period that: 'They came *(Advenerant)* from three very powerful Germanic tribes',[10] but this fundamentally historical description is now in danger of being sucked into the vortex of archaeological explanation. As John Hines has recently suggested, this term:[11]

> may be not so much superseded but transformed into an archaeo-logically-defined 'beginning of the Ango-Saxon Period', which in simple terms is the start of the connected series of Germanic contexts, features and artefacts in Britain.

Disputes concerning chronology are a major problem of the period, with estimates of the 'beginnings of the Anglo-Saxon Period' flowing backwards and forwards across a century or so, which begins at some ill-defined date before AD 400. Again, ar-chaeological data is notoriously imprecise in this respect and the more cautious among archaeologists are loath to commit them-selves to a debate with historians concerning precise dates. The earliest strata of Anglo-Saxon material in Britain would seem to belong to the fifth century but it is still impossible to be sure whether or not any was deposited within the first quarter of it.[12] We are left, therefore, with an archaeologically defined 'beginning' of Anglo-Saxon England which floats in time across several gen-erations, and which we are incapable of placing in any particular social context.

If this was a prehistoric period, scholars would have no option but to accept the limitations inherent in archaeological methodo-logy and accept this amorphous and ill-defined 'beginning' as an event the main characteristics of which are barely accessible to us today. Fortunately, however, it is not quite prehistoric. Setting aside the small number of continental texts which make passing reference to events in Britain, there is one, near contemporary, insular work of literature which does offer an account of the period. This is the *De Excidio Britanniae* ('Concerning the ruin of Britain') of the enigmatic Gildas. Since the eighth century at latest, this short and difficult text has been quarried repeatedly by those wishing to reconstruct, for whatever reason, the events of that period which separates the collapse of Roman rule in Britain from

Introduction

the emergence of Anglo-Saxon England into history, *c.* 600. It is this text, almost alone, which offers the opportunity to examine the 'beginnings' of England as a historical, as opposed to an archaeological, problem.

The realisation that the answers to my own questions might lie here, rather than in the archaeological material, came to me only during the process of writing my own synthesis of the period and its problems, during the summer of 1990.[13] That volume gradually became ever more influenced by my own study of Gildas's work, but there was no room (nor was it appropriate) to offer a full discussion of my own views thereon. Nor were these then fully developed. With the benefit of further analysis of the text since, it is here my intention to offer a fuller discussion of Gildas, his purpose, and his value as a source for the historian. It is this text, therefore, which is the principal source on which this present work of history will rest.

Gildas's text has posed enormous problems for historians down the centuries, not least for Bede whose own chronology and characterisation of the initial *adventus Saxonum* was arguably forced into error by his misunderstanding of it.[14] Great strides have been made in recent years in elucidating Gildas's meaning: the edition and translation published in 1978 by Michael Winterbottom, with notes and a list of quotations used, has rendered the text far more accessible than hitherto and provides a fresh starting point for all further studies; a series of historical essays appeared early in the 1980s which offered new perspectives on, and approaches to, the text;[15] lastly, the monumental work of Francois Kerlouégan on the language used by Gildas was published as a monograph by the Sorbonne in 1987.[16] These studies have done much to make my own possible but this will not be a work of synthesis: on the contrary, it is offered as a new departure which argues for a fundamentally different interpretation of Gildas's locality, date and purposes in writing from those which have previously been proposed. In consequence, it will also suggest that the political and social context in which he wrote was very different from that which is generally assumed. From that, in turn, derives a very specific view of the 'beginnings' of Anglo-Saxon England and one which has an almost universal application to erstwhile Roman Britain. Gildas's perspective, it will be suggested, had more in common with the Roman and Norman conquests – hence the title

4

adopted – and the chronological and geographical contexts of this conquest can be established within comparatively narrow limits.

The fifth century is not, therefore, entirely a time lost to history, 'long ago in the quiet of the world',[17] but a period in which it is possible to establish the main shape of events, even after the failure of Roman protection. The most important single such event was the Saxon victory in the war which began with their rebellion against their British employers and ended *c.* 441. It was that victory which conditioned the peace during which Gildas lived his adult life, and which he sought, through his writing, a means to reverse. The repercussions of that victory shaped the political and cultural geography of Britain thereafter, causing Wales (and the south-west peninsula) and England to become separate from one another. Indeed, those repercussions are with us still.

This new study of Gildas's text as a historical source is offered, therefore, in the hope that it will make a positive contribution to the history of fifth-century Britain. As such, it may be of interest to those whose studies focus not only on the first few generations of Anglo-Saxon England but also those whose interests lie in either late Roman Britain or the medieval Celtic West, for these subjects are still too often investigated in comparative isolation from one another.[18] More particularly, it is my hope that this work will do something towards rekindling the respect of archaeologists for a historical approach to the period and so facilitate renewed cross-disciplinary discussions between archaeologists, historians and palaeobotanists with a shared interest in this most obscure of historical eras.

Notes

1 W. H. Babcock, *The Lost Centuries of Britain*, Philadelphia, 1890, p. 2.

2 C. Hills, 'The archaeology of Anglo-Saxon England in the pagan period', *Anglo-Saxon England*, VIII, 1979, p. 312.

3 J. N. L. Myres, *The English Settlements*, Oxford, 1986, pp. 85–103.

4 G. Copley, *Early Place-Names of the Anglian Regions*, Oxford, British Archaeological Reports, British series, CLXXXV, 1988, p. 19.

5 S. C. Hawkes, 'The south-east after the Romans: the Saxon settlement', in *The Saxon Shore: a handbook*, ed. V. Maxfield, Exeter, 1989, p. 85.

6 Most recently by A. S. Esmonde Clearly, *The Ending of Roman Britain*, London, 1989 – although even therein it was a 'migration'; and N. J. Higham, *Rome, Britain and the Anglo-Saxons*, London, 1992, *passim*.

7 Most recently by M. Welch, *Anglo-Saxon England*, London, 1992, pp. 11–12.

8 So the hypotheses which Myres based on his own interpretation of 'Romano-Saxon' pottery: J. P. Gillam, 'Romano-Saxon pottery: an alternative explanation', in *The End of Roman Britain*, ed. P. J. Casey, Oxford, British Archaeological Reports, British series, LXXI, 1979, pp. 103–18; W. I. Roberts, *Romano-Saxon Pottery*, Oxford, British Archaeological Reports, British series, CVI, 1982.

9 It occurs, for example, in the title of early editions of Gildas's *DEB*: 'On the downfall and conquest of Britain', for which see M. Winterbottom, *Gildas: the Ruin of Britain and Other Documents*, Chichester, 1978, p. 10, note 3. See also note 1, above.

10 *HE*, I, 15. See also *HB*, XVI: *'Saxones venerunt in Brittanniam . . .'*. Gildas did not use the term in this context: his text would justify *intromissus* or *eruptus* (or some similar part of speech) as alternatives: *DEB*, XXIII, 1, 3.

11 J. Hines, 'Philology, archaeology and the *adventus*', in *Britain 400–600: Language and History*, eds A. Bammesberger and A. Wollmann, Heidelberg, 1990, p. 20.

12 *Ibid.*, p. 25.

13 Higham, *Rome*.

14 *HE*, I, 12–16, 22; see below, pp. 139–40.

15 Principally P. Sims-Williams, 'Gildas and the Anglo-Saxons', *Cambridge Medieval Celtic Studies*, VI, 1983, pp. 1–30; M. Lapidge and D. N. Dumville, eds, *Gildas: New Approaches*, Woodbridge, 1984.

16 F. Kerlouégan, *Le De Excidio Britanniae de Gildas: Les destinées de la culture Latine dans l'Ile de Bretagne au VIᵉ siecle*, Paris, 1987.

17 J. R. R. Tolkien, *The Hobbit*, London, 1937, p. 13.

18 As pointed out long since by S. Haselgrove, 'Romano-Saxon attitudes', in *The End of Roman Britain*, ed. Casey, pp. 4–13; R. Reece, 'Town and country: the end of Roman Britain', *World Archaeology*, XII, pp. 77–92, and more recently by M. E. Jones and P. J. Casey, 'The Gallic Chronicle restored: a chronology for the Anglo-Saxon invasion and the end of Roman Britain', *Britannia*, XIX, 1988, pp. 367–98.

1

The rationale of Gildas's
De Excidio Britanniae

The sole extant, sequential account, by a near contemporary, of the phenomenon which is widely termed the 'English Settlement' occurs in the 'historical' introduction of the *De Excidio Britanniae* ('The ruin of Britain', henceforth *DEB*), a Latin text attributed to the enigmatic British Christian, Gildas.[1] Unless he was responsible for the letter fragments and Latin Penitential which were later attributed to him,[2] we have no other work by Gildas to assist us in interpreting the *DEB*. It is, therefore, primarily with reference to this piece of literature that modern scholars debate his place both in history and in historiography,[3] and the relationship between his writing and the 'English Settlement'.

As regards Gildas the man, it would be overly optimistic to imagine that our knowledge has progressed far at all. When introducing his 1841 translation of Gildas, J. A. Giles remarked that: 'We are unable to speak with certainty as to his parentage, his country, or even his name, the period when he lived, or the works of which he was the author.' These same issues remain today either beyond resolution or, at best, hotly debated. Since his locality and the date at which he wrote are critical to any use of the text as a source by the historian, these will be discussed in detail below. Giles left to others recognition of the need to explore the reasons which motivated Gildas to write.

Gildas's work belongs to a tradition of late Classical, Christian history which begins in many respects with Eusebius,[4] friend of Constantine I. Constantine's triumph over his enemies, his strong favouring of Christianity and the apparently permanent omnipotence of Rome stimulated Eusebius to construct a new model of history which was designed to reconcile both the history and the destiny of the newly Christian Empire with the Bible-centred historical perceptions of early Christianity.[5] From being an occasional persecutor of Christians, Rome was converted to the sole legitimate ruler of the world, under God's protection.

Eusebius's optimistic view of the destiny of this Christian realm was sustained by Orosius,[6] St Augustine's younger contemporary and disciple, whose work confirmed that vision of a Roman history in accord with the God of the Christians and underlined the legitimacy of Roman rule. In contradiction of contemporary pagan claims that the barbarian-infested Empire was in crisis because its rulers had abandoned its native gods, Orosius insisted that the early fifth century was, by the standards of Roman history, an epoch of comparative peace, and anticipated that the Empire would successfully withstand or absorb its barbarian attackers.

Sidonius Apollinaris, born *c.* 430, preserved Orosius's faith in the destiny of Rome long into the second half of the century,[7] but the facts were by then pointing irresistibly in other directions, and other commentators abandoned this increasingly untenable position. After several decades of unchecked barbarian activity, with Roman Gaul supine before them, Salvian, a southern Gaullish commentator, found it impossible to share Orosius's complacency. Following a path which had been clearly marked out by Eusebius, he sought Old Testament precedents for the present, but, unlike Eusebius, it was Roman failure which he felt obliged to explain:[8]

> If therefore, they enquire, God reflects on mankind, if he cares, if he loves, if he directs, why does he permit us to be weaker and more miserable than all the peoples? Why does he suffer [us] to be defeated by the barbarians? Why to be subjected to the authority of the enemy?

Salvian's answer was simple: men's affairs remained within the control of an omnipotent Christian God. If He had withdrawn His protection from His people, it could only be because they had sinned. The disasters which had befallen Roman Gaul were therefore interpreted as a sign that its inhabitants had departed from their proper obedience to God and fallen into sin, and it was to that moral failure that Salvian addressed his energies:[9]

> I will speak of the infirmity and misery of the Romans ...

> the very barbarians are offended by our impurities. To be among the Goths is not a licence to be a whore of the Goths ...

The situation confronting Gildas had much in common with that faced by Salvian and his response to it was in many ways similar,[10] although there is no reason to think that he had read this work.[11]

There are even similarities in the vehicles chosen by Salvian and Gildas. Salvian's *De Gubernatione Dei* was addressed to a bishop,[12] and was implicitly written as a form of extended sermon. The *De Excidio* is self-evidently an *epistola* – a 'letter', a literary form familiar to its author from the Bible, and perhaps elsewhere,[13] and used by him for purposes comparable to those of St Paul,[14] who addressed sermons to distant churches by correspondence. Like the Christian congregations among the Ephesians or Corinthians, Gildas's audience consisted of gentiles far distant from the Holy Land: again like St Paul, Gildas was quick to confront and face down any doubts that this gentile audience might entertain concerning the universality of Christ's message.[15] Like St Paul's audience, those whom Gildas addressed lived in a world dominated by heathens.[16] Given the dependence of his text on Biblical images and precedents and his exclusively Christian theories of cause and effect, Gildas can only have aimed his message at Christians – as did St Paul. The vehicle he chose – the *epistola* – was, therefore, apt for his purpose.

We may reasonably assume that the *DEB* was a contribution to a debate current at the time of writing, concerning the ills affecting Gildas's own generation and the means by which these should be addressed. This he made clear in his *exordium*, or opening comments:[17] 'I am distraught at the damages and afflictions of the fatherland and rejoice in remedies to relieve them.' He was to return to the same theme thereafter.[18] His intention was, he claimed, to be helpful, but at the same time to 'prosecute with tearful complaint' those whom he held responsible. That Gildas conceived the whole as some sort of proactive 'lament' is obvious from his repeated return to this theme. The text is characterised by its pompous oratory and was written in an inflated rhetorical style.[19]

It was formally addressed to the leaders of insular, British society – its kings (or here 'tyrants') and priests, with the apparent purpose of inducing in them a moral reform and return to obedience to God and His law.[20] This form was probably, however, a rhetorical device and Gildas's immediate audience rather more restricted. His reference to what was apparently a well-known pre-existing text, written by 'one of us', in chapter ninety-two, verse three, which had an obvious relevance to the same debate that Gildas himself addressed, conjures up an image of a small, salon-style group of Britons each offering his own opinion on this same subject. The considerable erudition that Gildas required of his audience certainly supports the view that he was writing for a group whose Roman style of education equipped them to understand and appreciate his offering. If an education of that kind was accessible only to the rich in fifth-century Britain, Gildas himself, and his putative debating group, were all presumably members of the land-owning elite.

The *DEB* is, in a sense, a text which has a moral purpose – to address the moral failings of contemporaries. It is, however, far more than this. The primary, and interlocking, objectives of the *DEB* are established in the opening lines:

1 To rehearse and so establish the 'damages and afflictions' suffered by the 'fatherland' (by which he apparently meant what had been Roman Britain). This could be achieved very briefly because they were contemporary and not at issue within Gildas's circle.
2 To explain why those same 'damages and afflictions' had come about, and enable responsibility to be assigned where appropriate.
3 To mount an offensive against those responsible. Since Gildas adopted an explanation that was couched entirely in terms of morality and obedience to God, this took the form of complaints against the moral and spiritual condition of those responsible, whom Gildas believed it essential to bring to contrition and back to obedience to God.
4 With the relationship between God and His people restored, He would automatically renew His protection of His people and assist them in remedying those same 'damages and afflictions'.

To these we might perhaps add a fifth objective – that of entertaining his audience – for Gildas wrote with wit, irony and sarcasm, as well as complaint and invective. His was, by fifth-century standards, a highly erudite piece of composition, designed to arrest the attention of an audience of similar educational background to himself and persuade them of the veracity of his own views. This was, however, most probably a subordinate objective, intended to render the means by which his message would be delivered as compelling as possible. It seems unlikely that Gildas was writing primarily for literary purposes.

The fundamental interpretational problem today is to establish precisely to what 'damages and afflictions' Gildas was referring, since the context in which he wrote was so obvious to himself and his immediate audience as to warrant only the most subtle allusion in his own text. Once remote from that context, such allusions – largely offered in this text in the form of cleverly manipulated biblical extracts – are as difficult to identify as they are to interpret, and most have not hitherto been discussed.

To summarise, it will here be proposed that Gildas wrote against a backdrop of barbarian (that is Saxon) domination, with the ultimate purpose of freeing his people from their grip. Borrowing his stance as a providential historian from the Bible and from Church histories, he conceived this Saxon domination not as a political and military problem, *per se*, but as a consequence of the breakdown of the perpetual treaty between God and His people, as a consequence of their iniquity. His means of rectifying the political impasse was therefore to persuade the leaders of British society that their immorality and disobedience to God were responsible for the unfavourable relationship then existing between the Britons and the Saxons.[21] Only by their repentance and return to obedience would it be possible to restore divine protection to His people (the Britons[22]). With that protection restored, Gildas had numerous biblical precedents on which to base his assumption that the wrath of an omnipotent God would sustain the forces of the righteous and sweep away those who were oppressing them, for the Lord God was the Lord of hosts.[23]

To a modern audience, such thinking seems naive – perhaps even puerile – but it must be stressed that the intellectual environment of the late Classical world assumed just such a relationship between an omnipotent God and his worshippers.[24] History was conceived as the working through of divine will, with human agents enjoying little freedom of action beyond the ability to please, or offend, God. Orosius expressed this view succinctly at the inception of his *Histories*:[25]

if the world and man are directed by a Divine Providence that is as benign as it is just, and if man is both weak and stubborn because of the changeability of his nature and his freedom to choose, then man must be guided in the spirit of filial affection when he has need of help; but when he abuses his freedom, he must be corrected according to a spirit of strict justice.

Such a view is fundamentally biblical in its inspiration and Gildas naturally turned repeatedly to the Bible both for precedent and for proof of his thesis – to an extent and in a style which is today insupportable to most readers, even in translation. Yet Gildas's view of the history and political condition of his own people as a simple extension of the Bible was a commonplace of the period, the historian's role being to explain this relationship and graft on the experiences of Christian gentiles to the Testaments.[26] So too was his interpretation of history solely in terms of Christian virtues and an unwritten but perpetual contract – an 'eternal treaty' between the Christian and his God.[27] Closely comparable reasoning was to be evident among English Christians under attack from the Vikings. In both circumstances, Christian thinkers proposed moral reform as a matter of urgency, but in neither was that reform, in itself, the ultimate objective. It was, rather, a means to an end – that of renewing divine protection against a pagan foe whom Christian observers interpreted, in part at least, as an agent of divine wrath.

This perception of contemporary politics through spirituality and morality was sustained by circular reasoning, since it was the enemy attacks – ultimately their domination – which provided the most obvious *prima facie* evidence of God's displeasure. That they could have occurred while divine protection was in place was not, of course, considered possible, since God was omnipotent. Successful attacks on His people, particularly by heathens, *must*, therefore, be a consequence of God's withholding His protection. Within the bounds of his own system of faith, Gildas's perception of the Saxons was self-sustaining and beyond reasonable challenge. It was only that system which he was obliged to explain and sustain, and much of the early chapters of the *DEB* was given over to this purpose. Indeed, that is the function which his 'historical' introduction was designed to perform.

Gildas's 'damages and afflictions' were generally implicit rather than overtly stated, in a piece of oratory composed for present purposes. It was an attempt to influence contemporaries, but not to claim for himself a new and more influential role in the politics of the day.[28] Gildas was no politician and made no obvious effort in that direction.[29] Nor was he, by any definition now in use, an historian, despite Bede's reference to him as *historicus*,[30] and his own reference to the earlier part of his work as an *historia*. His interest lay in providential, not secular, history, the function of which was to substantiate a particular system of historical explanation by reference to divine providence. Gildas was familiar with some continental Church history,[31] and treated it as a quarry from which to extract the material through which he proposed to establish his own system of causation for contemporary purposes, but we treat him as a conventional historian at our peril.[32] The model which he followed was closer by far to the Old Testament prophets, through whom the Bible informed him that God had been used to address His people of yore and goad them to revert to the straight and narrow. Those prophets who sought to avert, or lamented on, heathen oppression of the Israelites were most favoured by him, as being most relevant to the present condition of his own people.

Gildas used his 'historical' introduction to the 'complaints' as a vehicle by which to place Britain and the Britons in their own special niche within a more general history of salvation which had reached him both from the Bible and from continental Church histories,[33] but that was not his primary objective. His 'history' was, first and foremost, the means of persuading contemporaries that there was an inescapable causal relationship between their own morality (essentially their obedience to God's laws), the attitude of God towards them and their success in withstanding or evicting their enemies. He adopted a chronological structure: this was perhaps natural, since he found such in the Latin writings he used;[34] it was also convenient to his rhetorical purposes, and Gildas was careful to develop, through various literary devices, the tension of his 'history' towards a crescendo calculated to coincide with the recent experience of his people and their current plight. Thus did he lend urgency and compulsion to his message.

His view, and use, of the insular past was, therefore, always subordinated to more fundamental purposes. It is essential that the 'historical' introduction be read not as a consecutive narrative of British history written by a man whose interest lay in recording

13

events through time, but as extended dialectic contrived to sustain a particular view of causality for present purposes, and so a particular explanation of the factors which conditioned that present.

Gildas laid his message before his readers in a logical and coherent form. He opened with a conventional preface, in which he set the scene, explained his purpose and excused his own temerity in undertaking the task. He then offered a precis of the stereotypical and anecdotal cycle of sin and retribution by which he proposed to characterise the past moral experience of the Britons, as a guide to the contents of the 'historical' section.[35]

He then opened his account with a geographical description of Britain. This was based ultimately on Orosius's work, but Gildas adapted and augmented it to such a point that the end result displays considerable originality and offers important insights into the state of Britain at the time of composition. Its inclusion was in part a concession to orthodox Classical style, but it was more than this: throughout this passage Gildas idealised Britain to such an extent that he must have had in mind a fundamental analogy of biblical origin. Just as God had made the Garden of Eden for Adam and Eve, so too had Britain been an Arcadian paradise before the introduction of the Britons.[36] It was original sin which had led to the expulsion of Adam and Eve from the Garden. So too were the Britons intrinsically sinful, as he had already asserted in verse thirteen of the introduction (chapter one). Gildas could assume his (obviously Christian) audience to be familiar with the doctrine of original sin and he invoked this image from the very beginning in an insular context, as a fundamental explanation of the moral failings underlying Britain's 'loss':[37]

> Ever since it has been inhabited, this ingrate [the island of Britain, so the Britons] has risen up, stiff-necked and haughty, now against God, on occasion against its own citizens, sometimes even against kings and their subjects from across the seas.

Continuing in this vein, Gildas laid before his audience his own views (or prejudices) regarding contemporary morality: the most heinous of crimes in his opinion were:

> to deny due reverence to God, charity to worthy fellow-citizens, honour to those of higher rank (*altior dignitas*), for that is their due provided there is no harm to the faith: to break faith with God or

14

man, to abandon respect for heaven and earth, and to be ruled each by his own contrivances and lusts.

As one might expect of a man with his education and training,[38] Gildas is revealed as a conservative as regards the structure of society, with an innate respect for established, Christian authority. His is a very aristocratic, Roman view of the body politic, which omits, of course, any reference in such a context to the barbarians. Gildas may have felt it necessary to excuse the attacks which he was about to launch against the contemporary British authorities, both secular and spiritual, but such was necessary to a self-appointed prophet keen to follow precedents, which he had already quoted in his own introduction, set by Jeremiah in his attacks on the Israelite king and by Christ in his condemnation of the scribes and pharisees. Beside this reactionary attitude, he was taking the opportunity to stress the importance to his own scheme for the deliverance of the Britons of proper obedience to God and legitimate authorities – among whom his immediate audience may well have been prominent.

Following on from this, Gildas informed his audience what he would omit: he was aware that, in pre-Roman times, Britain had been heathen but this was a condition which it had shared with the remainder of the Roman world; he hinted at some knowledge regarding the topography of British paganism,[39] but forbore to pursue a characteristic which, while it could be portrayed as erroneous, was not peculiar to the Britons. It was the crimes which were exclusive to his own countrymen to which Gildas wished to bring attention, not those which they shared with their continental neighbours, since only these could be deemed relevant to the present 'damages and afflictions' which were likewise peculiar to the Britons.

Roman Britain

Setting aside only his implicit comparison of Britain with the Garden of Eden, therefore, it was with the Julio-Claudian era of Roman world dominion and peace that Gildas began, confident perhaps that his audience would associate this period with the life of Christ.[40] That association may indeed have done much to bolster Gildas's perception of Roman rule as intrinsically virtuous and God-sanctioned.[41] There then begins an episodic and anecdotal unfolding of the moral relationship between the Britons, the Romans and the Christian God, beginning with the conquest (of Claudius: AD 43). Gildas's dialectic throughout was to be dominated by his desire to portray the past experiences of the Britons in terms of these relationships, and so establish the universality of their relevance. By so doing, he proposed to sustain his premise that only through moral reform and strict obedience to God could the Britons expect to solve the 'damages and afflictions' of the present. Since his reasoning conformed with – indeed, derived from – the pre-existing body of Hebrew, and Christian Roman, providential history, anecodotes from these sources would also be marshalled in defence of his thesis.

As the 'contents list' of chapter two had promised, the 'historical' account was therefore couched from its inception in terms of morality: the Britons were consistently portrayed as unwarlike and treacherous cowards, in contrast to the brave and virtuous Romans. It was the innate iniquity – the original sin – of the Britons, as expressed in chapter one, verses thirteen and fourteen, and chapter four, that made them in this pagan period fit only to be slaves of the Romans. Their inherently subordinate character was to recur repeatedly throughout the 'historical' introduction, and feature prominently also in a present context, so it was essential to Gildas's dialectic that it be explained from the beginning by reference to the moral and spiritual shortcomings of the Britons. Only through God's aid could it be overcome.

Gildas's development of the relationship between the Britons and the Romans is one of two fundamental themes of his introduction, paralleling (but never equalling) the interaction between the Britons and God: the Romans played a central and (almost) uniformly virtuous role in his perception of a properly ordered, Christian world.[42] It was from Rome that Christianity eventually reached Britain.[43] Implicit in his account is the assumption that, had Roman protection not collapsed – owing, of course, to the criminal folly of the Britons – the triumph of the Saxons could not have occurred, since the Britons would have remained under the protection of a more virtuous people, whose rule was divinely sanctioned.

Gildas registered his disapproval of the Britons in his choice of language – the Britons were 'faithless' 'rebels', who 'slaughtered' the Roman governors in the absence of their army. He condemned them also through a distinctive selection of metaphors: they were 'little foxes' (so tricky, rather than brave) and, like the Saxons (with whom his 'historical' account would end), they (or perhaps more specifically Boadicea or Boudicca, their queen) were described through a pejorative leonine metaphor.[44] Gildas had a conventional Christian's dislike of lions, presumably because of their role in early martyrdoms.[45]

He described the Roman response in terms which demand comparison with his comments on the present and more recent past: as the Saxons were to do, he envisaged the Romans killing some Britons and keeping the rest as slaves, in servitude under the whips and yoke of foreign domination.[46] Since it was the consequences of the later episode with which Gildas was familiar, and in which he was primarily interested, it was presumably with that in mind that he described the disasters of the early decades of Roman Britain. These were, therefore, images the potency and clarity of which derived from the present, but which were projected into the past for purposes of comparison.

If this foreign servitude of the Britons had a relevance to the present, that relevance lay primarily in the manner of its ending. Implicit in Gildas's account is some sort of reconciliation between Romans and Britons at the conversion. Roman persecution was relieved by Christ's gift of the true faith to the Britons, which Gildas dated to the reign of Tiberius.[47] He took this, the first of several opportunities, to emphasise God's charity towards the Britons, as a chance to portray the British adherence to Christianity as unenthusiastic,[48] as befits such an innately sinful people, but the dawn of Christianity could be deemed to have ended the cruel British servitude which had preceded it. Gildas's message here is simple: God had in the past succoured the Britons when slaves to foreigners. He might be persuaded to do so again in similar circumstances, if only Christ's precepts be followed. A long era of blissful security might then ensue, just as Gildas suggested that it had in the past.[49]

The next onslaught to which Gildas referred was likewise from abroad, in the person of Diocletian, arch-persecutor of Christianity.[50] That his assumption that persecution occurred at this date in Britain is unhistorical is immaterial. Gildas here took his brief from the universality of the persecution associated with Diocletian, with which he was familiar from Church histories,

17

and applied it on his own authority to Britain. He emphasised the constancy and endurance of the saints whom he represented as resisting the onslaught:[51] 'The whole church (*tota ecclesia*), in dense ranks, competed to reject the shadows of this world and hurried to the pleasant realm of heaven.' By portraying massed Christian resistance to a heathen master on the heroic scale in the past, Gildas was establishing a yardstick against which he invited his audience to measure the British *ecclesiae* of the present, so his Christian contemporaries, now faced by foreign, pagan persecutions of a similar kind.[52] Would they but display comparable fortitude, Gildas implied, God would intervene as He had done in the past by lighting 'the brilliant lamps of holy martyrs'.[53] He reinforced the contemporaneity of his message by stressing the relevance of the shrines and places of martyrdom of that age to the present: they would, he suggested, 'strike a great flame (or "love") of divine charity in the minds of participants', had they not been made inaccessible due to the partition with the barbarians which was a consequence of 'our sins'.[54]

Gildas reinforced his message by a lengthy account of a miracle credited to St Alban of Verulamium, a martyr whose shrine was prominent in 429, or at least thought to have been so in Gaul a half century later.[55] The veneration of St Alban was clearly not something which owed its inception to Gildas, who apparently had access to a tradition concerning this saint, or perhaps even a work of hagiography – a *Vita Albani*.[56] By recounting this miracle,[57] Gildas was able to portray St Alban as responsible for the conversion of his executioner (*carnifex*) 'from a wolf to a lamb', ready for martyrdom with him. Once more his message is contemporary: if the Britons stood firm in their faith at the present, then the 'wolves' of the present and more recent past (the Scots and Picts, Saxons, Satan and even Maglocunus)[58] might also be converted to lambs.[59] The glorious martyrdom of St Alban, and others, and the constancy of the survivors in their faith in God earned them relief, and 'the serene light of the breeze of heaven' restored a Christian peace.[60] Once more a just and charitable God had succoured His people when they were deserving of His aid, and a long and blissful peace ensued. This anecdote has an obvious relevance to the present.

Gildas culled one more exemplar from his literary sources: he characterised Arianism – 'vomiting foreign poison' – as just the first of a rush of heresies from abroad to infect the Britons, who took them up eagerly, inclined as they were (in his opinion) to inconstancy.[61] He associated this outbreak of disobedience to God with parallel disobedience towards Rome, so characterising Magnus Maximus as a cunning, perjured and wicked British tyrant in revolt against the legitimate authority of the Empire.[62] The consequence was the collapse of Roman rule in Britain, the end of divine protection and the beginning of barbarian attacks.[63]

Gildas had, therefore, used his scant literary resources to good effect. He had employed specific episodes concerning Roman Britain as exemplars by which to establish an entire system of causation of fundamental relevance to the present. Diocletian alone excepted, he had throughout sustained a virtuous characterisation of the Romans – as regards their courage and military qualities, and the legitimacy of their rule. The Roman Empire was God-sanctioned and part of the divine order. The Britons were, in his eyes, the antithesis of the Romans, sinful from the very beginning, weak-willed, craven in war, and unreceptive to the truth. These qualities had led them into early disobedience towards the Empire, but their rebellion brought down harsh punishments upon their heads. This parlous condition was relieved only through the charity of God, whose protection was extended over the Britons once they had accepted Christianity, provided only that they displayed the appropriate constancy of faith. This they had done to a triumphant conclusion during Diocletian's reign, only to fall away thereafter due to fresh outbreaks of their own fundamental moral failings. The fall of Roman Britain was the consequence of those failings, and these opened a new and frightening chapter in the experience of the Britons, the consequences of which conditioned the present, where Gildas's concern was chiefly centred.

Each episode which Gildas deployed served a specific function in his exposition of his philosophy of causation, and answered a particular question, each of which could have been deployed against his thesis. Question: 'Why were the Romans successful in conquering and ruling Britain, even when they were still pagan?' Answer: 'Because of the innate iniquity of the Britons and the superior virtues of the Romans, which led God to select their rule as a setting appropriate to the first coming'. Question: 'Why, in that case, did Roman persecution of Christians occur?' Answer: 'So that God could test His people'. Question: 'Why did that

19

persecution fail?' Answer: 'Because He found His people worthy and aided them against their enemies'. Question: 'Why did Roman protection of Britain fail?' Answer: 'Because of a dual rebellion by the fundamentally iniquitous Britons against both God and Rome, which made them unworthy of continuing protection by either party.'

This is not good history, if only because it is not secular history, but it is providential, or salvation, history of high quality, which offers a fundamental and rational explanation of universal relevance to the experiences of the Britons. If the blows which befell them in the past were a consequence of their moral inadequacies, so too were the 'damages and afflictions' confronting the Britons in the present. Each anecdote which Gildas selected was couched in a fashion intended to add something to his own solution to the Saxon menace. Just as those past reverses were corrected only by a renewal of the relationship between the Britons and God, so too was that the sole salvation available to them, in Gildas's opinion, in the present time. His rationale was by no means unique: it broadly coincides with that which Salvian invoked in reaction to similar problems in Gaul. In each instance, it is sustainable only within the belief system and philosophy of history to which these two writers both adhered.

One further factor is significant. Although their own 'original sin' was clearly relevant (in Gildas's opinion) in rendering the Britons peculiarly vulnerable to disobedience, all the disasters which befell the Britons derived from overseas:[64] the Roman conquest and subsequent suppression of rebellion; the persecution of Diocletian; the advent of heresy. From these Gildas was about to turn to the maritime attacks of the Scots and Picts,[65] and this theme was to continue into the present, when the latest of 'the fatherland's damages and afflictions' would be the arrival and successful rebellion of the Saxons.

By such means, as well as through recurring imagery and analogy, Gildas sought to weld into a single message a half millennium of very diverse historical experiences. That message concerned the present, and the 'damages and afflictions' of the present, not the past.

Britain without Rome

Although his reading of Latin literature could have afforded Gildas some information concerning the next quarter century or so,[66] it was with Magnus Maximus that he abandoned his sources, although whether from choice or from inadequate attention to them is difficult to judge. It is far from certain that Gildas was ignorant of either the existence of the Pelagian heresy or the career of Constantine III – to take only the most obvious examples which he omitted to mention in detail. Either or both could easily be implicit in his generalised references to 'every heresy'[67] and 'tyrant thickets'.[68] There is a good case for supposing that Gildas's very generalised comments on the *mala* – 'evils' – inflicted by the Britons on other citizens of the Empire derived from his reading of Orosius's indictment of tyrants set up by Britain and Gaul;[69] similarly, his comments on successively more evil tyrants ruling in Britain after Magnus Maximus may well derive from Orosius's more extended comments on the wickedness and incompetence of Gratian, Constantine III, his son and Caesar, the erstwhile monk, Constans, and their various slayers and successors.[70] Orosius's view that the Emperor Honorius successfully resisted these tyrants and various disobedient *duces* – 'military leaders' but probably referring primarily to Gerontius, Constantine's *magister militum* – by virtue of his own religious piety and the diligence and quickness of Constantius is reflected in Gildas's advice to, and condemnations of, his own people.[71]

It seems likely, therefore, that Gildas knew of, but preferred not to comment on, such a plethora of individuals. His work did not, after all, make any attempt to utilise every possible example for his rhetorical purposes, so the omission of specific names or particular anecdotes is far from proof that they were unknown to him: the *DEB* was never intended to offer a connected historical narrative.[72] He perhaps chose, in Arianism and Magnus Maximus, the first instances of which he was aware of each 'affliction', much as he later offered the name of the British commander in only the first victory over the Saxons.[73] Gildas's business was with examples and anecdotes, not the continuous warp of history and his case might well have been weakened by reference to more than a single exemplar of each sort.

His literary sources had provided Gildas with considerable

opportunity to develop his theme but they had also acted as a strait-jacket, since the better educated of his audience might be familiar with the same texts. From chapter fourteen onwards, until he reached the more recent past of contemporary memory, Gildas had no such guidance but nor was he fettered by the written word. He was, therefore, free to pursue his oratorical purposes, provided only that he reconstructed a past which was credible to his own generation. He needed, therefore, to remain within the limits imposed by folk-memory but the notion that the results are, in detail, based on oral traditions still alive at the time of writing is implausible,[74] at least from chapters fourteen to nineteen wherein there are none of the personal- or place-names which one might expect from such a source. There is necessarily a degree of historicity to the underlying character of the period as one in which the Roman and externally authorised government of Britain came to an end, exposing the diocese to barbarian raids, but Gildas's reconstruction is clearly retrospective and fundamentally false. It was almost certainly, in detail, his own work.

Gildas therefore created a basically fictional sequence of events, focusing on the interplay of raids launched by the Picts and Scots and a continuing dependence of the Britons on Roman protection. Neither barbarian attack, nor British military dependency is unlikely in itself: attacks by Picts and Scots are well known in the second half of the fourth century,[75] when a Roman garrison was still at its post; so too is the military incompetence of Roman provincials very widely evidenced in the fourth and fifth centuries.[76] Gildas was, therefore, probably right to infer a context for sub-Roman Britain with these characteristics, but his fabrication of two Roman expeditions to Britain and his appropriation of the two northern walls to this epoch are fundamentally unhistorical.[77] Since these are the central events of this section of the *DEB*, that must be considered a fabrication.

His writing was not, however, devoid of purpose. Gildas used these chapters to amplify one of the two themes – Britain's relationships with God and with Rome – which had so far dominated his writing, reinforcing his contrast between the virtues and warlike qualities of the Romans and the cowardice and military incompetence of the Britons.[78] The superior morality of the Romans, as God's designated rulers of the world, was sufficient to enable them, on occasion, to protect Britain, despite the continuing collapse of the relationship between the Britons and God in consequence of their admitting heresies to the island. It was the Britons (through Magnus Maximus) who had terminated their pre-existing relationship with the Empire: thus the efforts which the Romans made thereafter to protect the Britons were a matter of charity, undertaken not from duty but from compassion. Charity towards the Britons was, therefore, a facet not just of God's attitude towards His errant people but also of that of the Empire. By such means did Gildas emphasise the depths of iniquity into which the Britons had fallen. It was in that trough that they remained still in the present time, wrapped in crimes so heinous that their erstwhile, charitable protectors could not now overlook them.

The actions of virtuous Romans were adequate to drive out the barbarians but the sins of the Britons were such that, whenever the Romans departed, they were incapable, without assistance, of effective resistance. The introduction of this relationship between British morality and barbarian oppression was arguably a fundamental motive for Gildas's conception and development of these passages.

He took this opportunity to credit the Romans with advice to the Britons that they should defend themselves against their enemies,[79] in so doing using language redolent of his description of earlier British cowardice in the face of Roman rule.[80] It is a mistake to read into this account evidence that Gildas knew of the 'Honorian Rescript',[81] whether that be historical or not,[82] since these words were intended to have a universal – so contemporary – currency. As such it was one strand of Gildas's own advice to his countrymen.[83] That it was conveyed in this instance via Roman soldiers was arguably a device intended to lend his counsel added stature by association with that same military virtue and divinely sanctioned authority with which he had consistently invested Rome. This construction is, therefore, a literary device rather than an historical event.

Other aspects of this account are also of contemporary relevance: I have argued elsewhere that Gildas used the Roman walls in the north, concerning which he was poorly informed, as a vehicle through which to criticise recent or current dyke construction further south by British authorities;[84] his comments on the abandonment of towns (*civitates* – his mistake for the Hadrianic wall forts) presage and so contextualise in a causal sense his lament concerning the sack of cities by the Saxon,[85] and their current desertion;[86] starvation, supposedly experienced by the Britons under attack from the Picts and Scots,[87] had already been implicit as a feature of the Roman suppression of British rebellion, when Roman forces had to return home for lack of wine and oil, and would recur at the hands of the Saxons.[88] Much of the detail offered by Gildas was, therefore, included so as to sustain the closeness of parallels between the past condition of the Britons and that of the present time. These were literary embellishments included for dramatic and rhetorical effect, rather than historical details.

More important, perhaps, to Gildas's dialectic, was the opportunity to twice replicate the recent barbarian onslaught on the Britons in the more remote past. This enabled him to adopt rhetorical techniques designed to reinforce those aspects of his own characterisation of the current situation which he wished to stress: one such was the military ineptitude of the Britons; another was their sinfulness, but there were additional and purely rhetorical advantages. Replication of the appeal to the Roman 'Agitius' – albeit addressed more vaguely 'to Rome' – enabled him to emphasise and direct attention to the moment when Roman protection finally failed – that is when 'Agitius' failed to respond to the last appeal – by adopting successively more impelling rhetoric for these several episodes: in the first instance,[89] the Britons merely sent envoys to Rome asking for protection and promising loyalty in return; on the next occasion, envoys were portrayed as suppliants as if to a God, and as frightened chicks seeking protection from their parents, with reported speech conveying the wretchedness of their plight.[90] Gildas clearly based much of the imagery used in this passage on Jeremiah:[91] 'they have cast up dust upon their heads, they have girded themselves with sackcloth' – and this source is not without its own significance. The third appeal was to a named recipient, one 'Agitius',[92] and in this, the only one likely to be in any way historical,[93] Gildas resorted to direct speech, a rhetorical device of which he made carefully controlled use in this work. By such means he invoked a sense of gathering doom by progressively escalating the scale of the difficulties which the Britons faced and the emotional qualities of the appeals by which they sought to escape them. As he remarked in his 'contents list' (chapter two), the last enemy to afflict Britain was 'more savage even than the first' and it was towards that 'affliction' that his 'historical' introduction was directed.

The effect is a sustained and continuous escalation in the level of tension, from the introduction of the theme of British rebelliousness (in chapter four) towards a climax in chapters twenty-two to twenty-six, wherein occurs the Saxon *adventus* ('arrival') and rebellion. The imaginations of Gildas's audience were focused, thereby, on the terrible moment when Roman aid failed – a failure which led directly (in this reconstruction of events) to the invitation to the Saxons.[94] Gildas emphasised this moment not by bombast but by a resort to the starkest possible terms in a style which was the very antithesis of that which he normally used:[95] 'But they had no help from them.'

With this episode Gildas concluded his examination of the relationship between Romans and Britons. He had apparently drawn from it all that his rhetorical purposes required. Whether or not they took the advice he had opportunely placed in the mouths of the heroic Romans, the Britons would henceforth have to face the barbarians without Roman aid, since the protection of Rome was, by the time of writing, a dead force and presumably recognised so to be by his own audience.

With Roman intervention at an end, Gildas returned to the more fundamental of his two themes – the relationship between the Britons and God. He had last explored this in the context of the fall of Roman Britain, when he characterised the Britons as receptive to a series of heresies, so in rebellion against God.[96] Since that point, the Britons had failed to renew their allegiance to the Lord, and the ease with which the barbarians were able to raid and devastate all Britain was a consequence of that fact. Ignoring God, they turned repeatedly instead to the Romans for assistance, which that generous, and virtuous, people had on occasion provided. But such intervention was inadequate since, whenever Roman forces withdrew, the immorality and disobedience of the Britons left them once more at the mercy of the barbarians.

In the aftermath of their last, failed appeal, the Britons were therefore outside divine protection and at the mercy of the barbarians. Gildas now depicted the Britons as achieving military success, but only through divine aid. His account has many of the Britons afflicted by famine,[97] and prepared to accept slavery as the price of life.[98] These images are redolent of an 'affliction' which he had already described – the British servitude under Rome[99] – and continue the theme of Britain's disarray and the servitude of her people under later barbarian assault.[100] But just as the Britons had stood firm, fortified by God, through the persecution of Diocletian, so did Gildas portray them now beating off the barbarians with God's aid, once they had returned to their proper obedience. Similarities between these two episodes are clearly signposted: the Britons had resisted Diocletian from 'woods, desert places and secret caves'; so did they now fight the barbarians from 'mountains, caves, heaths and thorny thickets'. Just so would Gildas later depict British resistance to the Saxons,[101] and it is surely in support of his account of that episode that Gildas contrived both this one and the earlier example. It is, therefore, another instance of his replicating his own portrayal of recent events pertinent to current problems in the more distant past, for rhetorical effect. That effect was drawn out to its logical conclusion only in the 'complaints', wherein he castigated contemporary clergy for shirking the example of their forebears, who: 'endured wandering in the mountains and caves and caverns of the earth, suffered stoning, cutting and every manner of death, in the name of the Lord'.[102]

In developing this picture of interaction between God, the Britons and their barbarian enemies, Gildas's message is both clear cut and of obviously contemporary relevance. Indeed, the entirety of this section may well have been developed by Gildas in order to lay before his own audience examples of such episodes which were specific to barbarian oppression of the Britons, since it was that dimension which was lacking in the anecdotes available to him from continental sources.

With the barbarians repulsed by the Britons by virtue of their new found accord with God, Gildas was free to further explore this same relationship between God and 'His people' and bring it up to date. Preparatory to introducing the Saxons, in chapter twenty-three, it was essential to his thesis that he place the entire onus of responsibility for the final disaster with which they were associated on the Britons. That the Saxons could have achieved success against the Britons while they remained under divine protection was, for Gildas, an impossibility. The present plight of the Britons could, therefore, only be explained in the context of God's withholding such protection. Indeed, their impact was so profound that Gildas found it necessary to interpret the Saxons not merely as an evil which God had failed to deflect but, additionally, as one which He had Himself deployed. The mechanics of this were two-fold: in one sense, the Saxons were to be characterised as 'just punishment for the crimes which had gone before';[103] in another, they were self-inflicted in the sense of being invited by the Britons, albeit in a fit of blindness.[104] The Britons must, therefore, have lapsed from their true obedience and turned away from God to an extent which was wholly unprecedented in their historical experience.

In the closing lines of chapter twenty, and in a long chapter twenty-one, Gildas therefore indulged in a fulsome, but anonymous and highly generalised, condemnation of a time of peace and plenty which he interpreted as undermined by sin.[105] In this respect it should be contrasted with the periods of Christian peace prior to, and then post-dating, Diocletian, which had been sustained by a bare adequacy of virtue. For greater effect, he reintroduced the *epistola* theme with which he had begun his work, by quoting from the opening line of chapter five of St Paul's *Letter to the Corinthians*. St Paul's role as a self-proclaimed apostle to the gentiles had, of course, a clear relevance to Gildas's own perception of his own role.

Once more, his comments concerning the past mirror the present: his condemnation of sexual immorality echoes his attacks on the five tyrants of his own day;[106] the perversion of peace by civil war mirrors his comments on his own lifetime;[107] the welcoming of Satan replicates the appearance of the devil in chapter twenty-six and thereafter; his comments on the fate of mild kings is perhaps reflected in the murder by Maglocunus of his uncle,[108] and perhaps even the decline of the church as a *princeps*.[109] Even the rhetorical devices recur. The use of thesis and antithesis in chapter twenty-one, for instance, was to be taken up once more in those carefully crafted passages in which Gildas would generalise concerning the shortcomings of contemporary British kingship, in chapter twenty-seven, and priests, in chapter sixty-six.

Gildas concluded this condemnation by first appealing to the authority of the prophet Isaiah, from whose opening words he quoted at length.[110] His gloomy utterings in expectation of the disasters about to befall Judah for her disobedience to God fitted precisely with Gildas's anticipation at this stage of Britain's destruction by the Saxons for reasons which he believed were directly comparable.

At the last, he reinforced the currency of this condemnation: 'then as now, contempt was being poured on the princes, so that they were being seduced by their follies and wandered in the trackless desert'. The term 'princes' (*principes*) recalls Gildas's lament in his opening chapter, that the church had been a 'prince over provinces'.[111] So did he represent the British leadership already far-gone on its steep decline to the moral basement wherein it was resident in his own day.

Behind the rhetoric, therefore, Gildas was using this section (chapter twenty, verse two, to twenty-one, six) of the *DEB* to remind his audience once more that God was disposed to aid his people only when they were obedient to Him. By rehearsing their sins, he was able to place the full responsibility for later disasters on the wickedness into which the Britons had fallen. So as to reinforce that message, he spent more time and effort than hitherto in defining those sins, and called on biblical authority to underline the inexorable nature of their consequences. There can be little doubt that the sins which Gildas foists on this anonymous community are no more than a literary device required by his own rhetoric, so as to sustain his argument that God's aid in current circumstances was being withheld on account of the moral failings of the Britons. Only the period of peace itself is, perhaps, historical, since by this stage Gildas was approaching the present sufficiently closely to be cautious of gross misrepresentation of the body of knowledge concerning the recent past which was presumably common at the time of writing.[112]

Gildas had, therefore, explained away the protection once afforded by the Romans by reference to British rebellion. He had underlined the incompetence of the Britons when set free of both Roman tutelage and divine protection, drawing out and emphasising his message by a description of subsequent (but unhistorical and unavailing) efforts by Roman forces to protect Britain by expedition. The Britons were as if little children – even chicks – devoid of the protection of their parents, the stalwart

Romans. In chapter twenty-one he claimed that God, too, had been rejected by His people, leaving the Britons defenceless in the face of their enemies. Both these disasters stemmed directly from the unnatural and wicked disobedience of the Britons.

Having turned once more away from God, the Britons would again appeal to Rome (via 'Agitius'), but on this occasion to no avail. In Gildas's opinion, the Britons had been slow to take what he portrayed as Roman advice and take courage themselves,[113] although even military virtues required the complaisance of the Lord. Without such virtues the Britons were even more heavily dependent on divine protection than they would otherwise have been – and Gildas repeatedly emphasised the martial qualities of the God of the Hebrews which could have sustained them if only they had not thrown away His aid through disobedience. It was Gildas's opinion that the restoration of British obedience to that muscular God, in combination with a renewed fortitude in war, offered the only hope of success against the barbarian oppressors of the present.

At this point, therefore, Gildas had set the stage for the appearance of the Saxons, and the 'damages and afflictions' of the present of which they (under God) were the cause (or perhaps in his view rather the symptom). Their arrival and breakout would be his subject in chapters twenty-two to twenty-four.

Notes

1   M. Winterbottom, ed. and trans., *Gildas: the Ruin of Britain and Other Works*, London and Chichester, 1977, pp. 87–142.

2   Winterbottom, *Gildas*, p. 10, footnote 6; M. W. Herren, 'Gildas and early British monasticism', in *Britain 400–600: Language and History*, eds A. Bammesberger and A. Wollmann, Heidelberg, 1990, p. 66.

3   C. E. Stevens, 'Gildas Sapiens', *English Historical Review*, LVI, 1941, pp. 353–73; T. D. O'Sullivan, *The De Excidio of Gildas, its Authenticity and Date*, Leiden, 1978; E. A. Thompson, 'Gildas and the history of Britain', *Britannia*, X, 1979, pp. 203–26 and XI, 1980, p. 344; P. Sims-Williams, 'Gildas and the Anglo-Saxons', *Cambridge Medieval Celtic Studies*, VI, 1983, pp. 1–30; M. Lapidge and D. N. Dumville, eds, *Gildas: New Approaches*, Woodbridge, 1984; F, Kerlouégan, *Le De Excidio Britanniae De Gildas*, Paris, 1987.

4   Eusebius: *Eusebius, the Ecclesiastical History and the Martyrs of*

Palestine, trans. H. J. Lawlor and J. E. L. Oulton, London, I, 1927: Gildas had access to the Latin translation of Rufinus.

5 R. W. Hanning, *The Vision of History in Early Britain*, New York and London, 1966, pp. 23–32.

6 Orosius, *Histories*.

7 R. P. C. Hanson, 'The Church in fifth-century Gaul: evidence from Sidonius Apollinaris', *Journal of Ecclesiastical History*, XXI, 1970, pp. 1–10.

8 Salvian, *De Gubernatione dei libri viii*, in *Salviani Presbyteri Massiliensis Opera Omnia*, ed. F. Pauly, Vindobonae, 1883, pp. 1–200. This work dates from the years 439×451. The extract quoted is IV, 54.

9 Salvian, *De Gubernatione*, VII, 1, 24.

10 Hanning, *Vision*, pp. 46–8.

11 Kerlouégan, *De Excidio*, pp. 92–3.

12 Salvian, *De Gubernatione*, opening line of the preface.

13 Kerlouégan, *De Excidio*, pp. 31–5.

14 Gildas used this term in the opening line of his prologue, *DEB*, I, 1, and referred to the Epistles of St Paul in chapters I, 10; XXI, 2, then more extensively in C–CV. For discussion, see M. Winterbottom, 'The Preface of Gildas' *De Excidio*', *Transactions of the Honorary Society of Cymmrodorian*, 1974–5, pp. 278–80.

15 As in *DEB*, I, 7–10, quoting Matthew VIII, 11, 12; XV, 24, 26, the Epistle of St Paul to the Romans, XI, 17, and Acts, IV, 32, each of which offer this message. See discussion, p. 80.

16 See below, p. 52.

17 *DEB*, I, 1: the reference here to *miseriae* ('miseries') is one to which Gildas was to allude repeatedly, as in XVIII, 2 (*miserabilis*) and XXV, 1 (*miserae*).

18 E.g. *DEB*, XXVI, 4.

19 Winterbottom, *Gildas*, p. 8; M. Lapidge, 'Gildas's education and the Latin culture of sub-Roman Britain', in Lapidge and Dumville, *Gildas: New Approaches*, 27–50; N. Wright, 'Gildas's prose style and its origins', *ibid.*, pp. 107–28.

20 Specifically, kings in *DEB*, XXVII–LXV and the clergy in LXVI–CX. Compare the approach of Salvian, who did not distinguish between Romans and Gauls but impugned the morals of the entire Romano-Gaulish population and its leaders.

21 Kerlouégan, *De Excidio*, p. 547; see below, p. 77.

22 *DEB*, XXVI, 1.

23 As he was keen to emphasise: e.g. *DEB*, LXXXIX, 3–4.

24 Hanning, *Vision*, pp. 46–7.

25 Orosius, *Histories*, I, 1.

26 Cf. Eusebius, who began his Imperial *History* with Christ's birth:

I, 5. By contrast, Orosius began with Adam and Salvian with reference to the philosophers of ancient Greece.

27   *DEB*, XLIV, 2; Hanning, *Vision*, p. 6.

28   Cf. arguments of D. A. Brooks, 'Gildas' *De excidio Britanniae*: its revolutionary meaning and purpose', *Studia Celtica*, XVIII–XIX, 1983–4, pp. 1–10.

29   Hanning, *Vision*, p. 57.

30   Bede, *HE*, I, 22, which has found recent support, for example, in C. E. Stevens, 'Gildas Sapiens', pp. 572–3.

31   See above, and *DEB*, IX, 2. This was, of course, likewise providential history.

32   Thompson, 'Gildas', comes dangerously close to so doing: *passim*.

33   Hanning, *Vision*, p. 57.

34   Be they the Testaments or Church histories. For recent comment, see N. Wright, 'Did Gildas read Orosius?', *Cambridge Medieval Celtic Studies*, IX, 1985, pp. 31–42.

35   *DEB*, II: his ten 'plagues' therein approximate to the plagues affecting Egypt in Exodus and the ten persecutions of Christians under Rome, in Orosius, *Histories*, VII, xxv, 13.

36   *DEB*, III, 3–4: compare Genesis II as the probable inspiration for this paradisal landscape; for discussion of its originality, N. J. Higham, 'Old light on the Dark Age landscape: the description of Britain in the *De Excidio Britanniae* of Gildas', *Journal of Historical Geography*, XVII, 1991, p. 368. See also above, note 26: in this respect Gildas offered lipservice to Orosius's example but, in selecting a starting point for his own sequence, followed Eusebius.

37   As laid out in *DEB*, I, 13–14, and IV, 1, which was a condition to which the Britions easily returned: viz, XII, 3, XXI, XXII–XXIII, XXVI. The quotation is from IV, 1. This and, unless otherwise stated, all other translations are the author's.

38   Lapidge, 'Gildas's education', pp. 27–50.

39   *DEB*, IV, 3.

40   Thompson, 'Gildas', p. 203.

41   As Eusebius; cf. the views of Salvian.

42   E.g. *DEB*, V, l.

43   *DEB*, VIII.

44   *DEB*, VI, 1; XXIII, 3, 4.

45   E.g. *DEB*, XXXIII, 4; LXXIV, 1, but see p. 55.

46   *DEB*, XXV, 1; XXVI, 4.

47   *DEB*, VIII, based on Rufinus's translation of Eusebius.

48   So sustaining his fundamental characterisation of the Britons as sinful; see note 37 above.

49   I.e. from Tiberius (AD 14–37) to Diocletian (284–305). whether

31

or not he knew their precise dates, his readings in Church histories require that Gildas knew that a long period had elapsed.

50 *DEB*, IX; see Orosius, *Histories*, VII, 25, 13.

51 *DEB*, IX, 2.

52 E.g. *DEB*, LXXIII–LXXV.

53 *DEB*, X, 1. Note the similarity of imagery in VIII, 1.

54 *DEB*, X, 2. See discussion of this passage, p. 103.

55 Constantius of Lyons, *The Life of St. Germanus*, in *The Western Fathers*, ed. and trans. F. R. Hoare, London and New York, 1954, XVI.

56 But this would require that he did have one insular written source, despite his assertion to the contrary in *DEB*, IV, 4, but he may have been making reference to this under 'Church Histories', *DEB*, IX, 2. An oral source is entirely adequate as an explanation of Gildas's familiarity with this miracle story. See also Kerlouégan, *De Excidio*, pp. 64–5.

57 Which was based in turn on Joshua, III, 14, 17.

58 *Lupus* as Scots and Picts: *DEB*, XVI, 1; as Saxons, XXIII, 1; as the devil, XXXIV, 3–4; as Maglocunus, XXXIV, 3–4.

59 Gildas makes repeated use of the shepherd-sheep, wolf-lamb analogies so beloved of New Testament authors.

60 *DEB*, XII, 1.

61 *DEB*, XII, 3, but obviously referring back to I, 13–14, IV.

62 *DEB*, XIII, 2. Magnus Maximus was, of course, of Iberian extraction but Gildas fails to acknowledge that fact and may well either have been ignorant of it or have chosen to ignore it. For further comment, see p. 155.

63 *DEB*, XIV.

64 Hanning, *Vision*, p. 51.

65 *DEB*, XIV, 1; see discussion in N. Wright, 'Gildas's geographical perspective: some problems', in *Gildas: New Approaches*, pp. 86–96; N. J. Higham, 'Gildas, Roman walls and British dykes', *Cambridge Medieval Celtic Studies*, XXII, 1991, p. 2, particularly footnote 3.

66 E.g. Orosius, *Histories*, VII, 43, for Constantine III.

67 *DEB*, XII, 3, although his quotation from the Pelagian text, *De Virginitate*, VI, in *DEB*, XXXVIII, 2, betrays no recognition that Pelagianism was heretical, nor what it was: Winterbottom, *Gildas*, p. 153.

68 *DEB*, XIII, 1.

69 Cf. the sentiments expressed in *DEB*, IV, 4, and Orosius, *Histories*, V, xxii, 7.

70 Cf. *DEB*, XIII, XXI, 4, and Orosius, *Histories*, VII, xl, 4–7; xlii, 1–6. Gildas may have been confused by the appearance of a second Maximus as Caesar in succession to Constans: *Histories*, VII, xlii, 15.

71 *Ibid.*, VII, xlii, 15.

72   As Wright, 'Orosius', p. 35.

73   Ambrosius Aurelianus: *DEB*, XXV, 3. See below, p. 45.

74   As argued by M. Miller, 'Stilicho's Pictish War', *Britannia*, VI, 1975, pp. 141–50; see also Thompson, 'Gildas', pp. 206–7; Sims-Williams, 'Gildas', p. 15; D. N. Dumville, 'The chronology of *De Excidio Britanniae*, Book I', in Lapidge and Dumville, *Gildas: New Approaches*, p. 64; Higham, 'Gildas, Roman Walls', p. 6.

75   Ammianus Marcellinus, *Historia*, ed. T. E. Page, trans. J. C. Rolfe, London, 1935, XXI, 1, XXVII, 8. In terming Britain a 'watchtower', Orosius may have been signalling a general perception of the island diocese as the outer bastion of the Gaulish Prefecture against barbarian attack: *Histories*, I, ii, 70.

76   N. J. Higham, *Rome, Britain and the Anglo-Saxons*, London, 1992, pp. 216–26.

77   Cf. Orosius, *Histories*, VII, xvii, 7, who followed the widespread late-Roman practice of attributing at least one of the northern walls to Septimius Severus; Thompson, 'Gildas', p. 206, footnote 19. That Gildas offered an entirely different origin for both walls suggests either that he overlooked this reference or that he was confident that others would be ignorant of it.

78   Kerlouégan, *De Excidio*, pp. 548–53.

79   *DEB*, XVIII, 1.

80   *DEB*, VI, 2.

81   Cf. Thompson, 'Gildas', p. 207.

82   Thompson, 'Zosimus 6.10.2 and the letters of Honorius', *Classical Quarterly*, XXX, 1982, pp. 445–62; Higham, *Rome*, p. 73.

83   Cf. Sims-Williams, 'Gildas', p. 29.

84   Higham, 'Gildas, Roman walls', *passim*.

85   *DEB*, XXIV, 3.

86   *DEB*, XXVI, 2.

87   *DEB*, XIX, 4.

88   *DEB*, VII, 1; XXV, 1.

89   *DEB*, XV, 1.

90   *DEB*, XVII, 1.

91   Lamentations, II, 10.

92   *DEB*, XX, 1.

93   See pp. 120–37.

94   *DEB*, XXIII, 1.

95   *DEB*, XXI.

96   *DEB*, XII, 3.

97   *DEB*, XX, 2; as in Israel, for example, before the Exodus.

98   As were the Israelites in Egypt or Babylon, and Gildas probably had biblical analogies in mind here.

99   *DEB*, VI, 2; VII, 1.

100   *DEB*, XV, 2; XIX, 3, 4.

101   *DEB*, XXV, 1–3.

102   *DEB*, LXXII, 4. For discussion of the topographical context, see p. 44. The stoning refers to St Stephen (I, 11, *et al.*) and the other forms of martyrdom to St Alban (X, 2 to XI, 2) and others variously mentioned in the text.

103   Opening lines of *DEB*, XXIV, 1.

104   *DEB*, XXIII.

105   The passage is reminiscent of Orosius's comments on Sodom and Gomorrah (*Histories*, I, V, 8) and may well have been influenced thereby.

106   *DEB*, XXVII–LXV; see pp. 174–90. Gildas probably drew his inspiration from Jeremiah, III, 1–9.

107   *DEB*, XXVI, 2.

108   *DEB*, XXXIII, 4 and see above, p. 21.

109   *DEB*, I, 5.

110   Isaiah, I, 4–6.

111   See note 109 above, and p. 71.

112   Sims-Williams, 'Gildas', pp. 18–19; see p. 35.

113   Although his reference to 'bravest soldiers' in *DEB*, I, 2, may imply that Gildas recognised some contemporary Britons as valorous. He was, however, perhaps here using *miles* metaphorically in the Christian sense of 'soldier of Christ', so as a committed and virtuous believer, as opposed to soldier in the literal sense. The metaphorical sense is certainly uppermost in I, 16, where Gildas refers to 'excellent military recruits of Christ', using the term *tirones* which is similarly literal only in a military context. See discussion, p. 158.

2

Gildas and the Saxons

As already established, Gildas was not writing an objective, historical account of British history but a piece of dialectic which utilised the past to establish a system of causality appropriate to the present. The historicity of case studies which Gildas drew from the remote past were conditioned only by the possibility that members of his audience were familiar with the same anecdotes as he had drawn from the accessible literature. Where such did not exist – from chapter fourteen onwards – the only test of his accuracy is the general knowledge of recent events which we can safely assume that Gildas shared with his audience, with whose experiences and recollections his examples needed to be consistent if he were not to lose credibility.[1]

This test is valid only for his geographical introduction (chapter three) and for that later section of his 'historical' introduction which apparently derives either from oral traditions only one or two generations old at the time of writing, or from retrospective reconstruction on the basis of observation of the current situation.[2] The assumption that the sequence of events which Gildas offered is broadly correct from chapter twenty onwards may be justified, despite the fact that no part of it can be verified from an alternative source. The following outline may, therefore, be historical, but it is important to note that Gildas only lost the freedom to manipulate, or even invent, the past, as his episodic narrative approached the present. The historicity of the earliest elements in this sequence may be extremely generalised,[3] and the moral context in which he placed each was clearly of his own making, but the actual sequence commands some respect:

1 At the start of this recent, 'historical' account, the Britons were threatened by attacks from the Picts and Scots.
2 They therefore appealed to 'Agitius' for aid but without success.
3 They then themselves repulsed their enemies, although raids never entirely ceased.
4 In the expectation of renewed assault and devoid of Roman aid, a British ruler, in consultation with his counsellors, hired Saxon mercenaries to bolster their defences against the Picts and Scots.

Arrival and revolt: the coming of the Saxons

With the benefit of hindsight, Gildas interpreted the invitation to the Saxons as the most fundamental act of stupidity for which the British leadership had, to date, been responsible. He did this in a philosophical context which focused on his interpretation of the relationship between the Britons and God, bringing that to a long premeditated crisis at this point in his account.

As he approached this goal, Gildas was at pains to build his sense of climax, and expectation of imminent disaster, to the steepest pitch possible. To that end he first re-emphasised the charity of God,[4] portraying the Lord by analogy as both doctor and father of the Britons: God wished to 'purge' (or 'make well') His family, which was 'infected' by 'evil'.[5] He would later extend this metaphor, interpreting what may have been a memorable pestilence (if an opportune one) as another God-sent warning.[6] Total responsibility for their later 'afflictions' lay, therefore, with the Britons, who had ignored the advice of a God here exemplified by two figures of benign and charitable authority, both as their doctor and father.

Gildas continued to build expectation of imminent disaster by biblical quotation, first turning to the Proverbs of Solomon to emphasise the inherently rough, unresponsive and servile character of the Britons,[7] then with reference to a plague such as bears comparison with those instruments of divine will which are commonplace in the Old Testament.[8] Thereafter, he turned to the Book of Isaiah, a prophet whose anticipation of the catastrophe of the Babylonian sack of Jerusalem was particularly appropriate to his context. He quoted at length, from his comments concerning Judah, a passage pregnant with foreboding.[9] Any of his readers

who were familiar with this passage would perhaps have known
how it would continue:[10]

the Lord will carry thee away with a mighty captivity ...

He will surely violently turn and toss thee like a ball ...

I will drive thee from thy station, and from thy state shall he pull
thee down.

The gloomy predictions of Isaiah preface Jeremiah's Lament on
the fall of Jerusalem and the Babylonian captivity of the Israelites.
Gildas used it to introduce, and so characterise the magnitude of
the ruin and conquest of Britain which was about to occur at the
hands of the Saxons. That ruin was, in Gildas's opinion, consequent upon the criminal stupidity of the Britons and their invitation to the Saxons. Pausing only to make a brief reference to the
dark and apocalyptic vision of Abraham,[11] he then offered a
highly rhetorical and condemnatory interpretation of the decision-
making process which brought the first Saxons into Britain, which
almost obscures, under a wave of rhetoric, what was necessarily
an essentially factual basis.

Gildas still retained his medical metaphor to this point: the
Britons were 'struck blind' by a 'blindness of the mind',[12] but God
(apparently now out of patience with His patients) made no new
effort to treat their complaint sympathetically. It was at this point
that great rents begin to appear in His charity and the protective
role in which He had hitherto been invested in this text.

Like the Picts and Scots,[13] the Saxons were portrayed as wolves
attacking the flock of (Christian) sheep,[14] but Gildas now went far
further in his use of animal imagery, pulling together the several
references already made to savage beasts such as lions[15] and
dogs,[16] and depicting Britain and its inhabitants under attack
from the claws of brutal carnivores. Their extreme ferocity –
ferocissimus – was one characteristic which Gildas chose to highlight. Another was a criminal duplicity which he attributed to
them even at this early stage, and emphasised by thesis and antithesis. In his imaginative repertoire, the Saxons were not fully
human but rather savage animals, devils or brutal heathen: hence
their name was taboo; they were 'hated by man and God';[17] they
were 'sacrilegious ones of the east',[18] equivalent to the brutal
Assyrians and heathen oppressors of the Israelites in the Old
Testament.[19]

Notwithstanding the rhetoric and the moralising content of this passage, the *DEB* provides a basis of sorts for the historical reconstruction of these events. The employment of a small contingent of Saxons was a decision taken by a British council and implemented by a 'proud tyrant', so (with the pejorative element stripped out[20]) by an individual whom Gildas might otherwise have described as a king.[21] His play on *superbus tyrannus* may mean that the ruler concerned was indeed the Vortigern of Bede's narrative and the Amiens text of the *DEB*.[22] That this was no petty local chieftain ruling a small locality is implicit in Gildas's parallelling of the council and tyrant by the 'petty princes of Zion . . . giving foolish advice to Pharaoh'.[23] He consistently generalised concerning Britain and the Britons,[24] and seems to have seen the whole of what had been Roman Britain as a single political system at the point when Magnus Maximus led it into a sinful rebellion against Rome. He had been careful to represent the 'age of tyrants' as a continuum, through arboreal metaphors, in chapter thirteen: Britain was overwhelmed by 'tyrant thickets' which were growing into a 'savage forest', of which Magnus Maximus was merely one seed, albeit the only one named. He was certainly not the last, since Gildas attacked five of his own contemporaries under the same title. 'Vortigern' is the next such figure in Gildas's text after Magnus Maximus and he had certainly not anywhere stated that any fundamental division of Roman Britain had occurred in the interim. On the contrary, his very generalised comment on civil wars (in chapter twenty-one) implies that he thought of Britain as still under single rule to this point:

> If anyone of them [the kings] seemed gentler and somewhat more inclined to the truth, he was characterised as an overthrower of *Britannia* and the hatred and weapons of all were hurled [at him] without respect.

Given the universality of this image, such a king could only be ruler of all of what had been Roman Britain, Gildas's *patria*, or 'fatherland'. 'Vortigern' was the next ruler named. Whether or not he was in control of the old diocese or only a large part of it must remain uncertain, if only because it is not clear that Gildas had knowledge sufficient to sustain the accuracy of his own text, but there are no grounds whatever within that text to imagine that 'Vortigern' was king only over part of Britain. He was presumably, therefore, a man whose rule Gildas was content to portray as universal. It necessarily included that east coast of Britain, where the Saxons were about to be established,[25] and Gildas may well have been correct in portraying it as all-encompassing.

Had a Roman general in Gaul sent troops to Britain in the first half of the fifth century, they would almost certainly have consisted predominately of barbarian cohorts. With such aid withheld by 'Agitius', it was but a short step for a British ruler to make a direct approach to the barbarian world to hire soldiers. By so doing, he and his advisors were exhibiting a continuing adherence to a long-established system of government, and military recruitment, within the Empire.

Options did exist: Roman forces were also recruited from provincials in the late Empire, but demands on their estate manpower are likely to have been resisted by the landed aristocrats who were probably a powerful lobby in 'Vortigern's' council. Additionally, such raw recruits needed both training and arms – neither of which were obviously available once Constantine III had led parts of the British garrison to Gaul (in 407) and ceased to pay the remainder (at latest, at his death in 410–11). On several counts, therefore, there are grounds for thinking that 'Vortigern' and his advisors may have decided that the recruiting of barbarian mercenaries was the optimum method of improving British security.

Barbarians from different backgrounds were used by the Romans for different military tasks. The British government first required that they could themselves make contact and deliver an invitation, then that their mercenaries could reach Britain over the sea. That alone may have necessitated hiring men from a nearby, sea-going people. Furthermore, the attacks which the British council sought to deter were consistently portrayed as sea borne,[26] so the troops they required needed experience of boats and the capacity to intercept enemy raiders in coastal waters and to threaten their ships, once beached, from the sea, much as late Roman coastal garrisons seem to have done. Given that the Britons would presumably have preferred not to employ Picts and Scots against their own kin, the 'Saxons' – in late Classical writing a generic term for the seafaring peoples of Atlantic Germany – were the only obvious and available source of suitable barbarians. The Romans had deployed other units of marines in Britain, but no other source of ship-using mercenaries was accessible to the

Britons and their rulers, so the Saxons it had to be. If they were to be deployed against sea-borne Pictish – but not Scottish – raids, the obvious place for them to be stationed to defend the coasts of southern Britain would have been on the North Sea coast, perhaps at the northern end of the 'Saxon Shore', so in East Anglia, quintessentially 'on the east side of the island'.[27]

That the Saxons were then already 'feared worse than death'[28] is entirely incompatible with the decision to employ them. Indeed, Gildas recalls no earlier example of Saxon attack. Since comment on such would have massively reinforced his condemnation of the stupidity of the *superbus tyrannus*, and his advisors, this may mean that he knew of none. The British decision to employ Germanic soldiers itself implies that Britain had seen little of Saxon incursions since the putative attack of 410, a long time before, supposing this to have been an historical event – something which is in any case now in question.[29] Gildas's condemnation must therefore be his own, highly retrospective, judgement on a decision which, at the time, may have appeared of little consequence and only of marginal interest. That decision was entirely in accord with whatever recent Roman precedents as were pertinent to these matters are likely to have been familiar to Britain's rulers, and this circumstance, in turn, is likely to have reduced any debate on the issue to a formality. Even at this stage, therefore, the government of Britain was apparently conditioned by Roman practices.

That the Saxons were, *ab initio*, to be treated as if Roman soldiers is implicit in Gildas's comments: they were to be 'invited under one roof' – a phrase reminiscent of the standard late Roman practice of 'hospitality' – *hospitalitas* – by which soldiers on temporary placements or when travelling were normally billeted on provincials. The second, uninvited and larger group of Saxons who followed on were similarly accommodated by *hospites* and given *annona* ('grain tax') and *epimenia* ('monthly doles of provisions') – terms with a technical meaning both in the tax system and in the quartermaster's office of the late Roman army.[30] They were additionally subject to a *foedus* – a 'treaty' – which allowed them provisions in return for frontier service. Such arrangements imply that 'Vortigern' and his advisors were familiar with the detail, as well as the generality, of standard Roman practices of the day and modelled their own employment of barbarian mercenaries directly on recent Roman practice. The Saxons were *foederati*.[31] Given the maritime nature of the attacks they were employed to deter, the British coastline, not the northern wall, was naturally the frontier on which they were deployed.

The initial group was small. If the number is not apocryphal,[32] it was no more than could be carried in three ships, so perhaps scarcely more than 100 men. Late Roman fort garrisons along the British frontiers were often of this order, so such a force would presumably have been considered viable in the first half of the fifth century, for the purpose stated. That Gildas knew of auguries – such as would certainly have been undertaken before departing from Germany[33] – and the Germanic term for ships,[34] implies considerable familiarity on his part with Saxons and things Saxon,[35] if not necessarily personal acquaintance with individual Saxons. The three hundred years of Gildas's version again suggests a folklore element, but this may be other than Saxon in origin. If Gildas took it upon himself to reconstruct an augury of which he knew little or nothing except the probability that such had been taken, he may have sought inspiration in Virgil, in which case it is possible that he noted a passage very similar to his own, which occurs in book I (lines 272–3): '*hic iam ter centum totos regnabitur annos gente Hectorea*' ('this now will be ruled for the entirety of thrice one hundred years by the people of Hector'). Comparison of Gildas's: '*ter centum annis patriam*', and his own later use (in chapter twenty-four, verse two) of *gens* in the context of the Saxons, suggests that his text depends more on the *Aeneid* than on the actual wording of whatever augury had actually been taken in distant Saxony, before the first mercenaries even set sail.

Gildas's reconstruction of this detail may, therefore, betray a greater general knowledge of the manner in which contemporary Saxons set about making decisions concerning important events, than a specific knowledge of the original. Even so, such putative fabrication is confined to a theatre of activities which is exclusively Saxon. Concerning those matters which could have been reported to him by well-informed Britons – such as pertain to the decision-making process and the conditions of Saxon employment – Gildas's account is devoid of the miraculous, and of elements which are obviously derived from folklore. On the contrary, his information betrays considerable comprehension of late Roman practice, both in the generation which invited in the Saxons and that for which

he himself wrote. Gildas's contextualisation of the British employment of Saxons is, therefore, generally plausible, and lends a
significant degree of historicity to the entirety of this episode.

The second group of arrivals was larger than the first, but not
so large as to be beyond the means of 'Vortigern' and his advisors
to employ them and attempt their maintenance. Large numbers
are not even implicit in Gildas's comments, which are relatively
clear on this point.[36]

The Saxons eventually rebelled. Gildas offered three explanations for this rebellion:

1 It was a consequence of their inherent duplicity, but this is
really no more than a literary device of his own fashioning
designed in retrospect to emphasise the folly which he had
already caused to become attached to the initial decision to
employ them, so underlining the 'self-inflicted' nature of subsequent disasters. This entire argument was part of Gildas's
moral contextualisation of the Saxon *adventus* and has no
claim to be historical.

2 The Saxons complained about specific incidents – presumably
incidents which involved both Britons and Saxons and which
had inflamed feelings on both sides. Gildas loyally supported
the British interpretation, so represented the Saxons as 'colour-
ing incidents purposely', but he did not go further into detail,
leaving a modern audience with the analogy of similar incidents
between foreign garrisons and the indigenes in other, later,
war zones.

3 The Saxons complained also of the insufficiency of their
supplies.

Collectively, the latter two of these complaints provide a realistic
context for the rebellion, but Saxon demands may have stretched
to more than these, for Gildas reported that: 'they declared that
they would break the treaty and ravage the whole of the island
unless a more generous benevolence (*profusior munificentia*) be
heaped up for them'.

With Roman control of Britain in abeyance after 410, her rulers
had little or no coinage, so no obvious means of paying troops
short of collecting precious metal in the form of bullion. A 'more
generous benevolence' perhaps implies not so much more food-
stuffs as payments of a different kind, equivalent to the sort of *ex*

gratia payment in coin or bullion which a Roman general might make to his troops – or the booty that the Saxons might hope to gain by raiding. In his own reconstruction of these events, based exclusively on Gildas's testimony, Bede quite logically assumed that the mercenaries would have received *stipendia*,[37] and in this he may well have accurately reflected the expectations of the soldiers themselves. The bulk of the stock of precious metals then in Britain appears, from hoard evidence, to have been in the form of obsolete coinage, of table ware and similar vessels in aristocratic households,[38] or of religious accessories.[39] Such goods were not easily accessible to a government which arguably depended heavily on the support of the wealthy, landholding aristocrats – the natural councillors to whom Gildas had perhaps already referred – even should it wish to be more generous towards its barbarian soldiery. The result was a breakdown of the relationship between British authority and Saxon warriors. Their revolt was a direct consequence of the several grievances which had developed during their period of service in Britain, which Gildas characterised as 'a long time' – whatever such an imprecise period actually signifies.

Gildas described the Saxon rebellion in lurid terms. He pressed into service a series of graphic biblical parallels,[40] emphasised the barbarity and sacrilegious quality of the initial Saxon raid from 'sea to sea',[41] and highlighted their destruction of the towns of Roman Britain.[42] The employment of an extended metaphor concerning fire to describe the Saxon impact is reminiscent of hell, and was surely intended so to be.[43] To Gildas, the Saxons, like the Picts and Scots, were responsible for the destruction of the 'Romanity' of Britain, which was a quality to which he attached a high value. Within that 'Romanity' towns clearly played a focal role.[44] He had a consistently urban and suburban view of the Romano-British Church,[45] and here portrayed the fall of the British cities from a specifically ecclesiastical and congregational standpoint:[46] 'thus all the towns (*coloniae*) were overthrown by the repeated battering of enemy rams; and all the townsfolk with the leaders of the church, with the priests and the people.'

The damage wrought by the Saxons was portrayed as analogous with those other archetypal disasters familiar to Gildas and those of his audience who shared his Classical and biblical education – the sack of Troy, the fall of Jerusalem to Nebuchadnezzar,[47] to which Gildas referred in chapter twenty-four, choosing a line which made specific reference to the *templum sanctum* – 'the holy temple', and the destruction of Sodom and Gomorrah, which may also be relevant here, given Gildas's insistence that few if any souls were worthy of salvation and that the 'vineyard had degenerated into sourness'.[48]

At the opening of chapter twenty-five, Gildas sensationalised the consequences for the Britons: in language clearly reminiscent of his comments on the impact of the Romans,[49] and then the northern barbarians,[50] he described some as being killed by the Saxons and more as surrendering themselves into slavery in the hope of finding food; of these some too were slain – a fate which Gildas thought preferable to the notion of perpetual slavery to barbarians.[51] Others migrated overseas and Gildas put into their mouths a particularly apt extract from psalm 44:[52]

> But thou has cast off, and put us to shame;
> And goest not forth with our armies.
> Thou makest us to turn back from the enemy:
> And they which hate us spoil for themselves.
> Thou hast given us like sheep appointed for meat;
> And hast scattered us among the heathen.

Others escaped into the wilderness. Just as Gildas had portrayed the Britons resisting Diocletian,[53] then the Picts and Scots,[54] from the wild, so did he now portray the Britons as capable of resistance to the Saxons only from a comparable station, albeit only with God's aid. That the wilderness was an appropriate place to find shelter from small numbers of marauding barbarians seems reasonable enough, but Gildas was more interested in other aspects of this association: that the wilderness or desert was the proper place for the Britons to renew their relationship with God was an attractive concept which was familiar to him from the Bible,[55] and perhaps also from his acquaintance with the ideals and practice of contemporary insular monasticism.[56] It is at this point, therefore, that Gildas was able to reintroduce the notion of God's charity towards the delinquent Britons (last experienced briefly in chapter twenty, verse two, in directly comparable circumstances), and his capacity to succour those who had renewed themselves spiritually and returned to obedience, in the wilderness. He did this in what were by now entirely conventional terms which were already familiar to his audience through repetition in the context of the more distant past.

With the Saxons returned to the east from their initial, devastating and almost universal, cross-Britain raid, the Britons organised a resistance which was partially successful. Since it was essential to Gildas's dialectic that all British victories be attributed to God, those responsible had necessarily to be portrayed as worthy recipients of His help. Hence his portrayal of the Britons in the wilderness, who 'burdened heaven with unnumbered "prayers" that they should not be altogether destroyed'.[57] The survivors rallied around one Ambrosius Aurelianus and offered resistance to their tormentors.

Ambrosius Aurelianus was the first insular figure certainly named by Gildas since Magnus Maximus,[58] and he plays an important role in the text. Since he was the grandfather of (apparently) prominent contemporaries of the author he was necessarily an historical figure,[59] and was, potentially at least, familiar as such to his own audience. If those grandsons were much younger than Gildas himself – and they could easily have been up to twenty-three years his juniors while still being adults in the modern sense – it is not inconceivable that Ambrosius Aurelianus was still alive, if an old man, at the time of composition. But Gildas's treatment of him was not an exercise in historical biography, however brief. It was an essential of his dialectic that British leaders who were known to have achieved victory over barbarians be portrayed as deserving of divine aid on grounds of their superior Christian virtues, else their deeds might threaten the causal relationship between divine approbation and British success which Gildas was here seeking to sustain: for his victory to be consistent with the logic internal to the *De Excidio*, it was essential that Ambrosius Aurelianus be portrayed as a leader of exceptional virtues whose obedience to God had persuaded the Lord to give him victory. He was depicted, therefore, as a model leader in harmony with God's will and obedient to it, a *vir modestus*, in contrast to the *superbus tyrannus* who had invited them in.[60]

The late Roman aristocracy had long memories concerning illustrious antecedents and connections, however distant.[61] If Ambrosius Aurelianus's grandchildren were still influential at the time of writing, their lineage may have been known to Gildas. It is possible that Ambrosius was a distant relative of one of the imperial families sprung from the west, such as the house of Theodosius which had branches flourishing in Spain, at least until

45

the campaigns of Constantine III.[62] It may be that he was of continental (so 'Roman') descent or had come to Britain thence himself.[63]

This does not, however, explain Gildas's interest in him or his descent. The claim that Ambrosius Aurelianus enjoyed a Roman lineage which was then virtually unique in Britain was designed rather to associate him with the God-derived (so legitimate) authority and military virtues which Gildas consistently ascribed to the Romans.[64] The allusion to imperial descent placed his authority on a par with that of the emperors who had been the victims of the iniquities of that 'British' rebel, Magnus Maximus,[65] so beyond the criticism of immoral or amoral British contemporaries, whose own rule lacked the proper sanction of moral legitimacy.[66]

Such characterisation need not have been literally true, even supposing Gildas's portrayal of Ambrosius conformed with whatever facts were then a matter of public knowledge. What is important is the use which Gildas made of this British leader. It is safe to assume that his dialectical purposes here, as elsewhere, dominated his characterisation of historical figures, rather than the reverse. The living descendants of Ambrosius Aurelianus were unlikely to challenge Gildas's glowing report of their own ancestor, even supposing that they resented his guarded criticism of themselves.[67]

Gildas was here reconciling past events and personages already familiar to his audience with his thesis that the Saxon domination of the present day was a consequence of the Lord's having turned His face from the descendants of Ambrosius Aurelianus, their countrymen and contemporaries, in consequence of their disobedience to Him. The successes in war initiated under the leadership of the virtuous Ambrosius Aurelianus depended, in Gildas's view, entirely on God's valuation of that virtue. By describing him in such glowing terms Gildas was deliberately establishing an insular exemplar against whom to measure contemporary British leaders, to their disadvantage.[68] Ambrosius was, therefore, a convenient vehicle to encapsulate the image of the virtuous insular leader of the 'fatherland', whom God might support should he arise in the future. His virtues were not, however, exclusive to himself. It was essential to Gildas's dialectic that the generation of Britons active in the war be portrayed as morally superior to their descendants,[69] and that this contrast had its consequence in the 'damages and afflictions' of the present.[70]

Mount Badon

It was not Gildas's purpose to describe the subsequent war in any detail. He arguably knew no more about it than did those of his audience who were of approximately similar age and/or experience, and less perhaps than older contemporaries, so to offer them an historical account was pointless. It was his intention rather to draw from it fuel for his dialectical purposes. To that end, he referred to a period beginning with the victory of Ambrosius in which there were shifting fortunes, through which (as he interpreted it) God made trial of the British nation:[71]

> From that time now the citizens, now the enemy, were victorious as in that people the Lord could make trial (as is his custom) of his latter-day Israel to see whether it loves him or not. This lasted right up until the year of the siege of mount Badon (*obsessionis Badonici montis*) and almost the most recent slaughter of the convicts, and certainly not the least. That was the year of my birth; as I know, one month of the forty-fourth year since then has already passed.

Gildas did not state that the siege was decisive. Nor did he state, nor even imply, that it brought warfare to a close. Nor was it even the last British victory, since his use of *ferme* – 'almost' – necessitates at least one later success.[72]

The siege of mount Badon is, in a sense, the climax of Gildas's description of the conflict between Britons and Saxons,[73] if only because it is the point at which he broke off his description of that war, and it is couched in comparatively clear-cut terms which offer the much-later reader – who is naturally by this point highly exasperated by the very generality of Gildas's 'history' – a beguiling illusion of significance and certainty. Indeed, it is the only conflict which Gildas chose to name and that alone has been taken to suggest that it was a victory of real significance.[74]

For these reasons, mount Badon has been taken up by later writers and elevated to a pivotal position in most interpretations of Dark Age history.[75] Later medieval writers felt obliged to offer a fuller historical context for what rapidly became the culminating conflict of the war in which England was born.[76] Their comments have too often since been credited with an independent value which they do not deserve, thus further confusing the history of this period.[77] There is, today, an unfortunate tendency for the siege to be interpreted as an event which terminated the war,[78] with the subsequent period of peace a consequence of that victory.[79] The tide of English settlement, we are told, was thereby temporarily stemmed, only to be set once more in motion by renewed Anglo-Saxon aggression, or a second rebellion, in the mid- to late sixth century.[80]

Current knowledge of Badon and the events surrounding it are, however, woefully defective: although there has been much speculation concerning the locality,[81] as Sir Frank Stenton wisely opined, mount Badon cannot be located without the improbable advent of further evidence;[82] nor is it clear which side was the besieged and which the besiegers.[83] There is consensus that it was a British victory – indeed, this conclusion is almost inescapable.[84] Although a minority have considered that *mons Badonicus* need have been no more than a local incident,[85] most would concur with Peter Salway's view that it was a 'British victory that at the end of the fifth century was to set back further Saxon aggression in Britain for fifty years or more.'[86] The extent of the present consensus makes it legitimate to speak of an 'orthodox' view of mount Badon. This consensus has survived even the most recent re-appraisal of the *DEB*: the British victory remains a 'significant military event' which led directly to 'the present long-lasting relief from Saxon attack'.[87]

The mount Badon of later historiography has, unfortunately, become detached from Gildas's brief reference to it, and it is to that that we should return. That *mons Badonicus* was the sole conflict named by Gildas seems to have been conditioned by five factors:

1 The siege coincided with the year of Gildas's own birth in the forty-fourth year preceding that of composition. It was, therefore, an event which marked a year of personal significance to Gildas. He allowed himself the indulgence of associating the last significant occasion on which (to his mind) divine aid succoured the Britons with the start of his own life. Had he been born a year or so earlier, or later, Gildas might well have used an alternative (but now long forgotten) conflict to make his point. By making this link, Gildas was implying that his own birth occurred in the

last year in which the Britons experienced, even momentarily, the benefits of God's full support in their endeavours. By comparison with younger men he could therefore claim, as one born in a happier age with closer links to God, to be better equipped morally to lecture his contemporaries concerning their disobedience to God. This is a literary contrivance with some of the characteristics of a birth-related miracle, such as occur widely in the Bible and in much early hagiography, the purpose of which was arguably to sustain Gildas's own authority as a commentator on the present.

2   His purpose was to mark a specific year, not a particular battle. He did this by reference to a victory which he described as 'not the least'. This is a euphemism capable of a variety of interpretations. *Mons Badonicus* was necessarily still remembered at the time of writing and was presumably the best known British success of that year, forty-four years ago. Given the absence of dates from Gildas's text it may be that he considered the siege to be a clearer distinguishing mark of the year than a date, although it should be remembered that Gildas at least knew how many years before the present the siege had occurred.[88] More important, it was the siege's role as an indicator that divine support for the Britons was then still active that Gildas wished to emphasise. In that respect, reference to 'the year of the siege' offered a more pertinent characteristic than recourse to conventional dates of whatever kind.

3   Just as Gildas had provided an individual who seemed to enshrine the greater virtues of his generation (Ambrosius Aurelianus), so did he find it convenient for his rhetorical purposes to offer a single example of a British victory gained by divine aid in that long-gone era of superior (but still flawed) British morality.[89] Mount Badon was offered as just such an insular exemplar. It was to that specific victory which Gildas alluded in his contents list in chapter two.[90]

4   It may be significant that this was a siege, given his treatment of the war itself in terms of Saxon attacks upon British walled towns, and his preference for similarly urban parallels from existing literature. Had *mons Badonicus* not been a siege, Gildas might have preferred some other example by which to fix this particular year.

5   Most importantly, Gildas was looking back on the year in which the siege occurred from an historical perspective slightly

more than forty-three years distant from its close. With all the benefit of hindsight, he was offering his own phasing of the period of conflict, according to the criteria which he considered appropriate. Gildas was acting in some respects like a modern historian looking back on the Second World War and subdividing it into different phases according to those characteristics which he considers significant, but his criteria were not ones which a modern historian is likely to use but those of a scholar writing providential history for very specific, and contemporary purposes:

(a) he distinguished as his primary phase (I) the Saxon arrival, by invitation, their putative duplicity, their rebellion and their great raid. These events occurred when God and His people were estranged, on account of the blind stupidity and total immorality of the Britons. It is this moral condition which binds together these various events into a single phase;

(b) during a subsequent period (phase II), the Britons reacted to this disaster by seeking a reconciliation with God and He then tested His chosen people to see whether it loved Him or not. The result was a period during which the Britons enjoyed mixed fortunes in war, beginning with the victory won by Ambrosius Aurelianus. Almost the last British victory was the siege of mount Badon in the year of his own birth. For reasons discussed above, Gildas used this event to mark the year in which God ceased to test His people. Put simply, the Britons had failed the test and their relationship with God reverted to the impasse characteristic of phase I, above;

(c) after this there occurred the last phase (III) of the war, entirely within Gildas's own lifetime, so the most recent phase and necessarily the best known to his own audience. He forbore to describe it, but if the 'divine testing' of phase II had ceased, then the fortunes of war presumably swung one way.

What emerges from this account is of the utmost importance to our understanding of the war in which England was born: *mons Badonicus*, in the forty-fourth year before Gildas wrote, was not a decisive victory, yet it was almost the last victory vouchsafed by God to the Britons; the year in which it occurred – *annus obsessionis Badonici montis* – marked the end of what Gildas retrospectively interpreted as a specific phase of the war, but not

50

its end. Implicit in his account is the assumption that the balance thereafter shifted not in favour of the Britons but of their opponents, bringing an eventual peace on terms unfavourable to the indigenes.

Gildas subsequently refocused the attention of his own audience onto this second phase of the war by reference to 'mention of unlooked for aid' (*insperati mentio auxilii*),[91] referring once again to the participation of God in support of British soldiers more virtuous than those of his own day,[92] but still not so virtuous that ultimate victory was vouchsafed them. *Insperatus* here carries the meaning of 'beyond hope', either because the tactical position of the Britons was critical, or, more plausibly in this context, because the necessary divine assistance was insufficiently deserved, so should have been unexpected.[93] Gildas neither stated nor even implied that this 'unlooked for' victory had brought the Britons triumph in the war. In fact, he made it sufficiently clear that it had not.

Confusion over this issue stems very largely from consistently unfortunate translations of Gildas's anonymous reference to the same victory (or small group of victories) in chapter two, in which he promised to write 'concerning the very last victory of the fatherland which in our times was granted by the will of God.' Rendering *postrema* as 'final', rather than 'very last' has fostered a fundamental misinterpretation of this passage, from which derives the quite false assumption that mount Badon was a terminal victory which conditioned the outcome of the war as a whole.[94] This was another and even briefer reference to the divine aid to which Gildas attributed British victory at *mons Badonicus* but it adds little to our knowledge other than to indicate that, when Gildas précised for the purpose of his own contents list, British victories after *mons Badonicus* were so trivial or so poorly remembered that they could be safely discounted. Notice of the 'very last' victory won by the Britons certainly does not require that they won the war – rather the reverse. To offer a modern analogy, the Ardennes offensive was the 'very last' German victory of the Second World War but it did not lead to a German victory, despite the peace that subsequently prevailed between the erstwhile combatants. Mount Badon was no cup-final conflict, but just one – and not the last one at that – in a series which saw the pendulum of success gyrate from one side to another before swinging inexorably away from the Britons.

By successive references to the divine aid to which he attributed these, by then, long past British successes,[95] Gildas was reinforcing his message that relief from the present difficulties of the Britons was only possible via military operations conducted with courage (as advised by the Romans) and, more importantly, in full obedience to God. This was aimed at his own contemporaries, who Gildas hoped might emulate the virtues he had ascribed to Ambrosius Aurelianus, so attract renewed protection from the Old Testament God of battles and go on to win victories against the barbarians of greater moment than those achieved in the phase of the war which ended in the year of mount Badon.

To the remainder of the war Gildas made no reference in his sequential account of the past, preferring to jump forward to the present for the remainder of chapter twenty-six. This was described in terms which make it quite clear that the war had not ended in British victory. The current situation had been peaceful for a generation or so, as regards barbarian attack, but this peace had, in his view, brought no other benefits. In consequence of the war the cities were deserted and ruined, the Britons divided and at war among themselves, the people and their leaders lost to proper order, truth, justice and God. Excepting only a very few who remained loyal to 'holy mother church', the Britons were slaves of the devil.[96]

There is, in the *DEB*, an unfailing correlation between periods of political disaster and disobedience to God. That Gildas portrayed the present generation as exceptionally wicked requires that their suffering at barbarian hands was similarly exceptional. It was on this note that Gildas concluded his introduction, closing it with language reminiscent of that with which it had opened; he would 'employ lament rather than analysis' in response to 'an accumulation of evil'.[97] This is entirely irreconcilable with the view that *mons Badonicus* was the terminal victory of the war. Rather, it requires a Saxon victory which had conditioned the subsequent peace.

Gildas moved on to analyse the iniquities of contemporary kingship in general,[98] and the shortcomings of five individuals in particular,[99] before resorting once more to extensive biblical analogies in support of his arguments. His last target would be the clergy, none of whom he named but concerning whom he had even more to offer in the way of biblical exegesis. The main thrust of his arguments had already been established in his introduction and insular exemplars constructed for comparative purposes.[100] These examples would then be reinforced by reference to biblical testimony.[101] By comparison with the models of virtuous leadership, true Christian faith and successful warfare he had established in his historical introduction, Gildas's own contemporaries would be shown to be inadequate, both as regards their own morals and their prospects for leadership against the barbarians.

These 'complaints' once more require a Saxon victory in the war. Had the Britons been victorious, their success would have indicated to Gildas that God's protection was active over a virtuous people in obedience to Himself. An immoral British community cannot be reconciled with military victory within the system of historical explanation which he had, to this point, been so anxious to explain and sustain.

Allusions to the Saxons

There is the possibility of a further gloss on much of the 'complaints'. When Gildas introduced the Saxons by name in chapter twenty-three, he remarked that they were *'nefandi nominis'* – so 'of an abominable name', or 'name not to be uttered'. True to his word, he never repeated the term thereafter but, in the remainder of the 'historical' introduction, he established a series of alternative terms which he could then, at need, use as pseudonyms or mnemonics. The Saxons were 'wolves', 'death', 'lions', 'dogs', 'barbarians', 'soldiers', 'the enemy', 'heathens', 'impious ones', 'easterners', 'cruel plunderers', 'villeins', 'victors', 'convicts', 'the belly', 'devils', 'Assyrians' and 'foreigners' (*gentes*). Additionally they were associated with 'hell', 'fire' and 'burning', 'ferocity', 'pollution', 'laying low', 'jaws' and 'terrible claws'. They were also described via horticultural metaphors,[102] so they were 'the seed of iniquity', 'the root of bitterness' and 'a virulent plant'.

It is the pun implicit in the first of this last group which may indicate that Gildas was consciously establishing a battery of pseudonyms, metaphors and mnemonics by which he could thereafter make less obvious reference to the Saxons: the word which he used for a 'seed' was *'germen'*, a term so reminiscent of *Germanus* – 'German' – that the pun is unlikely to have been unintentional.[103]

That Gildas should have sought such indirect means of approaching the subject may derive from his determination to mobilise extensive quotations from the Bible. The total absence of explicit references to Saxons therein obviously hampered him if this was his intention, in which case the establishment of numerous pseudonyms offered a means of circumventing the problem. His pun – if that is what it is – signals his intention, so enables his audience to follow the drift of his arguments.

He may alternatively have preferred a tangential approach to his subject out of fear of Saxon, or Saxon-inspired, reprisal. Supposing him to have been a resident of a region whose British rulers were vulnerable to Saxon influence,[104] Gildas may have had good reason for caution. He was apparently writing under a pseudonym, so perhaps protecting his own identity for similar reasons.[105] A text which was more explicitly hostile to the Saxons and openly preached revolt might, therefore, have posed a danger to himself.

The establishment of a suite of pseudonyms and metaphors by which he could refer less obviously to the Saxons therefore offered Gildas opportunities to comment on the political situation then current. If this was a highly sensitive subject, he may have felt that some intentional obscurity was preferable to the risk of incurring penalty.

The possibility must, therefore, be born in mind that Gildas's audience was intended to read into his subsequent use of these same terms coded reference to, and condemnation of, the Saxons. This suggestion finds some support in the context in which some of these terms appear but his agenda is so well hidden that it is now impossible to offer conclusive proof of Gildas's purposes in this respect. Notwithstanding, several examples will here be explored.

The first of these is Gildas's use of *canis*, the standard term for a dog. Nine instances have been identified, all of which imply that Gildas, unlike some contemporaries,[106] had a consistently low, and biblically inspired, opinion of the dog. *Canis* occurs first in the preface:[107] 'It is not good to take one's sons' bread and throw it to the dogs.' Having just referred to tribute paid by the British churches,[108] the possibility that Gildas was here using 'dogs' as a metaphor for the Saxons is very real. The pagan Porphyry was then described as 'the mad dog of the East',[109] so combining two of Gildas's Saxon-related terms in one phrase, and this terminology emphasises the extent to which Gildas interpreted the various westward-moving, transmarine plagues of his 'historical' introduction as just one continuing effort by the Lord to correct His people. As merely the last, albeit the most virulent, of these, it was entirely appropriate that the Saxons and all other continent-derived scourges should be characterised by the same sub-set of vocabulary.

Canis was used twice explicitly of the Saxons,[110] then occurs in the name of Aurelius Caninus, whose Saxon-like qualities are highlighted by Gildas's reference to him also as a 'lion-whelp'.[111] Gildas threatened the immoral British kings that their descendants would be eaten by dogs,[112] and quoted aggressive passages from Isaiah and Jeremiah which could well be interpreted as attacks both on the Saxons and their confederates, and on pagan sacrifice.[113]

Perhaps the most compelling analogy is Gildas's final reference:[114] 'Do not give a holy thing to the dogs, or throw your pearl before swine, in case they trample them underfoot and turn to rend you, something that happens frequently to you?' These animal analogies serve to establish the bad priests, whom Gildas was here ostensibly attacking, as moral equals of the accursed Saxons, who would be the most obvious recipients of such holy things (including church ornaments in precious metals), pearls, and such like – as tribute-takers or raiders – and the most obvious contemporary 'renderers' and 'tramplers' of contemporary Britain.

The term *catulus* – 'whelp' – is similarly indicative of the Saxons or 'Saxon-like' qualities: it was used first of the Saxons themselves,[115] then of the brutal tyrant, Constantine of Dumnonia, in association once more with 'lioness',[116] and of the disreputable Aurelius Caninus.[117] The most explicit reference is to the appearance in battle of the soldiers of Maglocunus's royal uncle, who were likened to 'lion's whelps',[118] in what must surely be a conscious comparison with Saxon warriors.

There are further apposite references to lions of one sort or another: Boudicca (or Boadicea) was dubbed such,[119] as was the Saxon nation overseas,[120] the Dumnonian nation,[121] and immoral British rulers in general.[122] Otherwise Gildas used biblical quotation which referred to 'lions' teeth that slay the souls of men',[123] 'the voice of roaring lions',[124] and, in an extended discussion of the martyrdom of Ignatius,[125] he contrasted the eagerness for martyrdom of such Christian heroes of yore, with the backsliding of his own generation. Clearly, when applied to Britons, references to lions were intended to be pejorative. There remains the suspicion that several instances were intended to serve as pseudonyms for, or allusions to, the Saxons, particularly when combined with other of these key words.[126]

Other examples are numerous: *ignis* – 'fire' – is a commonplace, often being used in association with divine wrath,[127] so appropriate to the Saxons when portrayed as a present-day agent of the same, but also in association with hell and hell-fire,[128] which is another image independently associated with the Saxons;[129] references to *bestiae* – 'beasts' – include Ignatius's fighting them,[130] and bad priests who were 'beasts of the belly', so again combining two terms relevant to Saxons.[131] The Saxons are probably implicit in Gildas's adoption of a quotation from Ezekiel:[132] 'If I bring evil beasts into the land and punish it and it falls into destruction and there is no one able to journey across it in the face of the beasts' and by reference to people who had transgressed the word of God, so were 'a prey to beasts, the sword and fire'.[133]

Despite, therefore, there being only a single explicit reference throughout the *DEB* to 'the Saxons', Gildas does seem to provide himself with a sufficient battery of pseudonyms, mnemonics and analogies to make repeated allusion to them, if only as a yardstick by which to measure immorality, ferocity and depravity. There are numerous biblical quotations which can be interpreted with ease as relevant to God's use of the Saxons as an instrument of his wrath. Otherwise there are powerful literary links between the Saxons, beasts of all kind, powerful biblical oppressors of the Israelites, hell-fire and hell and its residents – all of which serve to keep alive the image of the Saxons throughout a work which was probably intended *ab initio* to carry several layers of interpretation. In this sense, the inimical influence of the Saxons is as pervasive in the text as it was in the Britain in which Gildas himself lived and wrote.

Conclusions

It was Gildas's intention to impose a particular theory of causation on his contemporaries in order to sustain his view of their present 'damages and afflictions'. He used his 'historical' introduction as a means of achieving this end, employing successive episodes in the past to illustrate a relationship between the Britons and their God which he considered of universal, so of current, relevance. He brought that account to a climax at the point where he introduced the Saxons – by means of concentrated metaphor, imagery and biblical quotation, using a series of rhetorical devices to raise the tension in his account to a crescendo. There can be no doubt that the Saxons were the cause of those same 'damages and afflictions' affecting his countrymen in the present, which this text was intended to redress.

He divided the British experience of the Saxons into several periods, by reference to changes in the relationship which he divined between God and the Britons:

1   The Saxons arrived, were employed, rebelled and raided across almost all Britain while that relationship was in tatters, due to the blindness and obstinacy of the Britons.
2   A period of mixed fortunes in war, introduced by a reconciliation between some of the Britons and God and the victory won by Ambrosius Aurelianus, was interpreted by Gildas as a period when God tested his people, to see whether it loved him or not. This period, but not the war, ended in the year of the siege of mount Badon.
3   Gildas did not describe the remainder of the war, but turned instead to the post-war period.
4   The post-war period was one of peace between Saxons and Britons but was otherwise a period depicted by Gildas as disastrous. He couched this in moral and spiritual terms, describing the majority of the Britons as subject now to the devil – so utilising one of the several images – that of hell – which he had already established as appropriate to the Saxons.

Gildas's moral invective in this last chapter of the 'historical' introduction – and thereafter for the remainder of the work – was conditioned not by the expectation of a Saxon revival following comprehensive defeat at *mons Badonicus*, but by the reality, and currency, of Saxon domination. No other explanation is consistent either with the structure of the 'historical' account, or with the specific nature of his complaints concerning the present.

This parlous situation is obscured by two circumstances: the more obvious is that the nature of the current 'damages and afflictions' were not at issue between Gildas and his immediate audience – as is made quite clear as regards one of these contemporaries whose work he was to quote with approbation in chapter ninety-two; the second is Gildas's interpretation of these 'damages and afflictions', which diverts the entire issue onto the moral and spiritual status of the Britons. The 'damages and afflictions' are, however, a reality which can only derive from a Saxon triumph over his own countrymen. That was, in turn, viewed by Gildas as consequent upon their own moral inadequacies and obstinate rebellion against God's will and it was, therefore, that relationship which was the focus of his work. The Saxon victory he could take for granted, confident that his own audience were as painfully aware as he himself of the outcome of the 'War of the Saxon Federates'.[134] Indeed, if his work was a direct consequence of some collective decision among a small assembly of the better educated to explore remedies to the maladies from which they collectively recognised that the *patria* was suffering, a direct description of those same maladies was obviously redundant at this point.[135] Such an omission has caused enormous difficulties for later historians seeking to utilise Gildas's text, but it was probably quite clear in meaning to contemporaries.

Gildas's ultimate solution to the problems of his *patria* was, in part, to induce whatever military leaders were still present among his own countrymen to accept moral correction. Thereby he believed they would obtain the divine aid which was an essential prerequisite of the defeat and ejection of the barbarian oppressors of his people. If this was Gildas's 'remedy' to the 'damages and afflictions' which beset the 'fatherland',[136] it follows that – providential history aside – it was the Saxons who were currently at the root of their problems. In order to pursue his concern at their influence a stage further, it is necessary to return to Gildas's preface, where he briefly characterised those problems and whither the concluding sentences of his 'historical' introduction should already have long since dispatched us.[137] If doubts still remain at this point concerning the specific nature of those same 'damages and afflictions', it is there that these will be resolved.

Notes

1 N. J. Higham, *Rome, Britain and the Anglo-Saxons*, London, 1992, p. 157.

2 So *DEB*, XX–XXVI.

3 For discussion, see P. Sims-Williams, 'Gildas and the Anglo-Saxons',

Cambridge Medieval Celtic Studies, VI, 1983, pp. 19–25.

4 Recall *DEB*, IV, 1; IX, 1; X, 1; XI, 1 and likewise the charity of the Romans towards the undeserving Britons implicit in XV, 2 and XVII, 2.

5 *DEB*, XX, 1.

6 *DEB*, XX, 2: *pestifera*. When considering God as a father-figure, recall that Gildas has already emphasised the child–parent relationship of Britons and Romans in XVIII, 1, and seems heavily influenced by Roman-style notions of the husband's authority over wife and children alike. Concerning plagues, the Old Testament offers such numerous parallels (as in note 8 below) that it must be recognised that this very opportune instance could have been entirely apocryphal.

7 Proverbs, XXIX, 19: *servus durus*, recalling and emphasising the sequence of characterisations throughout the   *DEB*, beginning at I, 13–14.

8 E.g. Numbers, XXV, 8–9, with which Gildas was certainly familiar, or Exodus, VII, which, given his allusion to 'Pharaoh' in *DEB* , XXIII, 2, might be the analogy which he here had in mind.

9 Isaiah, XXII, 12–13.

10 Isaiah, XXII, 17–19: quote from the authorised version.

11 Genesis, XV, 13–18: see p. 138.

12 *DEB*, XXIII, 1–2.

13 *DEB*, XVI, 1.

14 *DEB*, XXIII, 1.

15 *DEB*, XXIII, 3–4: see also VI, 1 and p. 55. His ultimate inspiration was probably the Book of Jeremiah.

16 *DEB*, XXII, 4–5; K. H. Jackson, '*Varia*: II. Gildas and the Names of the British Princes', *Cambridge Medieval Celtic Studies*, III, 1982, pp. 31–2.

17 *DEB*, XXIII, 1.

18 *DEB*, XXIV, 1.

19 *DEB*, XXIV, 2, quoting from Psalms, LXXIII, 7; LXXVIII, 1.

20 *DEB*, II, 16; IV, 3, 4; VII, 4; IX, 1; XIII, 1; XIV, 1; XXIII, 1, 4; XXVII, 1; XXXI, 1; XXXIII, 1; XLIX, 2; LXII, 5; LXVII, 2; LXXV, 3; LXXVI, 1.

21 As he had legitimate, Roman rulers, e.g. *DEB*, IV, 1; V, 1. For comment see B. S. Bachrach, 'Gildas, Vortigern and constitutionality in sub-Roman Britain', *Nottingham Medieval Studies*, XXXII, 1988, pp. 126–40, but recall that 'constitutionality' is unlikely to have been the determining factor in Gildas's choice of terminology.

22 Jackson, '*Varia*: II', pp. 35–6.

23 Isaiah, XIX, 11. For the view that Vortigern was an insular emperor, see S. S. Frere, *Britannia*, Oxford, 1974, pp. 411–12, but his reasoning is not particularly convincing.

24 Sims-Williams, 'Gildas', pp. 18–19; 29–30.

25 E. A. Thompson, 'Gildas and the history of Britain', *Britannia*, X, 1979, p. 217; P. Salway, *Roman Britain*, Oxford, 1981, pp. 472 ff.; Sims-Williams, 'Gildas', p. 20; D. N. Dumville, 'The chronology of *De Excidio Britanniae*, Book I', in *Gildas; New Approaches*, eds M. Lapidge and D. N. Dumville, Woodbridge, 1984, p. 71, and see, p. 40.

26 *DEB*, XIV; XVI; XIX, 1; XX, 1.

27 *DEB*, XXIII, 4. Gildas's allusion is alone insufficient to localise the first Saxon settlement, but archaeological evidence makes East Anglia the clear favourite. Recall the impact of Picts and Scots in general in 365, and not so very far from London in 367; Ammianus Marcellinus, *Historia*, ed. T. E. Page, trans. J. C. Rolfe, London, 1935, XX, i, 1; XXVII, viii, 1–10. For recent comment which emphasises the poor quality of Roman defence, E. A. Thompson, 'Ammianus Marcellinus and Britain', *Nottingham Medieval Studies*, XXXIV, 1990, pp. 1–15.

28 *DEB*, XXIII, 2. This reinforces the view which Gildas offers in several places in the text that death is preferable to servitude under the barbarian yoke: *DEB*, XIX, 2; XXV, 1.

29 Zosimus, *New History*, translated and with a commentary by R. T. Ridley, Australian Association for Byzantine Studies, Sydney, 1982, VI, 5; Gallic Chronicle of 452, 410, and particularly the doubts of R. W. Burgess, 'The Dark Ages return to fifth-century Britain: the "restored" Gallic Chronicle exploded', *Britannia*, XXI, 1990, p. 191. Even the most uncritical reading of this entry does not justify the claims of some modern scholars that the 'Saxon settlement' began at this date, since it is a raid, not a migration, to which these texts refer and those are fundamentally different phenomena.

30 C. E. Stevens, 'Gildas Sapiens', *English Historical Review*, LVI, 1941, pp. 368–9; Thompson, 'Gildas', p. 217; Sims-Williams, 'Gildas', p. 20, note 86, and p. 22, note 89; Higham, *Rome*, pp. 160–4.

31 W. Goffart, *Barbarians and Romans AD 418–584: the Techniques of Accommodation*, Princeton, 1980, *passim*; H. Sivan, 'On *Foederati, Hospitalitas* and the settlement of the Goths in AD 418', *American Journal of Philology*, CVIII, 1987, pp. 759–72. I see little reason to avoid the term for fear of technicalities, as does Sims-Williams, 'Gildas', p. 20, footnote 86.

32 Sims-Williams, 'Gildas', pp. 22–3; Higham, *Rome*, p. 165. The three shipfuls do suggest a folklore element but it *need* not be inaccurate, nor, if it is, need it be grossly inaccurate.

33 Cf. the Germanic use of auguries in Tacitus, *Germania*, trans. and ed. M. Hutton, London 1914, X; Procopius, *History of the Wars*, ed. H. B. Dewing, London, 1914–40, VIII, xx, 13–14; *The Earliest Life of Gregory the Great, by an Anonymous Monk of Whitby*, ed. B. Colgrave, Cambridge, 1985, XV.

Gildas and the Saxons

34 Cf. Gildas's knowledge of the Scottish term: *DEB*, XIX, 1. He otherwise referred to British shipping as *classis* (VI, 1) and Roman and Saxon vessels as *rates* (XV, 2; XXIII, 4).

35 Which is the more comprehensible if Gildas lived under the ultimate authority of the Saxons; see p. 57. Note also his apparent familiarity with the appearance and customs of the Picts and Scots: *DEB*, XIX, 1.

36 Cf. Bede's escalation of the numbers involved: *HE*, I, 15, from which originate later interpretations of this event as a mass migration. On the basis of the *DEB*, hundreds should be preferred to thousands.

37 *HE*, I, 15, based on *DEB*, XXIII, 5. This is the standard Latin term for a soldier's pay. This is likewise the sense of Winterbottom's translation: 'more lavish payments', *Gildas*, p. 27.

38 S. Archer, 'Late Roman gold and silver hoards: a gazetteer', in *The End of Roman Britain*, ed. P. J. Casey, British Archaeological Reports, LXXI, Oxford, 1979, pp. 29–64.

39 As in, for example, the Water Newton Treasure.

40 *DEB*, XXIV, 2.

41 *DEB*, XXIV, 1.

42 *DEB*, XXIV, 3.

43 *DEB*, XXIV, *passim*. The language used conjures up visions of hell, with British immorality punished by fires overseen by the sacrilegious Saxons, concerning whom diabolical and bestial metaphors are used, as in *DEB*, XXIII, 1, 3, 4, 5; XXVI, 4.

44 E.g. *DEB*, XXIV, 3–4; cf. XIX, 3. Gildas's initial description of Britain's cities, in III, 2, was based, most appropriately, on Orosius's description of Babylon: *Histories*, II, vi, 10; N. Wright, 'Did Gildas read Orosius?', *Cambridge Medieval Celtic Studies*, IX, 1986, p. 35.

45 E.g. *DEB*, I, 5; X, 2; XII, 2.

46 *DEB*, XXIV, 3–4.

47 *Aeneid*, II. For the crucial parallel of Jeremiah's Jerusalem, see pp. 71–9.

48 Genesis, XVIII–XIX; Gildas made further references to Sodom (and derivatives) in XXVIII, 4; XXXIII, 1; XLII, 2, 3; LXVIII, 2, and LXXXII, 3, and Gomorrah in XLII, 2 and LXXXII, 3, so the analogy was certainly in his mind. He described the tyrants of the present as 'princes of Sodom' in XLII, 3.

49 *DEB*, VI–VII.

50 *DEB*, XIX, 3–4; XX, 2.

51 Cf. *DEB*, XIX, 2, where the miserable fate of some was presumably slavery of comparable kind.

52 *DEB*, XX, 1; Psalms, LXXIII, 7, not Psalms, XLIII, 12, as in M. Winterbottom, ed., *Gildas: The Ruin of Britain and Other Documents*, Chichester, 1978, p. 156. The following extract is XLIV, 9–11, from the Authorised Version. Note the portrayal of God as the very antithesis of the 'Lord of hosts' whom we meet elsewhere in *DEB*.

53 *DEB*, XI, 2.

54 *DEB*, XX, 2.

55 E.g. Exodus, XVI; Luke, IV. Matthew, XIV, 13–15 cannot have been unknown to a writer who quoted so extensively from this section of this Testament. See also Jeremiah, III, 23.

56 E.g. *DEB*, XXVIII, 1; XXXIV, 1.

57 *DEB*, XXV, 2, adapting Aeneid, IX, 24. Gildas was probably attracted to this quotation in part because Turnus was depicted as being in a wood set in a glen, but the primary analogy for this topography remains biblical, as in notes 55 and 56 above. The context is moral and conventional, rather than literal. In consequence, the landscape features of *DEB*, XXV, 1, do not necessitate a geographical context in upland Britain: cf. Dumville, 'Chronology', pp. 74–5. For other literary parallels to Gildas's sensationalist style, see Sims-Williams, 'Gildas', pp. 10–12.

58 *DEB*, XIII, 1–2; that is excepting only 'Vortigern'. For comment on Ambrosius, see Dumville, 'Chronology', p. 76.

59 *DEB*, XXV, 3.

60 *DEB*, XXV, 3. See discussion in R. W. Hanning, *The Vision of History in Early Britain*, New York, 1966, p. 56.

61 J. F. Matthews, *Western Aristocracies and the Imperial Court, AD 364–425*, Oxford, 1975, *passim*.

62 Zosimus, *New History*, V, 43; VI, 4.

63 Higham, *Rome*, p. 160. For speculation on his parentage, H. Williams, *Gildae De Excidio Britanniae*, London, 1899, p. 60, note 2.

64 *DEB*, V, 1; VI; VII, XV; XVI; XVII; XVIII, 1. The latest parallel, with 'Agitius' in XX, 1, was perhaps the most relevant here and was emphasised by use of *vir* in both. See Hanning, *Vision*, p. 56, who described Ambrosius as the 'historiographical descendant of Constantine [the Great]'.

65 *DEB*, XIII, 2. Note Gildas's use of *rector* both for God (XI, 2) and for legitimate, secular governors, whether British (I, 14) or appointed from Rome (VI, 1).

66 As portrayed by Gildas in *DEB*, XXVI, 3, and thereafter.

67 *DEB*, XXV, 3: 'of whom in our time the progeny has degenerated very far from the grandfather's goodness'.

68 As, for example, the five tyrants: *DEB*, XXVII–XXXVI.

69 *DEB*, XXVI, 3. All those associated with Ambrosius Aurelianus's success had sought 'desert places' and turned to God *en masse* in XXV, 2.

70 *DEB*, XXVI, 3–4, with resonances of I, 1.

71 *DEB*, XXVI, 1.

72 *DEB*, XXVI, 1; Sims-Williams, 'Gildas', p. 25; Dumville, 'Chronology', p. 76.

73 *DEB*, XXVI, 1, and see Hanning, *Vision*, p. 51.

74 E.g. Sir F. M. Stenton, *Anglo-Saxon England*, Oxford, 1971, 2–3: 'a struggle on equal terms . . . was ended by a British victory . . . To Gildas the battle was a turning point in history, for it gave to the Britons a respite which, when he wrote his book, had already lasted for at least forty years'. See also R. G. Collingwood and J. N. L. Myres, *Roman Britain and the English Settlements*, Oxford, 1936, p. 379. For a note of caution, see Sims-Williams, 'Gildas', pp. 25–6.

75 See note 74 and A. S. Esmonde Cleary, *The Ending of Roman Britain*, London, 1989, p. 163: 'culminating in the battle of Mount Badon at which the Anglo-Saxons were comprehensively defeated and a generation of peace ensued'. Similar interpretations occur in P. H. Blair, *Introduction to Anglo-Saxon History*, 2nd edn, Cambridge, 1977, pp. 14, 30, 31; S. S. Frere, *Britannia* , Oxford, 1978, p. 427; S. Johnson, *Later Roman Britain*, London, 1980, p. 112; P. Salway, *Roman Britain*, Oxford, 1981, p. 484; C. Thomas, *Christianity in Roman Britain to AD 500*, London, 1981, pp. 245–51; J. Campbell, ed., *The Anglo-Saxons*, London, 1982, p. 23.

76 Less so Bede, *Historia Ecclesiastica*, I, 16, who merely paraphrased *DEB*, XXVI, 1, albeit leaving the battle suggestively at the chapter's end; more so the *HB*, LVI, and the *AC*, both of which offered spurious elaboration of Badon and assigned it to King Arthur. For discussion, see D. N. Dumville, 'Sub-Roman Britain: history and legend', *History*, LXII, 1977, pp. 173–92.

77 Most particularly by J. Morris, *The Age of Arthur*, Chichester, 1973, pp. 169, 212, 227, 280, 293, but see also C. E. Stevens, 'Gildas Sapiens', *English Historical Review*, LVI, 1941, p. 370.

78 See notes 74, 75.

79 E.g. Blair, *Anglo-Saxon England*, p. 30: 'we may accept as historical fact the winning of a major British victory over the invaders and the consequent enjoyment by the victors of a respite which lasted half a century or more'.

80 E.g. Morris, *Age of Arthur*, p. 293: 'The second Saxon revolt was no concerted national rising. . . . It began as a trickle and became a flood. The memory of Badon had contained the English within their borders for three generations; though the military strength of Arthur's empire soon dissolved, fear of superior British power long outlived its reality'; something similar is envisaged by S. C. Hawkes, 'The south-east after the Romans: the Saxon settlement', in *The Saxon Shore: a Handbook*, Studies in History, XXV, Exeter, 1989, pp. 94–5.

81 E.g. E. Guest, *Origines Celticae*, eds W. Stubbs and C. Deedes, 2 vols, London, 1883, II, p. 189; Williams, *Gildas*, p. 60, note 4; Stevens, 'Gildas', p. 371, particularly footnote 6; Thompson, 'Gildas', *passim*; J. N. L. Myres, *The English Settlements*, Oxford, 1986, p. 159; Hawkes,

'South-east', pp. 94–5.

82 Stenton, *Anglo-Saxon England*, p. 3; Myres made a similar disclaimer in Collingwood and Myres, *Roman Britain*, p. 379, and T. D. O'Sullivan, in *The De Excidio of Gildas: Its Authenticity and Date*, Michigan, 1974, p. 231.

83 Although evidence of fifth-century hill-fort refurbishment, apparently by Britons, may imply that the Britons were within: e.g. L. Alcock, *By South Cadbury Is That Camelot: Excavations at Cadbury Castle, 1966–70*, London, 1972; I. Burrow, *Hillforts and Hilltop Settlement*, Oxford, British Archaeological Reports, British series, XCI, 1981.

84 The context confirms the meaning of this phrase, but *stragis de furciferis* does not necessarily mean a 'slaughter' visited *upon* 'the convicts': it could be read as one attributable to them as agents or possessors, as, for example, in the use of *de* in *DEB*, XXVIII, 4: 'the bitter vine *belonging to* the men of Sodom.'

85 E. A. Thompson, *St. Germanus of Auxerre and the end of Roman Britain*, Woodbridge, 1984, p. 100; C. J. Arnold, *Roman Britain to Saxon England*, Beckenham, 1984, p. 7; Hawkes, 'South-east', p. 95; Higham, *Rome*, pp. 160–1. Thomas, *Christianity*, p. 251, suggested the conflict at Badon was 'isolated', despite inference in the text that it was a named example of more than one victory.

86 Salway, *Roman Britain*, p. 498.

87 Dumville, 'Chronology', p. 76; see also Sims-Williams, 'Gildas', pp. 25–6.

88 See p. 137 for discussion of dating.

89 Cf. his reference to a single late-Roman (putatively British) tyrant and a single heresy.

90 *DEB*, II. See discussion below, p. 51. His use of the lower case for *mons* may imply that this was not even then a compound place-name but rather a descriptive term dependent on some neighbouring place called Badon.

91 *DEB*, XXVI, 2.

92 See reference to virtuous soldiers in *DEB*, I, 1, 16, but note the reservations expressed on p. 34, note 113.

93 Such was consistent with Gildas's portrayal of the poverty of British faith throughout, as in *DEB*, IX, 1.

94 Williams, *Gildas*, p. 60, offered a marginal heading against chapter XXVI which reads: 'The final victory over the Saxons, Siege of Mons Badonicus'; A. W. Wade-Evans, *Nennius's 'History of the Britons' together with 'The Annals of the Britons' and 'Court Pedigrees of Hywel the Good' and 'The Story of the Loss of Britain'*, London, 1938, p. 151, inserted a heading: 'Of the final victory of the fatherland which had been granted by God's will in our times.' Both derive ultimately from *DEB*, II.

See the very different translation of J. A. Giles, *The Works of Gildas and Nennius*, London, 1841, p. 6.

95 Assuming the last to have occurred in the year of mount Badon. For comment, see Dumville, 'Chronology', p. 76, but *postrema patriae victoria* should be identified very closely with mount Badon, the sole named victory which Gildas used to close this phase of the war. There is no textual reason to connect it with the 'present long-lasting relief from Saxon attack'.

96 *DEB*, XXVI, 4.

97 *DEB*, XXVI, 3. Compare *'malorumque cumulum lacrimosis querelis defleam'* of *DEB*, I, 1. There is further reference to 'lamentation' in *DEB*, XXXVII, 1; LXXXIII, 1, and LXXXVIII, 3.

98 *DEB*, XXVII.

99 *DEB*, XXVIII–XXXVI.

100 Cf. the virtuous Ambrosius Aurelianus and the five named tyrants: St Alban and the martyrs of *DEB*, IX–XII, with the contemporary British clergy.

101 As for priests in *DEB*, LXIX, 2 to LXXV, 3, or CIX, 3.

102 Cf. *DEB*, XIII, 1.

103 For Gildas's penchant for puns, see Jackson, *'Varia*: II', *passim*, but note that *germen* also occurs with reference to Magnus Maximus in *DEB*, XIII, 1. *Germanus* occurs in Gildas's castigation of Aurelius Caninus (*DEB*, XXXII, 2), with regard to his second marriage to his own sister-in-law, who is termed 'a gallows-bird of the same parentage' (as her sister). Again a pun may be intended. See also in reference to British sins, XIII, 1; XXI, 2.

104 See p. 57.

105 Sims-Williams, 'Gildas', p. 3.

106 So the western kings: Jackson, *'Varia*: II', pp. 31–3.

107 *DEB*, I, 8, derived from Matthew, XV, 26.

108 See discussion, p. 75.

109 *DEB*, IV, 3.

110 *DEB*, XXIII, 4, 5.

111 *DEB*, XXX, 1.

112 *DEB*, XL, 1, 2.

113 *DEB*, LXXIX, 3. I do not share the confidence that Gildas's contemporaries were immune from paganism or apostasy of, for example, J. Evans, 'From the end of Roman Britain to the "Celtic West"', *Oxford Journal of Archaeology*, IX, 1990, p. 96.

114 *DEB*, XCIV, 3, quoting from Matthew, VII, 6.

115 *DEB*, XXIII, 3.

116 *DEB*, XXVIII, 1.

117 *DEB*, XXX, 1, once more with 'lion'.

118 *DEB*, XXXIII, 4. The possibility that some of these soldiers in western Britain were pagan Irish and Picts might explain Gildas's familiarity with their appearance and customs, as in *DEB*, XIX, 1.

119 Assuming this anonymous reference to be to her: *DEB*, VI, 1.

120 *DEB*, XXIII, 3.

121 *DEB*, XXVIII, 1.

122 *DEB*, LXXXVII, 2; XC, 3.

123 *DEB*, LXIV, 1, quoting from Ecclesiasticus, XXI, 2–3.

124 *DEB*, LXXXVIII, 3, quoting from Zechariah, XI, 3–6.

125 *DEB*, LXXIV, 1, quoting from Rufinus's translation of Eusebius *Ecclesiastical History*, in *Eusebius: the Ecclesiastical History and the Martyrs of Palestine*, trans. H. J. Lawlor and J. E. L. Oulton, 2 vols, London, 1927, I, ii, 9.

126 As in *DEB*, LX, 2, where it is combined with fire. Note its use in the Book of Jeremiah, II, 15, 30; V, 6, which may collectively have been Gildas's ultimate inspiration.

127 E.g. *DEB*, LX, 1, 2; LXXII, 2, 3; LXXXIX, 5.

128 E.g. *DEB*, XXIX, 3; XXXII, 5.

129 *DEB*, XXVI, 3–4.

130 *DEB*, LXXIV, 2.

131 *DEB*, LXVIII, 1. *Ventor* ('belly') is used repeatedly to convey a vulgar image, reflecting sin, lust or gluttony, and is associated with brute beasts. 'Claw' and 'throat' have similar roles, excepting only the claws of the Roman eagles (XVII, 2), which imply that Gildas was conscious that the eagle was a symbol of the Roman Empire and its soldiers.

132 Ezekiel, XIV, 12–16, in the context of the Babylonian sack of Jerusalem, for the relevance of which see pp. 71–9.

133 *DEB*, I, 3, quoting Numbers, XXVI, 51.

134 The term is Thompson's: 'Gildas', p. 219, but there is nothing in the text to support his assertion that it was a 'relatively minor' event.

135 See above, p. 30, note 17, and also pp. 67–79, following.

136 *DEB*, I, 1.

137 See above, p. 52 and note 97.

3

Gildas and Jeremiah

In order to explore further the conclusion of the 'War of the Saxon Federates', and so the political conditions current at the time of writing the *DEB*, it is necessary to concentrate attention on Gildas's exordium or prologue. He himself appears to have directed attention, through similarities of both style and phrase, from the end of his introduction back to his initial remarks in the prologue: *deflevero*, for example, at the close of chapter twenty-six clearly recalls the *deflendo* of the opening line and *defleverat* of chapter one, verse five. Such 'lamentation' was to be a potent image throughout but was particularly prominent as a theme in the introduction. These links were a literary device but they have a practical purpose, which is to refer the audience back from this final 'lament' concerning the present to his characterisation of the 'damages and afflictions' of the 'fatherland' which he had already established as its causes.

In those opening lines, Gildas claimed that, from modesty, he had refrained for ten years from the task he was now about to undertake.[1] This was not the sole reference to his own humility, which he elaborated at various later stages of his introduction, but all are probably conventional and tell us nothing about the actual personality of an author whose writing otherwise betrays little modesty.[2] While professing modesty, therefore, Gildas was also busy establishing the immediate context of his remarks, through the current 'damages and afflictions' of the 'fatherland'. He then elaborated further the purposes for which he wrote: he first justified and contextualised the *DEB* by reference to specific incidents in the Old Testament,[3] then spelled out the relevance of his readings to the present, using for the purpose a further series of quotations, allusions and metaphors.[4]

Thereafter Gildas transferred his attention forward to the New Testament,[5] alluding to episodes which he considered made points relevant to the solution that he was proposing, then once more linked this material to the present.[6] With the problem and his solution to it spelled out, he reverted thereafter to a justification of his own decision to write by forestalling the criticism that others were better placed than himself to correct the moral shortcomings of the Britons,[7] then, in terms which continued his self-justificatory theme, described his decision to proceed with the work and anticipated the reception which he believed it might receive.[8]

In his allusions to the Old Testament, Gildas pursued a single thread of argument and it was this which governed his selection of texts. There are six of them, of which it may be helpful to consider initially only the first five as a group:

1 A revered law-giver (Moses) was prevented by a single word's doubt from entering the promised land with the Israelites.[9]
2 The sons of the priest (Nadab and Abihu, sons of Aaron) died a swift death because they brought strange fire to the altar.[10]
3 A general, if somewhat contrived reference to the downfall of the Israelites on account of a transgression against the word of God, despite God's care for them in the crossing of the Red Sea, in the desert and in battle (with Amalek).[11]
4 Despite God's aid in destroying the walls of Jericho, a little money stolen from a cursed offering (that is an offering to a pagan God) brought the downfall of many.[12]
5 The Israelites' breaking of the treaty with the Gibeonites (though it had been wrung from them by a trick) brought destruction on not a few.[13]

The first four all belong to the latter stages of the Exodus from Egypt and subsequent establishment of the Israelites in the Promised Land but they have more in common than their propinquity in the Old Testament. Each refers to an episode in which divine support for the Israelites was clearly manifest but some transgression against divine will by one or more of them brought down a terrible retribution: Moses questioned the Lord his God; Aaron's children introduced variations in matters of ritual; a generalised but apparently associated condemnation even after all the aid vouchsafed the 'Chosen People' during the Exodus and, finally, ritual pollution and theft. If the affair of the Gibeonites be added, its message is much the same – namely that the Israelites were punished by God for Saul's breaking of his word, despite the extenuating circumstances in which this *foedus* (treaty) was made.

All instances, therefore, refer to divine punishment of His chosen people for transgressing His commandments, despite the general and very active protection otherwise afforded them. In each instance relations between God and the Israelites were thereafter restored and His protection renewed, once the Israelites returned to their obedience. Since Gildas believed the Britons to be a 'Chosen People' at the time of writing,[14] these instances were, in his view, directly analogous to the current relationship between the Britons and God. His message was here fundamentally optimistic – that a renewal of strict morality on the part of the British rulers and clergy would lead God to withdraw His anger and renew His protection of His 'latter day Israelites'. Their oppressors would presumably then, in Gildas's view, be swept away as effortlessly as those of the Israelites in successive episodes of the Old Testament.[15]

What Gildas was therefore doing here at the very outset of his text was establishing his own philosophy of history and historical explanation, so his own reasoning concerning the 'damages and afflictions' facing the Britons in the present. Since he perceived the current experience of his own people as merely an extension of the history of the 'Chosen People' as developed in the Testaments, the Old Testament offered him examples which were not only of unimpeachable authority but also of direct relevance for this purpose. In brief, his general message here is that even the Israelites, whose very special relationship with God is the principal theme of the Old Testament, suffered frequent punishment on account of specific failings in obedience to God, but no such punishment proved to be a terminal event and, once his people showed appropriate repentance, God's protection was invariably restored. It is the perpetual contract between God and His people which characterises the continuum of relations between them, against which the breakdown of that relationship should be viewed as occasional and episodic, albeit unfortunately of long standing at the present time.

It is significant that the *foedus* between Israelites and Gibeonites was the last of the biblical episodes to which he alluded in this passage. Although he probably had in mind specific analogies for each reference to the Old Testament, most are now necessarily obscure. Similarities between this *foedus*, however, and the first of those to which he referred in the *De Excidio* are too obvious to be coincidental:[16] both were between God's 'Chosen People' and a pagan tribe; both enabled the latter to settle in the homeland of the former; both led to war between them; in each instance God's people were discomfited in the war; in neither instance were the immigrants expelled.

There are, of course, differences – the principal one being that the biblical *foedus* was broken by the Israelites but the initial *foedus* between the Britons and the Saxons by the incomers (although a subsequent *foedus* was still in force at the time of writing)[17] – but it is difficult to offer a closer analogy than this from the Old Testament for the circumstances in which the 'damages and afflictions' of the present had come about.

It was not just the *foedus* and the status of the Gibeonites as incomers which appear to have attracted Gildas to this episode. God's attitude towards the war and its disastrous outcome were at least as significant and it was with the destruction which resulted from it that he terminated this, his fifth reference. This *exitium* – 'destruction' or 'ruin' – must be viewed as, in Gildas's opinion, an analogy of direct relevance to the present, so to the lament which he would offer concerning that present context in chapter twenty-six.

From this very apt allusion, Gildas turned in the last of his six references to the Old Testament in this passage,[18] to the plaintive voices of the prophets in general, but of Jeremiah in particular as he lamented the 'ruin of his city'. The text spells out Gildas's intention *ab initio* to emulate the prophets of the Old Testament. Just as the occasion of his speaking out was to be compared to theirs, so too would he pursue a comparable scheme of correction, by associating his complaints and lamentations concerning his own contemporaries with theirs.[19] By so doing, Gildas achieved several objectives:

1 He justified his own comments concerning powerful contemporaries by reference to precedents of unquestionable authority.
2 He re-emphasised his belief that the experiences of contempo-

rary Christians were a direct continuation of a comprehensive and divinely inspired, providential history which was rooted in the Bible.[20]

3   Lastly, but most importantly, he invoked as an analogy for his own times the entirety of Jeremiah's Lament, and the several descriptions of Jerusalem's sack by the Babylonians which contextualised that event. Just as the *exitium* – 'destruction' – of the Israelites at the hands of the Gibeonites was comparable to the present plight of Britain at the hands of the Saxons, so too was the *ruina* of Jerusalem at the hands of the Babylonians. Gildas therefore established at this early stage of his text that the 'damages and afflictions' of contemporary Britain were to be compared with the wreck of Jerusalem as lamented by Jeremiah, which constituted the most traumatic catastrophe to affect the Israelites throughout the Old Testament available for Gildas's use. It would not be an overstatement to describe the entirety of the *DEB* as a 'lament', the ultimate model for which was primarily Jeremiah's, reference to which would be a major theme of the text thereafter.

That Gildas passed from what appears to have been the most apt of his biblical analogies (concerning the Gibeonites) to his self-identification with Jeremiah was no coincidence. His reference to Jeremiah served to link these other disparate biblical episodes with the contemporary comments which were the theme of his next passage:[21]

> And I could see even in our own time, just as he [Jeremiah] had lamented, the city (that is, the church) sat solitary, bereaved; hitherto full of peoples, mistress of races, the prince of provinces, it was now placed under tribute. I saw that gold (that is, the lustre of the word of God) had been dimmed and the colour of the best things changed. I saw that the sons of Sion (that is, of the holy mother church), once glorious and clad in fine gold, had embraced dung. And I saw how – in a manner as intolerable to him in his greatness as to me for all my humility – things in one way or another came to a level of suffering where he so grieved for the nobility, once so affluent, that he said: 'Her Nazarites were whiter than snow, redder than antique ivory, more beautiful than the sapphire.'

This passage comprises another cocktail of biblical fragments and allusions which have been reassembled by the author for an explicitly current purpose. It is here, therefore, that Gildas proposed to spell out the relevance to the present of his Old Testament quotations, which had hitherto been implicit.

As might be expected of a text which so trenchantly evokes his authority, all references or quotations derive from Jeremiah's Lamentations.[22] That they were in order implies that Gildas was writing with Lamentations open in front of him, as also seems to have been the case when later composing chapters forty-seven and forty-eight. The passages used were so inappropriate to Gildas's purposes that, departing from his usual practice,[23] he explained each of his allusions. Jeremiah's Lament was therefore viewed by Gildas as so compelling and fundamental an analogy to his own text that he preferred to construct clumsy metaphors from quotations derived from this source rather than seek apter material elsewhere. This practice reinforces the universality of his reference to Jeremiah's Lament at the end of the previous paragraph and establishes beyond reasonable doubt that he saw the political context in which he was himself writing as peculiarly analogous with that confronting this particular prophet.

Gildas was, therefore, drawing heavily on two biblical analogies – the defeat of the Israelites by the Gibeonites and the sack of Jerusalem by the Babylonians. Each offered parallels to the recent war between Britons and Saxons and the circumstances under which it had ended. It was, however, the latter to which Gildas paid the more attention: not satisfied with a single reference to it, he established its relevance to the present in the most explicit terms and repeatedly quoted from it. It was this text, therefore, to which he here directed the attention of his audience with the utmost urgency. The matter of the Gibeonites was to recur in the *DEB* only once, but Gildas would return repeatedly to Jeremiah's Lament and also to related sections of the Bible which were likewise conditioned by Jerusalem's destruction.[24] The reader is left with little option but to accept that Gildas had chosen the sack of Jerusalem as the most appropriate and compelling parallel to be found in the Bible for the present condition of his own *patria*, the British 'fatherland'.

Jeremiah's Lamentation follows, and was consequent upon, the sack of Jerusalem by Nebuchadnezzar, King of Babylon.[25] Biblical accounts mark the following stages:

1 King Zedekiah did evil in the eyes of the Lord.[26]
2 He rebelled against Babylon.[27]
3 Nebuchadnezzar besieged Jerusalem, which suffered famine and from which the king and soldiers fled.[28]
4 Zedekiah was taken by the Chaldeans, judged by Nebuchadnezzar, then forced to witness the killing of his sons and kin before himself being blinded, carried off to Babylon and imprisoned.[29]
5 Nebuzar-adan (Nebuchadnezzar's captain) sacked and fired the temple, the palaces and houses in Jerusalem and demolished the walls.[30]
6 He carried off some of the poor, leaving others to work the land.[31]
7 He despoiled the temple of precious metals.[32]
8 He took captive the leaders of the Israelites, priests included, and they were executed by order of the king.[33]

In Jeremiah's view, this catastrophe was the personal responsibility of King Zedekiah, on account of his failure to obey God[34] and his rebellion against Nebuchadnezzar. He was also very critical in other passages of priests and prophets.[35]

Much of what Gildas found in Jeremiah either, therefore, paralleled his own complaints or was picked up in his 'historical' introduction to some degree as appropriate to the experience of the Britons: Zedekiah's rebellion against God parallels Gildas's comments on various British leaders, but most particularly those which preface and describe the 'proud tyrant' and his council, who invited in the Saxons;[36] the famine at Jerusalem was analogous to several famines which Gildas introduced to his 'historical' narrative, the literal instances of which were invariably in connection with foreign attack;[37] the irresolute Israelite soldiery mirror the consistent incompetence of the Britons concerning military matters;[38] the killing of selected captives calls to mind the treatment of the Britons by the Saxons – a treatment which Gildas apparently extrapolated back into the past as a characteristic of every type of foreign oppression;[39] the enslavement of the Britons compares with the deeds of Nebuzar-adan, who enslaved the Israelites.[40] The blinding of the Hebrew king parallels the collective blindness of Britain's rulers when the invitation to the Saxons was dispatched.[41] The British *superbus tyrannus* (or king) was depicted as *infaustus* – 'ill-starred' – and his (presumably) unpleasant fate was perhaps a fact shared by Gildas and his intended audience,[42] in which case it may have paralleled the end of Zedekiah. The physical destruction of Jerusalem is paralleled by Gildas's grandiose and apparently somewhat fanciful description of the Saxon sack of Britain's towns and destruction of *Britannia*, which had been introduced in chapter three as an island paradise. The analogy is spelled out by apt quotations from those Psalms which lament Jerusalem's fall.[43]

Gildas's preoccupation with the fall of Jerusalem is so profound that it seems to have acted as his paramount source of inspiration and paradigm, as his own text was born and then took shape. Indeed, it seems to have so influenced him as to make it a legitimate concern that it may have affected his own reconstruction of the fall of Britain. It seems likely, at least, that it was this analogy which persuaded Gildas to adopt such an overtly urban dimension, both in his general description of Britain and also with reference to its subsequent fall to the Saxons.[44] Even so, the analogy is so powerfully drawn that parallels between the sack of Jerusalem and the fall of Britain must have seemed compelling to him as an author, even without some manipulation of his British material and notwithstanding the topographical dimension. Furthermore, the entire construction must have appeared sustainable before his own, contemporary audience and this implies that Gildas was guilty of few open departures from the facts, to the extent that those were then known.

The account of the fall of Jerusalem shares with the episode with the Gibeonites the assumption that it was the morality primarily (even perhaps exclusively) of rulers and priests which conditioned the relationship between God and his people.[45] If Zedekiah's initial tributary status be considered a matter of treaty (as seems at least a logical implication), then, once again, his war against the Babylonians involved the breaking of a *foedus* by an Israelite leader. In both instances, failure in war resulted in the discomfiture of the Israelites but it was Jeremiah alone, confronted by a far greater catastrophe, who dwelt on the nature of that discomfiture. It was arguably for this that Gildas invoked what must count as his primary biblical authority for the status of Britain at the time of writing.

Similarities between the sack of Jerusalem in Jeremiah's

Lamentation and the 'ruin of Britain' are emphasised by a debt as regards both language and imagery, which numerically much exceed the more obvious quotations and paraphrases adopted by Gildas.[46] Such were highlighted in Gildas's explicit comments on the situation current over at least the previous ten years,[47] in verses five and six of the prologue. Since his comments here referred specifically to the present and the very recent past, Gildas had no room for misrepresentation or invention. He may well have omitted much that a secular historian might have included and coloured that which he incorporated to accord with his thesis, but one cannot doubt the fundamental veracity of his factual statements.[48] These were as follows:

1　The Church (*ecclesia*) had fallen from its pole position within British society and had lost much of its membership.[49] That it was 'widowed'[50] implies a collapse in the ability of the sub-Roman, Christian State's ability to protect it. The normal duality of Church and State is perhaps implicit in Gildas's juxtaposition of *rectores* (governors) and *speculatores*,[51] and implicit too in his juxtaposed complaints concerning the British 'tyrants' and clergy, from chapter twenty-seven onwards. His use of *urbs* – 'the city' – may have conjured up the image of Rome for some of his audience, as it might have done Orosius,[52] but Gildas regularly used Jerusalem as a metaphor for the Christian community.[53] Given the source of this quotation, this was necessarily the stereotypical city which he had in mind. The numerical decline of congregations could reflect either the general collapse of State protection or the onset of apostasy.[54] Whichever, his comments here, as in chapter twenty-six, require that congregations were much reduced and the Church's authority diminished in the Britain in which Gildas wrote.

2　The Church had been placed under tribute.[55] This was not paid to the British nobility since they were likewise represented as impoverished in the next verse. Given his insistent analogy with the situation confronting Jeremiah, Gildas was necessarily here comparing current tribute payments by the British *ecclesiae* to the Saxons with the outflow of valuables to Nebuchadnezzar from the temple at Jerusalem, which had been ransacked by Nebuzar-adan. The analogy was later reinforced by his simile concerning the *columnae ac fulcri* ('pillars and posts') of salvation – the architectural origin of which is highly reminiscent of Jeremiah's temple –

to which he compared the prayers of the few by whom he was sustained in the present, and his explicit reference to that same temple as raised and burned by the Saxons during the early stages of their revolt.[56] In Gildas's imagery, Solomon's temple represented the British Christian community and its despoliation was an apt metaphor for their continuing losses at Saxon hands.

Two references to gold occur in this passage. Mentions of precious metals are not uncommon in the *De Excidio*, although most are in quotation and should probably be read metaphorically,[57] as should these examples. Comparable, grouped references occur to bronze, silver and gold stamped with the image of Caesar,[58] and to gold, silver and *divitia* – wealth – in association with Maglocunus.[59] Both these instances were associated with authority, so perhaps with taxation. Gildas's selection of quotation, here in chapter one, verse five, seems conditioned by reference to precious metals, and this is unlikely to have been accidental. The literal reference is to the fall of Jerusalem, the sack of the temple and the enslavement of the Israelites,[60] but he probably here intended a *double entendre*. Gold had been the normal medium of late Roman taxation to the extent that that was paid in precious metals. His implication here may be that it constituted a part (at least) of the tribute paid by his own countrymen to the barbarians. That Christians had been forced to part with personal ornaments is expressly stated ('the sons of Sion . . . dung'). Gildas's ultimate choice of quotation in this passage refers to antique ivory, sapphires and, perhaps, fine white cloth. Once again there is a metaphorical meaning available, but it may have been his intention that these also should be understood as among the types of precious goods paid over in tribute to the Saxons. Collectively these references seem to establish an all-embracing and generic body of precious goods, the fate of which was common to all. If this be accepted, Gildas was here conditioning the reference which he had already made to current tribute paid by the Britons, by implication to the Saxons, by denoting the types of high-status goods which were used for this purpose. Given that Roman Britain had recently become a coinless society, such payments in precious goods of whatever kind seems plausible. The parallel between the Saxons of the present and the Babylonians of the biblical past was apparently an apt one.

With his sense here explored, it may be profitable to return to

Gildas's choice of biblical quotation in the previous verse. His references to improper (pagan?) rituals polluting an altar and to a 'cursed offering' (so a pagan sacrifice) are easily reconciled with his comments on Saxon domination of the British *ecclesiae*. Taken together they imply that some hitherto Christian Britons had abandoned God. It was precisely this charge that Gildas repeated at the close of his 'historical' introduction when referring to the 'devil' to whom the Britons were now 'slaves'.[61] It was the pagan Saxons – hated by man and God[62] – to whom this presumably referred.[63] Of the Britons 'a great multitude had been lost, as people daily rush headlong to hell',[64] presumably in part conditioned by their subjection to the Saxon 'antichrist'. Gildas was apparently referring to the decline of the city-centred church organisation of the lowlands of Britain, which late Roman authorities had initially established and then protected, under pressure from an unsympathetic (or even hostile) Saxon domination.

By close attention to Gildas's purposes and to his use of Old Testament analogies it is, therefore, possible to establish what he considered to be the principal 'damages and afflictions' affecting his own people at the time of writing. Since the present and recent past were conditioned by the result of the 'War of the Saxon Federates', those same 'damages and afflictions' must reflect the terms under which that was brought to an end, since ended it had: on that issue Gildas was quite specific in chapter twenty-six. As already outlined, he recognised at least three phases within the war: first came the invitation, the revolt and ravaging of the Saxons; then came a period of mixed fortunes, in which British victories were initiated under the leadership of Ambrosius Aurelianus. Gildas identified the year of the siege of *mons Badonicus* as the end of this second phase. If there is one single event which could be said to separate Romanised Britain from medieval England, it is this siege: up to this year there still seemed hope of a British victory (if only in Gildas's view under divine guidance) over their erstwhile mercenaries; excepting only a small coterie of lesser British victories thereafter (which Gildas forebore to name and which may also have occurred in this year), subsequent conflict (herein, phase III of the war) was necessarily won by the Saxons and the war ended in a peace conditioned by Saxon victory.

The conditions of the treaty by which the war was concluded included the payment of tribute by the Britons, perhaps more specifically by the churches or the Christian community, to the Saxons, and that tribute was considered by Gildas a principal 'affliction' of the present time.

It was presumably to the *foedus* (treaty) which brought hostilities to an end that Gildas referred elsewhere:[65] 'we much desire that the enemies of the church should be our enemies also without a *foedus* and our friends and defenders our fathers and lords as well'. Gildas included this as if quoting from an existing text known to his audience and even written by an acquaintance. Whether or not, there can be little doubt that, to an extent, it sums up his own view of the present, particularly since he introduced it by reiterating his own reliance on biblical authority.[66] His comments here imply that the British community within which he was himself resident was party to a treaty with the Saxons – the 'enemies of the church'[67] – which acknowledged their protection and so sundered it from Christian kingship such as still existed in the west, where British rulers were active as 'fathers and lords' of their peoples and 'friends and defenders' of the Christian community.[68]

Had this been a text of Gildas's own composition, his customary unwillingness to acknowledge the morality and royal virtues of these rulers might have meant that his 'fathers and lords' should refer back to the Romans, in his eyes the only truly legitimate protectors of Britain beneath God, whom he would portray in just such a parental role in chapter seventeen. However, his allusions to legitimate regality in the context of Maglocunus (in chapter thirty-three) somewhat detract from this logic and, in any case, the composition of this sentence by some other, contemporary, British commentator diminishes any tensions that it might otherwise set up with other sections of his work. The anonymous commentator whom Gildas was here quoting clearly viewed the British princes in the west (to whom this necessarily refers) in a far more charitable light than did Gildas.

In his concluding passages of the 'historical' introduction Gildas remarked in scathing terms on the changes which had occurred since the decease of the generation which had experienced the war. That generation had been sufficiently virtuous to at least be tested by God. Their successors were less virtuous, so unworthy of even divine scrutiny, let alone intervention. To this moral decay Gildas attributed many of the changes which had occurred during his own lifetime, which was necessarily a period of rapid readjustment to a new Saxon supremacy.[69] He noted, for example, the downfall of justice in terms which imply that it was only at this stage that Roman law was finally abandoned.[70] Such complaints, or 'laments', harp back once more to his introductory remarks in verses five and six of the prologue.

If political dominance passed at this stage to pagan barbarians, those social and political pressures that had hitherto encouraged the British establishment to conform with Roman culture – particularly the imperial religion of Christianity – may have begun to dissipate. Indigenous paganism was far from dead in the early fifth century, whether it be examined in Britain or in other parts of the Empire.[71] The military triumph of Saxon pagans presumably reversed the spread of Christianity in the British lowlands, where Saxon cultural influences rapidly became entrenched. Continuing 'English' domination thereafter may have had dire, if predictable, consequences for the Church as a land-owning corporation,[72] laid heavy demands upon it and encouraged apostasy and a resurgence of paganism, in the long run in favour of the more successful, so implicitly more powerful, gods of the conquerors.[73] At the time of writing, Gildas depicted the urban-centric church of the lowland zone and its aristocratic and Romanised allies as caught in a downward spiral of collapsing influence, dwindling congregations and declining wealth.[74] He was surely right, and there is no evidence that it ever recovered.

The New Testament

Having utilised Jeremiah's Lament to characterise and describe contemporary British society and its 'afflictions', Gildas turned to the New Testament in search of material through which to offer a solution.[75] He offered twelve quotations – perhaps consciously adopting the apostolic number by so doing, for rhetorical effect. They can be listed as follows:

1 Christ, travelling to Tyre and Sidon, was so impressed by the faith of a Canaanite woman that He cured her daughter of demonic possession.[76]
2 At Capernaum, He was so impressed by the faith of a Roman soldier, in comparison with that of the Israelites, that He promised that gentiles would attain the Kingdom of Heaven

while children of the Kingdom might be excluded.[77]

3 A second reference to 1, above.[78]

4 The 'Great Denunciation' of scribes and pharisees as hypocrites.[79]

5 A second reference to 2, above.[80]

6 An extract from the concluding passage of the Sermon on the Mount warning that not all those who profess the faith will enter heaven and attacking those who prophesy and do wonderful things in the name of the Lord.[81]

7 On the way to crucifixion, Christ addressed the daughters of Jerusalem in a lament in praise of virginity.[82]

8 The parable of the wedding, reiterating Christ's 'I know you not', which compares closely with 6, above.[83]

9 Christ's command to His assembled apostles after the resurrection to go out and preach the Gospel to all the world.[84]

10 Extract from the Epistle of St Paul to the Romans, concerning his role as apostle to the gentiles who were being grafted onto the Israelites as chosen ones through Christianity.[85]

11 The coming of the Holy Ghost to the apostles, in a scene which stresses the great communality and fellowship of the primitive church.[86]

12 The denunciation of Ananias and Sapphira, who kept back part of the proceeds of the sale of their property when they gave the remainder to the apostles, and died in consequence.[87]

These quotations offer a series of interlocking messages which Gildas proposed to make the foundation of his solution to his country's problems. Prominent is the reassurance offered in numbers 1, 2, 3, 5, 9, 10 and 11, that salvation through Christianity was at least as accessible (and perhaps more so) to the gentile as to the Jew. It was a central feature of Gildas's exposition that the Britons were God's chosen ones and these passages justifies his stance on this issue. But this position was to an extent conditional: in the first scene which he had chosen, Gildas was picking up a view of the Britons as Canaanites, whose relationship with Christ was that of dogs who obtained only the crumbs from the dining table of God's people. So too did he consider that the Britons had to overcome a much greater hurdle of 'original sin' than had the original chosen ones of the Bible. He made this clear at a later stage of his introduction:

when they strayed from the path of righteousness the Lord spared
not a people which was peculiarly His own among all the nations, a
royal lineage, a sacred race. . . . What then will He do concerning this
great blemish on our generation? It has heinous and awful sins like
unto all the wicked ones of the world; but in addition to that, it has
as though inborn a load of ignorance and stupidity that can neither
be removed or avoided.

Prominent, therefore, is his emphasis on the quality of faith required by God of British believers. It was only faith of the very
highest class, to which the supplicant was totally committed, which
was capable of persuading Christ to intervene and take action on
his or her behalf. The retribution which befell Ananias and
Sapphira was consequent upon the half-heartedness of their commitment to the Christian community. Gildas used the parable of
the wedding to stress the need for constant preparedness in case
the Judgement Day should arrive. In several references, therefore,
Gildas was stressing the need for wholehearted commitment to the
simple and unmarred faith of the primitive Church.

Alongside this was his condemnation of some, at least, of the
clergy, whom he attacked in references 4 and 6. The hypocrisy
and self-satisfied character of the scribes and pharisees were to be
revived in detail in Gildas's own complaints concerning the clergy,
but these passages serve to formulate the basis of his condemnation
or criticisms.

The subject of sexual morality was touched upon in extract 7.
Again, this was a favourite theme of Gildas's complaints, although
in this instance more specifically aimed at the laity and their
secular leaders than at churchmen.

Gildas's quotations conform with the general chronology of
Christ's ministry, passing from his life to his crucifixion and thence
to his resurrection and the Acts of the Apostles. He was, perhaps,
writing once more with a copy of the Scriptures open before him.

It is the passage linking his New Testament quotations with
those which he had just deployed from Jeremiah which is of
critical importance:

I gazed at these things and numerous others in the Old Testament as
if on a mirror reflecting our own life, then I turned even to the New
[Testament], and there I read more clearly what had hitherto perhaps
been dark to me, the shadow fell away and the truth dawned more
strongly.

This is a complex group of images: the darkness of his *obscura* was not just of Gildas's comprehension but also of the Saxon domination which he had just defined by biblical analogy. His juxtaposition of *clarius* ('more clearly') and *obscura*, and of *umbra* ('shadow') with *veritas* ('truth') and *inlucescens* ('the coming of the dawn') suggests a host of images: his solution (light) will follow his outline of the problem (shadow), much as the New Testament follows the Old; just so could the moral regeneration which Gildas urged on his countrymen bring salvation in the matter of their political predicament, leading to a blissful period of Christian peace free of barbarian oppression. By similar metaphors did Gildas later introduce Christianity to Britain in his 'historical' account.[88]

In this instance, Gildas's primary purpose is made clear in his first quotation from the New Testament, which this text directly introduces and which he then reinforced by a second reference to that same passage in his third selection. It seems clear that Christ's meeting with the Canaanite woman was considered by Gildas of special relevance to his own problems. He was probably attracted in part by the fact that Jesus was here depicted as being outside Israel and adminstering to a gentile (as noted above), but it was surely the boon that she asked of the Lord which was of primary interest to him: the daughter of the Canaanite woman was in the possession of a demon which, by her great faith – despite being gentile – she persuaded Christ to eject from her. So too was *Britannia* possessed by the Saxons. Only exceptional and un-questioning faith in God on the part of the Britons offered a means by which He might be similarly motivated to expel them in a fashion directly comparable with Christ's act in St Matthew's account. It may well have been his desire to emphasise the aptness of this, his first use of the analogy of demon or devil for the Saxons, that encouraged Gildas to use it in profusion at the end of his 'historical' account.[89]

His message was, therefore, a specifically Christian one. Salvation – in both the personal and collective senses – was feasible in Gildas's opinion *only* through unquestioning faith, fear-ful respect for the Lord and a stainless morality. The 'grafted branch of the olive which did not fear' the Lord was to be cut off.[90] Thus did Gildas propose to cut out from the Church all that was less than wholesome, from apostates and those prepared to make concessions to the heathen, or the devil,[91] at one extreme, to the morally lax and spiritually indolent at the other. Only by this path could the 'sack of Jerusalem' (so the Saxon domination over, and exploitation of, Britain) be undone, to be replaced by a community of saints, basking in the warmth of divine approbation and under God's protection. His admonitions to the British leadership would return repeatedly to precisely these issues and these texts, quoting, for example, extensively from the Epistles of St Paul,[92] and the Gospel of St Matthew,[93] just as they would from Jeremiah.[94]

Gildas was careful to spell out his hostility towards the British payment of tribute to the Saxons. This was the one clear-cut manifestation of British dependency on, and subordination to, the Saxons to which he had already directed attention in that series of quotations from the Old Testament in which his characterisation of the present 'damages and afflictions' had been framed. His third quotation from the New Testament, drawn like the first from St Matthew's account of the meeting between Christ and the Canaanite woman, made precisely this point: 'It is not good to take the bread of the sons and throw it to the dogs.' As has already been established (see above, pp. 54–5), Gildas invariably used 'dog(s)' in a pejorative sense and it featured prominently among those terms of which he made a metaphorical use to refer to the Saxons. He had already, in verse five, established the term 'sons of Sion' as specific to the Britons. The bread may here be standing in a generic sense for goods of all kinds, but Gildas might have exploited this particular quotation for its use of *panis*, for the additional dimension of the bread of the Christian mass. Whether or not this last suggestion is accepted, Gildas was making a specific recommendation: that his contemporaries should not pay over their own goods to the Saxon dogs in tribute.

Conclusions

Gildas employed his Old Testament analogies to characterise Britain's 'afflictions' as he perceived them at the time of writing. In so doing, he focused on Jeremiah's Lament concerning the fall of Jerusalem to the Babylonians as his principal text, to the extent that one can only conclude that the analogy was a close one. It is

Gildas's insistence on the relevance of this analogy to Britain's experience over the recent past which confirms, without the possibility of reasonable doubt, that the 'War of the Saxon Federates' ended in an almost universal defeat for the Britons and victory for the Saxons. The Britons were left, after that war, under Saxon domination and paying tribute to them.

Although his method of characterising this situation was fundamentally moral in kind, it was the political consequences of that Saxon victory which Gildas sought ultimately to address in his *DEB* and he did make quite clear statements to this effect in his exordium.

Even so, his eagerness to exploit this analogy *may* have led Gildas to over-emphasise certain aspects of Britain's ruin – particularly by introducing the notion that the towns of Roman Britain fell to barbarian assault.[95] In detail, the fall of Jerusalem differed in many respects from Britain's experience at Saxon hands. That Gildas chose to overlook, or overcome, such difficulties confirms his determination to utilise this analogy for his own purposes but the recognition that there were problems of comparison in turn strengthens the appropriateness of his use of Jeremiah's text as a means of offering a general characterisation of the 'ruin of Britain'. The method of delivery is obscure – particularly to a modern audience dependent on this text alone for some grasp of the context in which he wrote – but the basic message is clear enough.

Gildas's solution to this problem was that of a conventional, late Classical, providential historian. He explained the catastrophe as a consequence of a moral and spiritual failure on the part of the Britons, so turned his attention throughout the bulk of his text to this issue and away from the specific political circumstances of the present. He urged the relevance of Christian faith on his contemporaries and outlined the means by which they might prevail upon Christ – or the Lord – to intervene on their behalf, in precisely the same manner as He had on behalf of the Canaanite woman. A purity, totality and constancy of faith, therefore, was the solution which Gildas proposed.

He then hammered home his message in a sequence of contrasting allusions to figures from the early Church, choosing exemplars who personified blessedness (St Peter), wretchedness and greed (Judas), martyrdom (Stephen) and heresy (Nicholas). Their virtues, or antithetical sins, would later be taken up at length, both in the 'historical' introduction and in the complaints.

His message had here an optimism which not all his passages were to share. He wrote, only a few lines further on,[96] of his despair at the moral and spiritual inadequacies of the Britons. That perhaps betrays Gildas's prevailing mood and his despondency concerning the uphill task he faced, as a self-appointed, latter-day Jeremiah, seeking to set free his allegorical Jerusalem from the sins of his own countrymen, and so from the oppression of the Saxons, those latter-day Babylonians and Chaldeans, under whose whips his fellow-countrymen were currently in captivity.

Notes

1   *DEB*, I, 2. Had he written ten years earlier, he would probably have been the same age as is traditionally ascribed to Christ at his resurrection – thirty-three – and this analogy may have prompted Gildas's reference to a gap of ten years.

2   *DEB*, I, 2, 6, 14. Cf. St Patrick's similarly conventional *exordia* in both the *Confessio* and *Epistola*: *St. Patrick*, ed. A. B. E. Hood, Chichester, 1978, pp. 23, 35.

3   *DEB*, I, 3–4.

4   *DEB*, I, 5–6.

5   *DEB*, I, 7–12.

6   *DEB*, I, 13. This practice of grouping biblical references by Testament (even by book) was resumed by Gildas, for example in his condemnation of the priesthood: LXVI–LXXII; LXXIII–LXXV.

7   *DEB*, I, 14.

8   *DEB*, I, 15–16.

9   Numbers, XX, 12.

10   Leviticus, X, 1–2.

11   There are allusions here to Numbers, XXVI, LI, LXV; Exodus XIV, 22; XVI, 15; XVII, 6, 11. Gildas confused the Israelites *in toto* of Numbers XXVI and LI with the Israelites numbered in Sinai by Moses and Aaron (XXVI, LXIV). Moses and Aaron were presumably the 'truthful' men excluded by Gildas.

12   Joshua, III–VII.

13   Joshua, IX; II Samuel, XXI, 6. Gildas returned to this issue in *DEB*, XXXVIII.

14   *DEB*, XXVI, 1, and see also I, 13.

15   As, for example, Jeremiah LI, concerning his expectation of God's destruction of Babylon. Gildas cannot have been unaware of Jeremiah's views: see note 22, below.

16 P. Sims-Williams, 'Gildas and the Anglo-Saxons', *Cambridge Medieval Celtic Studies*, VI, 1983, pp. 27–8, but recall also Gildas's 'eternal treaty' between God and man: *DEB*, XLIV, 2.

17 *DEB*, LXXIX, 1; XCII, 3.

18 *DEB*, I, 4, drawing on Jerome's prologue to the Vulgate.

19 A theme to which he returned in *DEB*, XXXV, 1; XXXVII, 2; for discussion, M. Winterbottom, *Gildas, the Ruin of Britain and Other Documents*, Chichester, 1978, p. 5. See also references to 'tearful complaints' in I, 1, 'mourning' in X, 2, and 'groans' in XIV, XX, 1 and XXXII, 2.

20 *DEB*, I, 13.

21 *DEB*, I, 5–6.

22 Lamentations, I, 1; IV, 1, 2, 5, 7.

23 Although this is not unique: see, for example, his explanation of metaphor in *DEB*, LXXI, 3.

24 So by repeated references to Isaiah: e.g. *DEB*, XXII, 2; XXIX, 2; XXX, 1, Ezekiel and those psalms which also relate to the sack of Jerusalem.

25 Jeremiah, L–LII.

26 By planning rebellion against Babylon under the influence of false prophets: Jeremiah, XXVII, 12–15; LII, 2.

27 Jeremiah, XXVII; LII, 3.

28 Jeremiah, XXXIX, 1; LII, 3.

29 Jeremiah, XXXIX, 5; LII, 8.

30 Jeremiah, XXXIX, 8; LII, 13.

31 Jeremiah, XL, 8; LII, 15, 16.

32 Jeremiah, LII, 17–23.

33 Jeremiah, LII, 24–30.

34 See above, notes 26, 27.

35 The priests in the temple were characterised as rebels against God's true prophet: Jeremiah, XXVI. The analogy with the British clergy whom Gildas attacked in *DEB*, LXVI onwards is a compelling one, with himself playing the role of Jeremiah.

36 Parallel *DEB*, XXII–XXIII, in which a quotation from Isaiah, XXII, 12–13, introduces the invitation sent by a 'proud tyrant' to the Saxons. See also Vortipor, whose life was '*in dei offensam*' (*DEB*, XXXI, 2); Cuneglasus, '*dei contemptor sortisque eius depressor*' – 'despiser of God and oppressor of his rank' (*DEB*, XXXII, 1). Rebelliousness towards God and God-given authority was, in Gildas's opinion, an inherently British characteristic: *DEB*, I, 13–14; IV, 1, 3; V, 2; VI, 1; XII, 3; XIII, 1, which collectively contextualise XXII, 2: '*servus durus*'.

37 *DEB*, XIX, 4; XX, 2; XXI, 2 (a famine of morality); XXV, 1.

38 E.g. *DEB*, V, 2; VI, 2; VII; XIX, 3.

39 *DEB*, XXV, 1, with which compare VII, XI, XIX, 2–3.

40 *DEB*, XXV, 1, with which compare VII, XV, 2 and implicitly XIX, 2.

41 *DEB*, XXIII, 1–2.

42 *DEB*, XXIII, 4.

43 Towns: *DEB*, XXIV, 3–4; the island: XXIV, 1–2; the quotations are from Psalms, LXXIV, 7; LXXXIX, 1, *contra* M. Winterbottom, *Gildas: the Ruin of Britain*, Chichester, 1978, p. 156.

44 The urbanity of Jeremiah's account is emphasised in *DEB*, I, 4–5. See also III, and the implausible notion of Saxons taking British towns by assault, in XXIV, 3. For further consideration of their abandonment in the present, see p. 165 below.

45 A view which Gildas adopted to an extent in his own complaints, but see below, p. 147.

46 See, for example, parallels between *DEB*, XXIV, 3 and Lamentations, II, 12.

47 For problems of interpreting this passage, see D. N. Dumville, 'The chronology of *De Excidio Britanniae*, Book I', in M. Lapidge and D. N. Dumville, eds, *Gildas: New Approaches*, Woodbridge, 1984, p. 84, and see above, p. 85, note 1.

48 Which might otherwise have critically undermined his general thesis.

49 *DEB*, I, 5; Lamentations, I, 1. *Ecclesia* here may bear the meaning of 'congregation' or 'Christian community', as is implicit by analogy with Lamentations, I, 10, but it may also have encompassed both the fabric and the ecclesiastical organisation. See also *DEB*, LXVI, 1: *ecclesiae domus*, presumably referring to the church more in the sense of a building, although Jeremiah used *domus* for the Hebrews: e.g. III, 18. For discussion, see R. W. Hanning, *The Vision of History in Early Britain*, New York, 1966, p. 55.

50 Winterbottom, *Gildas*, p. 5, preferred 'bereaved', but this is not the literal meaning. Gildas may have used the term in the sense of the Church as a widow losing the protection hitherto afforded by the husband (the State). For parallels see *DEB*, XVII, where the Romans were 'parent-like'; *Britannia* appears as a 'chosen bride', in III, 3; see also, XXVII; XCII, 3. The image of a 'divorce' in X, 2, may also be relevant.

51 *DEB*, I, 14. Gildas was familiar with *speculatores* from the Bible (*DEB*, XCI, 2–3), quoting from Ezekiel, XXXIII, 1–9, wherein the term means 'watchmen' and this may be the sense here, in which case it is paralleled by the virtuous *duces* of L, 1. Some doubt must arise, however, owing to the seventh- to eighth-century use of this term as polite address to 'bishops'. I assumed a literal meaning in 'Gildas, Roman walls and British dykes', *Cambridge Medieval Celtic Studies*, XXII, 1991, pp. 11, 14.

52 E.g. Orosius *Histories*, I, xiv.

53 Explicitly for the 'Church' *in toto*, in *DEB*, XI, 2, and the individual 'soul': *DEB*, LXXXVII, 1, and implicitly in eleven further instances.
54 See below, p. 77.
55 *'sub tributo fuisse factam'*. Compare that of Jerusalem in Lamentations, I, 1: *'fact est sub tributo'*. Gildas presumably wrote the former with the latter open in front of him.
56 *DEB*, XXVI, 4 and XXIV, 2.
57 *DEB*, LV, 1; LIX, 5; LXXX, 3; LXXXIX, 5.
58 *DEB*, VII.
59 The paraphrase is from Lamentations, IV, 1–2. For Roman coining of British metals, *DEB*, VII; for Maglocunus's association with precious metals, *DEB*, XXXIV, 2.
60 It has resonances for the fall of the towns of Roman Britain: *DEB*, XIX, 2; XXIV, 3; XXVI, 2.
61 *DEB* , XXVI, 4.
62 *DEB*, XXIII, 1.
63 See F. Kerlouégan, *Le De Excidio Britanniae de Gildas*, Paris, 1987, p. 274, for terms by which Gildas referred to the devil, but note the substantial overlap between these and those he used for the Saxons. See above, p. 53, and below, p. 160.
64 *DEB*, XXVI, 3.
65 *DEB*, XCII, 3, quoting from a pre-existing text written by 'one of us'. For recent comment on this passage, see Sims-Williams, 'Gildas', pp. 21–2; Dumville, 'Chronology', pp. 81–2.
66 *DEB*, XCII, 3. Note here the use of the ambiguous *hostes* – 'enemy' – which could variously mean either the barbarians (including Saxons) or the devil. This *foedus* recurs in LXXXIX, 1, for discussion of which see p. 191.
67 *Hostes* occurs in reference to barbarians of all sorts: *DEB*, IV, 4; XV, 1, 2, 3; XVIII, 2; XIX, 3; XX, 3; XXI, 1; XXVI, 1, and was also used in a pejorative sense for British kings: XLIII, 2.
68 Note the ironical reference to *vindicantes et patrocinantes* – those 'avenging and defending' – in *DEB*, XXVII. The rulers of the Celtic west clearly saw themselves in this light: for the use of such terms on a memorial stone, see V. E. Nash-Williams, *The Early Christian Monuments of Wales*, Cardiff, 1950, p. 138.
69 *DEB*, XXVI, 3, 4. Gildas returned to this theme, e.g. LXXXIII, 3: 'do not allow the heathen to rule over your people, oh Lord'.
70 *DEB*, XXVII.
71 As may be implied by Gildas's awareness of it, even though he placed it in a past context (*DEB*, IV, 2, 3), but he may well have been unaware that Christianity had been less than universal prior to the Saxon *adventus*. For recent comment on the archaeological evidence, C. Thomas,

Christianity in Roman Britain to AD 500, London, 1981, fig. 48, p. 265. Both Orosius and St Augustine were writing in part to defend the Christian position against influential pagan critics, during the first three decades of the century.

72 For clergy as 'businessmen', *DEB*, LXVI–LXVII; for wealth of bishops, CVIII, 3.

73 In *DEB*, LXXIX, 3, quoting Isaiah, LXVI, 1–3; LXXXIII, 3, quoting Joel, II, 17.

74 *DEB*, I, 5, 6.

75 *DEB*, I, 7.

76 Matthew, XV, 24.

77 Matthew, VIII, 12.

78 Matthew, XV, 26.

79 Matthew, XXIII, 13.

80 Matthew, VIII, 11.

81 Matthew, VII, 23.

82 Luke, XXIII, 29.

83 Matthew, XXV, 10–12.

84 Gildas adapted Mark, XVI, 16.

85 Romans, XI, 17; the claim is made in XI, 13.

86 Acts, IV, 32.

87 Acts, V, 9.

88 *DEB*, VIII, employing once again the metaphor of the sun's rays.

89 *DEB*, XXIV, XXVI, and see above, pp. 53–6.

90 *DEB*, I, 10, quoting Romans, XI, 17.

91 Cf. *DEB*, CVIII, 4.

92 All quotations from *DEB*, XCVII–CIII are from St Paul's epistles.

93 *DEB*, XCII–XCVI.

94 *DEB*, LXXX–LXXXII.

95 *DEB*, XIX; XXIV, 3.

96 *DEB*, I, 13.

4

The locality of the
De Excidio Britanniae

To this point, our discussion of Gildas's text has been outside
any specific geographical setting, other than the assumption that
Gildas was a Briton who wrote from an insular perspective, so
inside Britain. This *Britannia* is, however, an extremely imprecise
concept, even within the text: in his geographical introduction
(chapter three), and elsewhere, Gildas was content to accept
Orosius's useage of the term for the whole island, yet it is clear
that, in practice, he assumed a rather narrower definition of the
term, which ignored those parts of Britain which had lain outside
Roman jurisdiction. His *Britannia* was, therefore, close kin to the
Britanniae – the provinces of the late Roman British diocese. He
may even have been ignorant of the survival of free indigenous
communities in the far north throughout the Roman period, if he
ever considered the question.

Britannia is such a broad geographical concept that there have,
over the last millennium or so, been numerous attempts to localise
Gildas, and so place the *DEB* more precisely. This has been attempted more recently as an aid to using his text more effectively
as a historical source, but earlier assays owed more to the desire of
monks at St Gildas de Rhus, in south-east Brittany, to invest him
with antecedents appropriate to his sanctity.[1] The earliest Breton
Life gave Gildas royal antecedents in Strathclyde, then had him
educated in Wales,[2] so providing him with both geographical
and social terms of reference which were appropriate to a tenth-
century perspective on the Celtic world. That this explanation
of Gildas's origins and early career is apocryphal is now fully
accepted,[3] but folk traditions of this sort have combined with his
self-evident familiarity with the politics of contemporary Wales to

encourage several modern scholars to assume that he wrote in some part of the medieval principality.[4]

In contrast, both Molly Miller and Professor Edward Thompson noted Gildas's apparent knowledge of, and interest in, the north of Roman Britain.[5] Miller proposed that the 'northern' content of the 'historical' introduction was such, between chapters fifteen and twenty, verse one, that Gildas was here referring specifically to the north of erstwhile Roman Britain, and pointed to the *Interea* ('Meanwhile') which begins chapter twenty, verse two, as the point at which this 'northern' section ends. Professor Thompson developed this argument a stage further, proposing that there was sufficient reason to place the period of luxury and even the Saxon *adventus* ('arrival'), which were recorded in subsequent chapters, in the north east of erstwhile Roman Britain, and Gildas himself somewhere in the north west.[6]

Thompson's thesis has exercised some influence over Patrick Sims-Williams, and far more over David Dumville.[7] It has the advantage of being based primarily on evidence internal to the text. It may therefore be worth considering it in some detail:

1 As regards locality, Thompson opens with the assumption that Gildas was writing 'in the West in the mid-sixth century', and characterises him as a 'provincial historian'.[8]

2 His locational hypothesis is founded primarily on interpretation of *DEB* chapter nineteen, verse one, which reads: 'They [the Scots and Picts] seized the whole of the extreme north of the island from its inhabitants (*indigenes*) up to the wall.' To Thompson, this *must* mean Britain south of the wall and *cannot* refer to Scotland north of the wall, because the subsequent actions of the raiders necessarily occurred within Roman Britain.[9]

3 With this established as a 'fact' to his own satisfaction, Thompson then juxtaposed Gildas's account of attacks on the Britons by northern barbarians with what he believed to be a broadly contemporary account of a successful Saxon invasion and settlement in southern Britain, in the Gallic Chronicle of 452 under the year 441 (he offered 441–2). A northern Gildas with interests in Picts and Scots and the great walls was therefore juxtaposed with a southern Gaulish account of Saxon activity in the south of Britain.

91

4   When Gildas described the consequences of these barbarian
    attacks as causing a famine throughout the whole *regio*,[10] this
    necessarily refers to the north because it was in the north that
    these attacks were taking place.[11]
5   Since the letter to 'Agitius' was written in response to these
    same calamities, it was necessarily written from the north and
    sought aid for a specifically northern community who were,
    alone, suffering attacks from the Picts and Scots.
6   The reintroduction of the term *regio* in chapter 22 of the *DEB*
    conditions the invitation to the Saxons and their settlement,
    which must therefore have occurred in the north. Swayed,
    perhaps, by the archaeological evidence (although he does
    not say so), Professor Thompson suggested that settlement
    occurred in the East Riding or Vale of York, but insisted
    on what would eventually become Northumbria as a general
    location. The great raid and 'War of the Saxon Federates' were
    then specifically and exclusively northern events.[12]

Professor Thompson's thesis was presented with his usual pithy
logic and an enviable enthusiasm, but it is far less robust than its
author avowed. That he may himself have sensed its inadequacies
is possible; hence the rhetorical flourishes by which he attempted
to sustain it.[13] In practice, his case is deeply flawed, both on the
general grounds that he omitted to consider much of the evidence
which is pertinent to Gildas's regional perspective, and as an
exercise in dialectic. Criticisms of the latter can be summarised as
follows, and are arguably sufficient on their own to undermine the
'northern Gildas' of Thompson's explanation:

1   As had already been noted before Thompson presented his
    thesis,[14] Gildas's comments on the seizure of land by the Picts
    and Scots, in *DEB* chapter nineteen, are easier reconciled with
    extramural Britain. As Thompson admits, an almost identical
    phrase occurs in chapter twenty-one, in a very similar con-
    text, which he is prepared to accept does refer to extramural
    Britain.[15] In Gildas's reconstruction (of what we must remem-
    ber are apparently fictitious events), the second occurrence of
    the *extrema pars* is dependent on the first, in the sense that the
    capacity of the Picts to return to the far north from raiding
    intramural Britain depended on their having already seized
    precisely that region of Britain, two chapters previously. That

initial seizure of territory preceded their attack on the stone wall, a sequence which is incomprehensible if they were already located south of it. Both the sentence order and sequence of events in this account require that Gildas was initially, in chapter nineteen, verse one, establishing his Picts in extramural Britain, then imagining them thence launching a frontal assault on the wall and its 'towns' (by which he meant the wall forts), but only then its hinterland, before retreating back to extramural Britain once more.[16] That the Scottish and Pictish raids were specifically or exclusively directed against northern parts of the old diocese is not, therefore, established. Rather, arguments to that effect are unsustainable.

2   With Professor Thompson's interpretation of chapter nineteen refuted, or at least in jeopardy, there is no basis for the juxtaposition of a northern view of events in the *DEB* with a southern perspective in the Gallic Chronicle of 452, since Gildas was not 'certainly and explicitly speaking of the north'.

3   With this case at best unproven, Professor Thompson's argument unravels because it is entirely dependent on interpretation of just that one passage: reference to the *regio* affected by famine at the close of chapter nineteen need not be specifically northern; nor need the appeal to 'Agitius' have originated in the north; nor need recurrences of *regio* (chapter twenty-two) be specific to the north, and this, in turn, frees the Saxons of Gildas's invitation – their settlement, rebellion, raid and subsequent warfare – from an exclusively northern context. Indeed, that Saxon raiding was exclusive to any one region is expressly contradicted by Gildas, who depicted the Saxon fires as affecting 'almost the whole surface of the island'.[17]

Several more general observations can be added to these specific objections. Thompson's thesis depends heavily on his own view that Gildas saw himself, and should be accepted by ourselves, as a writer of 'provincial history',[18] despite the fact that 'history' – particularly in the modern sense – was never his principal objective.[19] Nor were his interests primarily 'provincial': Gildas was interested in the salvation of a community which he defined in terms which suggest that he had in mind at least the entirety of what had been Roman Britain. When his comments referred to less than the totality of 'Britain', he was generally careful to admit as much, albeit in the very general terms quoted above. His perspective was not 'regional' in a modern sense.[20] Nor was it 'provincial' in the late Roman sense, but rather 'diocesan' in scope. His concern was with the entire *ecclesia* of the Britons – so the total community – and any lesser construct is inadequate as a context for his text.

Thompson's thesis also depends heavily on Gildas's competence as a historian within that section of the 'historical' introduction of the *DEB* which has the poorest claim to historicity – that separating the battle of Aquileia (388) from the situation which prompted the (undated) appeal to 'Agitius'. If this section is fundamentally fictional, then any thesis based exclusively on it, but which is designed to explain Gildas's locational perspective *in toto*, is extremely vulnerable to challenge or correction if evidence which conflicts with it be found elsewhere in the text. Gildas's claim that the barbarians 'seized the whole of the extreme north part of the island as far as the wall' may indicate nothing more significant than his own ignorance of the whereabouts of the Picts during the Roman period,[21] as is, perhaps, implicit in his readiness to simply ignore the limits to Roman occupation of Britain throughout his treatment of Roman Britain: if the northern walls be misplaced after 388, then Gildas was free to imagine that hitherto Roman Britain had encompassed the entire island, and he certainly offers nothing which contradicts this interpretation.

In crucial respects, the issue hinges on Gildas's use of the term *regio*. Although normally translated into English as 'region', this word was used in a variety of senses by Gildas: he considered it appropriate to the district through which a British king might pursue a thief,[22] so to a kingdom or area of jurisdictional unity of whatever size; it was used, too, of amorphous territories beyond the sea, and of neighbouring parts of the Roman Empire.[23] If all Gaul, for example, is encompassed in this last remark, then there is nothing amiss with the view that Gildas saw all of Roman Britain as just one *regio* of the Roman Empire. It was initially just one *provincia* – a term which Gildas used alongside *pagus* – district – in chapter thirteen, in a context which implies that he was aware of the basic territorial organisation of the late Empire into provinces and 'districts'. He seems to have been unaware that Britain had begun as a single province but was successively subdivided: in a contemporary, British context he used the term in the plural (in chapter one, verse five) and regularly used the term *rector* – 'governor' in the plural (see pp. 151–5), although he accepted without correction the notion of a singular British province from St Jerome (chapter four) in an early post-conquest context.

Other Classical writers used the term *regio* for extremely wide-ranging purposes: thus the *Sugdianorum regiones* of Mela's *De Chorographia*. Gildas is unlikely to have had access to this text but he may have been familiar with Virgil's similar useage of the term in the *Aeneid*, in a very broad sense as the 'regions of the earth'. If Gildas was familiar with, and influenced by, the practice of any particular, pre-existing text in his use of *regio*, it was surely that of Orosius, whose geographical material he drew on for his own description of Britain in chapter three of the *DEB*. Orosius introduced his account of the world by noting its division into three *partes* – the continents of Europe, Africa and Asia – then subdivided these in turn into *regiones*. The island of *Britannia* was one of these.[24] Supposing that Gildas had not rejected the useage of the term *regio* which he found in the writings of Virgil and Orosius, it can safely be assumed that he employed it either of all Britain or, at the very least, of all that part of Britain which was inhabited by Britons and/or which had been Roman. This is certainly the natural interpretation of the term in the *DEB*, for example, where Gildas refers to the threat of barbarian settlement 'from the border even to the boundary of the *regio*'.[25] It is the universality of this threat which concerns him, albeit in a comment which presumably has far greater relevance to the Saxon settlements of the present than putative Pictish and Scottish activity in the past. It was this geographical and social concept of *Britannia* and *patria* which interested him, not just one part of it – hence his personification of 'Britain' as a collective noun applicable to all the Britons.[26] Similarly it is all Britain – or at least the entire Christian community of Britons – whose salvation was his concern.[27]

There is therefore no warrant to the assumption that, in chapter nineteen, Gildas was necessarily using the term *regio* for any territory smaller than that same 'fatherland' of ex-Roman Britain, concerning which he was wont to generalise. His theme was the downfall of all Britain, not just its northern parts. Thompson's view is based on the unfounded expectation that Gildas meant something quite different, and far more specific, in his use of *regio*, than that with which he was familiar in Orosius and Virgil. Such a view is unsustainable.

Nor does Gildas's insistence on the significance of Pictish and Scottish raids inevitably identify the north as the theatre of his interests, even in chapters fourteen to twenty two.[28] There is no literary evidence of Saxons raiding in late Roman Britain, excepting only in 410,[29] until the eventual establishment of a permanent Saxon presence in Britain. That such raids were frequent and a matter of current knowledge when the invitation was dispatched to Gildas's Saxons is implausible in the extreme, if only because if such were the case the Britons would surely have looked elsewhere for mercenaries. There is, however, evidence of raids by the Picts and Scots, who were apparently active relatively close to London in 367.[30] They were the first mentioned threat to the diocese *c.* 400, in the eyes of a eulogist active at Ravenna, with the Saxons appended for good measure.[31] Saint Patrick, with others, was enslaved by Scottish raiders, albeit at an unknown (but apparently very late fourth or early fifth century) date and from an unidentified locality,[32] and he later commented on British contact with Irish and Pictish slave markets in his own *Letter to Coroticus*.[33] Once the Roman maritime defences had ceased operation, all Britain was vulnerable to sea-borne raids from Ireland or Pictland and the coastal waters of the North Sea coast – hitherto overseen by a system of watch-towers in Yorkshire – may have carried numerous raiders down to the Channel. Gildas's own perception of the raids besetting Britain post-Aquileia may be that of an observer distant in time, but he was quite clear in his own mind that the Scots and Picts were the aggressors across all Britain, and has nothing at this stage to say of the Saxons.

Locality and the *DEB*

If Thompson's 'northern Gildas' be placed to one side, so too must efforts to assign Gildas to any specific locality which rest on the hagiography and political propaganda of the early to central Middle Ages. The sole basis for discussion of the locality of Gildas's perspective is the text itself. Nowhere is it clearly or overtly assigned to any particular district, and the lack of clear guidance on this point has led to a growing pessimism concerning our ability to localise the perceptions inherent in its authorship.[34]

Such pessimism finds support in Gildas's efforts to generalise concerning Britain as a whole, and is further encouraged by speculation that he *could* have been itinerant, or a man who was eager to conceal his own identity, perhaps because he lived within the jurisdiction of one of the very 'tyrants' of whom he complained.[35] Certainly, the assumption that he *necessarily* lived and worked outside their orbit merely because he attacked them so openly is far from conclusive.[36] This dose of pessimism has provided a useful antidote to the hypotheses concerning a 'northern Gildas' which have already been outlined, but it may encourage even more negative conclusions than the evidence requires.

We can make some headway here: Gildas's comments at the end of his preface give the clear impression that the *De Excidio* was written with a particular audience in mind.[37] That intended audience apparently included men sympathetic to the most ascetic wing of the contemporary Church, whose support he anticipated, and others representing the majority (and perhaps also predominantly clerical) of whose hostility he felt assured. Gildas referred again to the prayers of the few remaining 'true sons of holy mother church' in the closing section of his 'historical' introduction.

There is some indication that Gildas may have been subject to some British authority which was itself under Saxon 'protection', as opposed to those communities ruled over, and protected by, the British kings of the far west.[38] If so, Gildas may have written in fear of the vengeance of the Saxons directly (supposing them to have been informed of his text), or alternatively of some British authority subservient to, or even complacent concerning, the Saxon domination. If it be considered original to the text, it may have been as a defence against retribution from some or all of these powerful potential critics that he used the unique, apparently meaningless and certainly non-Roman name 'Gildas', perhaps as a pseudonym or *nom de plume* behind which to hide his own identity. Yet his comments on his intended audience at least demonstrate that he had one, and so preclude any intent to keep the document entirely secret, even in the short term.

There is a little more that can be added on this subject without inviting controversy: Gildas was a Christian Briton, with strong sympathies for asceticism and the monastic movement, perhaps himself a deacon, from a background which was sufficiently wealthy to have afforded the luxury of a good Latin education –

hence he most probably sprang from a land-owning family; his training in rhetoric and his comments on the law courts of his own day imply a particular interest in Roman law and court practice,[39] as might have been expected in a scion of an aristocratic household in late Antiquity; his audience apparently included similarly cultured, Christian, aristocratic, Romanised Britons who enjoyed a level of education which can only have derived from estate-tenure, which in turn effectively anchored them to a particular part of Britain. Such men may well have shared Gildas's fundamentally conservative social and political values,[40] even if many were more accommodating than him as regards the changes then underway in the body politic.

Gildas and his audience knew precisely where they were. It is our misfortune in treating of the *De Excidio* that we do not share the vast backdrop of everyday knowledge which is taken for granted therein, other than that which can be reconstructed painstakingly from the text itself. So where was Gildas, and the audience for whom he wrote?

First, it may be helpful to rehearse the negative evidence: we can be certain that they lived outside those parts of Britain already by this stage under the direct control of Germanic rulers. Despite recent words of caution,[41] it does seem admissible to rule out on this basis the areas of primary Anglo-Saxon settlement as defined by artefactual remains, specifically in East Anglia and the central Thames valley; that the community to which Gildas apparently belonged had long been at peace with the Saxons at the time of writing,[42] under a treaty which acknowledged a partition between British and Saxon areas of control,[43] suggests that they shared some sort of frontier. This in turn would seem to rule out the far north and extreme west of Roman Britain, particularly southern Scotland, Cumbria, North Wales generally and the south-west peninsula of Wales, all of which were so far distanced from territory likely to be under *direct* Saxon control by the date of composition as to be inadmissible.

If the latinity of the *De Excidio* in any way mirrors local commitment to late Classical culture and education over a long timescale, we should expect this work to have derived from the more Romanised, lowland zone of sub-Roman Britain. Yet it was possible for a royal prince from Gwynedd to acquire, by whatever means, an education of the same type, apparently in the lifetime of

Gildas,[44] so Gildas's whereabouts is far from fixed by such considerations.

More positively but also more tentatively, within the *De Excidio* itself can be found a series of clues to the general location of both author and audience, which, while short of clear proof, may allow us to build up a pattern of probability. These will be examined in the order they are introduced in the text.

The geographical introduction

Given that he shared the scribal error of 200 miles for the width of Britain, Gildas necessarily derived his dimensions for the island from the *Historiae* of Paulus Orosius,[45] with which he seems to have been more familiar than sometimes thought.[46] Gildas, however, corrected the defective and highly erroneous figure which he found therein by excluding from it 'various large promontories'.[47] Although the argument is far from prescriptive, his correction is easiest reconciled with the southern coast of Britain (or documents relating to distances across the south of the island), so omitting the Kentish and Cornish peninsulas. This detail becomes progressively less appropriate to an author, and audience, beyond one or two days ride from the south coast. While it could still conceivably be applied to the width of Britain measured from one of the Welsh peninsulas to the North Sea coast, the plural of the text requires a second notable promontory on the east side of the island (figure 1). Such is conspicuous by its absence: there are no 'curving ocean bays' for many miles north of the Wash, and the ill-defined coastline of that embayment fits poorly with the visual image demanded by the text. The Thames estuary and the chalk cliffs of Kent and Sussex are the best fit in the east for 'large promontories of land which jut out' and 'curving bays'. In the west the indented coastlines of Dorset, Devon and Cornwall offer an appropriate context. North of the Welsh landmass, any correction to Orosius's figure for the breadth of the island would be more likely to re-evaluate it downwards, making a specifically northern perspective implausible in the extreme.

Gildas found in Orosius a description of the Channel crossings written from a continental standpoint.[48] He reversed this perspective, writing of the Channel from an insular stance. His adaptation and augmentation of the original implies that he was in Britain at

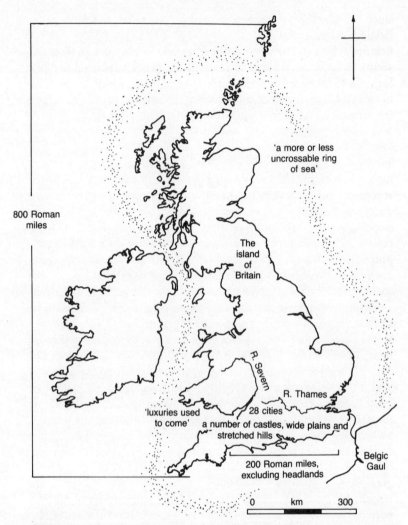

Figure 1 The spatial content of *DEB*, III: Gildas's 'geographical' introduction.

the time of composition and was writing for an audience which was still resident there, as opposed to the exiles whose departure overseas he later noted.[49] His interest in, and apparent knowledge of, these crossings may incline us to a southern context for Gildas, since he returned to them repeatedly. In his view, the crossing to Belgic Gaul was pretty well the only navigable route to and from Britain.[50] That this view was exclusive of barbarian shipping seems clear from his repeated, but implicit, assumption that the Scots and Picts used other sea lanes which were apparently beyond his knowledge. It was Britons and Romans, therefore, to whom the Channel crossings mattered, and there is no evidence in the text that Gildas envisaged that either had ever thought to cross any other of Britain's seas. Given his insistence that Britain's encircling seas were only passable along the Channel, it seems most improbable that Gildas envisaged refugees from the Saxon revolt to have been sailing to a destination other than Gaul, where we can at least confirm the presence of Britons in some numbers in the aftermath.[51] The prospect of psalm-singing Christian Britons fleeing in some numbers to an Ireland which Gildas uniformly portrayed as the home of savage and bestial barbarians,[52] has always been a weakness of all arguments for a western, and more specifically a north-western, Gildas.[53]

Gildas's interest in the Channel did not stop there: his reference to the lack of a fleet manned by Britons when rebelling against Rome is pertinent;[54] so too are his two Roman invasions, then his imagined sea-borne Roman expeditions crossing to Britain;[55] the various appeals for Roman assistance arguably crossed the other way to Gaul; since they were obviously perceived as migrating from within the Empire, the same route necessarily brought the plague of heresies that was spearheaded by Arianism, and took away the armies of Magnus Maximus.[56]

That these allusions to the crossings were not always historical is immaterial in this context. Gildas seems to have expected a great deal of the Kent–Gaul crossings and he was quite correct in envisaging a need to protect these crossings from sea-borne barbarians.[57] That this was to him the principal seaway of interest to the Britons suggests a southern geographical perspective.

Gildas named two great rivers, the Thames and Severn, in the context of the past import of luxuries to Britain by ship. In this context we should understand Gildas to be referring to Roman goods from continental Europe. Since neither was noted by Orosius, this passage would seem to be original to Gildas.[58] Any member of the sub-Roman community in Britain would be likely to note the Thames in this context, given its enormous past importance in cross-Channel trade. The Severn was of far less importance, serving only minor ports (primarily in the vicinity of Bristol and at Gloucester), although there is some evidence of a fourth-century fort of 'Saxon Shore' type at Cardiff. It may be significant that the Humber/Ouse/Trent waterways are ignored – but too much should not be construed from negative evidence. However, the equation of the Severn with the Thames in this context may imply that the *DEB* was the work of someone more familiar with the hinterland of that minor trade route than with other parts of the island. Such reasoning would place Gildas in some part of the fourth-century province of Britannia Prima, which was based on Cirencester.

To the Thames Gildas would later return in his description of a miracle performed by St Alban, who opened up an otherwise unknown route across the bed of the 'noble' river.[59] That it was 'unknown' has no bearing on Gildas's own familiarity with the river's course since it merely denotes the fact that this route was only accessible via this bible-derived miracle and not, either before or after, a ford in normal use. That the river was 'noble' once more suggests some familiarity with this, the greatest of Britain's rivers, so the most apt for such a description.

The description of vigorous agriculture on wide plains and 'stretched hills',[60] is consistent with widespread agricultural activity in a landscape of alternating downland-type hills and valleys. Celtic fields of known Roman date are a prominent feature of the southern chalklands, but almost entirely absent from hills which could be described as 'stretched' in the Midlands, Wales and the north, so primarily the Pennines. An exception is the widespread Celtic lyncheting of several of the Dales of western Yorkshire, but these are not sited on the hilltops in the fashion required by the text. Only the southern downs certainly fulfil the paired characteristics of Gildas's brief reference. This detail may point to a southern locality.

The practice of transhumance was probably widespread,[61] but reference here to 'mountain-pastures' suggests that some sort of upland was envisaged, although that certainly need be no more elevated than Bodmin or Dartmoor. It is quite possible that high downland would be sufficient: to a lowland community, mountains may be comparatively minor features of the landscape and a too literal interpretation of Gildas's employment of the term is clearly suspect, given, for example, his use of the term in his account of St Alban's miraculous crossing of the river Thames, or his analogy of a 'mountain torrent' for the Romans.[62] Mountains were clearly a fundamental part of the *DEB*'s rhetorical topography, the function of which was rarely geographical.

In other respects Gildas's view of Britain is that of a lowlander, conversant with the climate of the south. Hence the clear fountains of constant flow, the murmuring and brilliant rivers that send people to sleep,[63] which would be incongruous in upland Wales, for example, the north west or the Pennines. The remarkable whiteness of the stones therein similarly suggests a limestone or, better, a chalkland, environment.[64]

Martyrs

All three martyrs named by Gildas belong to the south of Britain – to Verulamium (St Albans) and, less certainly, to Caerleon.[65] Although this does not require that Gildas shared their locality, it certainly gives no grounds for any other, and it is a necessary assumption that the martyrs named were known, by reputation at least, to Gildas's audience, and particularly revered by Gildas himself. The fame of St Alban may exempt him from this part of the debate, but neither SS Aaron nor Julius are known to have enjoyed a far-flung following, either in the fifth century or thereafter.

It was Gildas's opinion that, were his fellow citizens able to visit their graves and places of martyrdom, they would benefit greatly.[66] He lamented that they were deprived of so doing 'on account of their numerous sinful deeds by the mournful *divortium barbarorum*'. The barbarians are necessarily the Saxons but the use of *divortium* requires some explanation, since it is not the obvious term for a 'partition'.[67] It may be that Gildas here had in mind another *double entendre*. He was to refer at several points of this work to the 'widowhood' or 'bereavement' of the British Church,[68] and to the duality of Christian leadership, with husbandly protection the role of the secular arm,[69] and the Church playing the female role.[70] The analogy of a marital breakdown for the loss of Britain seems to have been one which Gildas found attractive. This allegorical marriage is relevant to the entire relationship between Britain (always a feminine in this text) and the protective role of Rome, which was to be set aside by the Britons rebelliously seeking a *divortium* via the rule of tyrants. Relevant too is the repeated use of parent–child metaphors to define the same relationship.[71] In both instances, the Roman state is portrayed as the secular protector – so the dominant male figure – and the British Christians as its dependants.

This *divortium* has a similar relevance to Gildas's perception of the collapse of relations between Britain and God, to which the reference to the 'impious acts' of the Britons herein surely points.[72] In this case it is God who assumes the manly, protective but judgemental role, and the Britons the position of dependants bound to obey the will and strictures of a superior, wielding legitimate authority. It is possible to see a further interplay between such marital analogies and the sexual immorality which Gildas particularly highlighted among the contemporary rulers whom he chastised.

Whether or not these resonances should be sought, *divortium* apparently has two meanings: at one level, Gildas was making passing reference to the collapse of relations between the Britons, the Romans and God, which had led to this sorry situation; at another he was referring to a fact of political geography. British pilgrims seeking to pass through areas under direct Saxon control would presumably have left the protection of British authorities and their courts and passed into territory subject to the protection of customary, kin-centric, English law, within which they were kinless and without status, and so liable to attack, capture and enslavement.

The geography and chronology of early Saxon settlement in the mid- to upper Thames valley was arguably far better understood by both Gildas and his immediate audience than it is by modern scholarship, dependent as that is on the interpretation of archaeological evidence which lacks any clear indication of spatial influence. With that said, it is clear that a series of Saxon settlements and attendant cemeteries were established in that region by, and perhaps a little before, the mid-fifth century (figure 2). It is difficult to envisage any other area of archaeologically evidenced, Germanic control which can have posed a threat to British travellers journeying from any specific, fixed point outside immediate Saxon control, seeking access to both Verulamium and Caerleon – assuming that it was the latter which was here intended.

This textual construction concerning sites which are poles apart

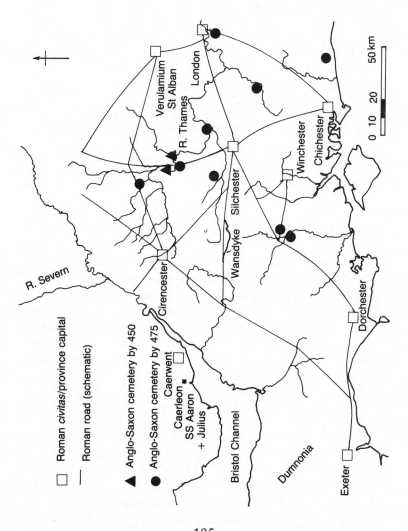

Figure 2 Central southern Britain in the fifth century: a map to illustrate the problem of localising Gildas (Anglo-Saxon cemeteries after J. Hines, 'Philology, Archaeology and the *adventus*', in *Britain 400–600: Language and History*, Heidelberg, 1990).

R. Severn

Verulamium
St Alban
London
R. Thames

Winchester
Chichester

Cirencester

Wansdyke

Silchester

Caerwent
Caerleon
SS Aaron
+ Julius

Dorchester

Bristol Channel

Dumnonia

Exeter

☐ Roman *civitas*/province capital

— Roman road (schematic)

▲ Anglo-Saxon cemetery by 450

● Anglo-Saxon cemetery by 475

0 10 20   50 km

requires Gildas to be writing from a perspective focused south of the middle or upper Thames. Indeed, his selection of the far-distant SS Aaron and Julius alongside St Alban may imply that he was intentionally defining the limits of the 'diverse places' associated with martyrs then inaccessible to his fellow citizens, at least without grave risk, in which case he was pointing to the mid- and upper Thames valley as the region where travellers might expect to experience difficulties. Whether or not, an author with a perspective focused in Wales, the midlands or the north is entirely inappropriate to this passage, since one or other of these shrines would be accessible without risk. The inference must be that Saxons in the upper Thames valley were in a position to impede travellers approaching south-east Wales or St Albans via the roads from the south. Once more, Gildas has a southern perspective.

The northern walls

Gildas combined a small amount of fact concerning the two walls in the north with a great deal of fiction, to construct a tale set in the past to suit his own moralistic and rhetorical purposes.[73] In the process he displayed a southerner's ignorance, and misunderstanding, of the actual remains, in particular in his confusion of the stone-founded forts of Hadrian's Wall with Roman towns.[74] To Gildas, forts seem to have been something which existed on the coast, as in chapter eighteen, where he refers with far greater accuracy to the forts of the Saxon Shore (albeit in a mistaken chronological context, and as an antidote to raids by the Picts and Scots). To Gildas, forts seem necessarily to have been constructed in coastal locations – which would be an accurate definition by criteria derived from the south of Roman Britain. Walled sites further inland were necessarily, therefore, towns. With this preconception in place, he naturally, but quite erroneously, interpreted the wall forts of the north as a line of *urbes* – 'towns' – which had been built inland 'for fear of the enemy', which the later wall linked together.

Had Gildas been familiar with northern Britain (where Roman forts were always far commoner than towns) this is precisely the type of error we might expect him to avoid. Similarly, his useage of the neutral term *indigenes* for the extramural population (in chapter nineteen) may imply that this northern community was not included within his own vision of the *patria* or 'fatherland' of the Britons. He may well have been ignorant of the presence of Britons and Brittonic speakers in southern Scotland at this or any other date, or simply uninterested in the fate of any part of Britain exclusive of that area which had been Roman, so intramural Britain. In either event, his unemotional notice of barbarian attacks on a community immediately beyond the wall has a recognisably distant, so southern, perspective.

The naïvety inherent in Gildas's comments on the walls does nothing for the view that he was familiar with the region even as a visitor – rather the reverse. On the contrary, he displays both here and elsewhere an interest in the wrecked towns of Roman Britain which is difficult to reconcile with the north or far west. Cities played a prominent role in his description of Britain,[75] over-shadowing the brief mention of other fortified sites. His vision of Diocletian's persecution was urban in context, with the Holy Scriptures being burnt in the town squares.[76] If his martyrs were buried in suburban cemeteries, then his vision of a subsequent phase of church building was also urban-centric.[77] His perception of the Saxon rebellion and devastation was likewise written from a profoundly urban and urban-Christian viewpoint,[78] as was his reconstruction of the ensuing peace.[79] Reference to Roman coinage may also imply that Gildas should be sought in the pro-vincial heartland, where coin-use was best developed and lasted longest.[80] All these factors, therefore, favour a perspective for Gildas deriving from the southern heartland of the civil diocese.

The Picts

The 'historical' section of the introduction to the *De Excidio* contains numerous references to the Picts, who are portrayed as barbarians who invariably attacked the Britons by sea.[81] It has been suggested that Gildas believed them to come from outside Britain up until the mid-fifth century, when he referred to them as resident in 'the far end of the island'.[82] In fact, the Picts had been resident in northern Britain throughout the late Roman period and (if this was his opinion) such a view betrays a gross ignorance of northern geography on the part of the author – again implying that he wrote from a perspective far removed from the north. Alternatively, Gildas may – as a southern commentator writing for a southern audience – have merely assumed that Picts always attacked Britain from the sea because that was the normal experience of southern Britain.[83] He certainly suggested that Pictish and Scottish attacks motivated Roman construction of forts along the Channel, so he does seem to have been confident that this occurred.[84] His assumption that the same kind of seaborne Pictish tactics were appropriate to a (fabricated) account of the northern walls as were commonplace when they raided southern Britain conforms with a belief system which is inconsistent with a 'northern Gildas'.

In either case, Gildas displayed an ignorance of the north which is difficult to reconcile with personal familiarity with the area. It is far easier to explain his thought processes as the product of a perspective which derived from the deep south of Roman Britain, than any part of the north. This view is confirmed by his description of the Picts as resident *in extrema parte insulae* – 'in the outermost (or "foreign") part of the island' – a phrase which might be ambiguous if used by a resident of what would one day become northern England, who was unfamiliar with events in the south, but which was crystal clear from the standpoint of a southerner.[85]

The tyrants

Using repeated instances of thesis and antithesis to good rhetorical effect, Gildas adressed the British kings in general terms before making a series of five personalised attacks on specific rulers. It has often been suggested that Gildas was writing outside the territory controlled by these kings but in an area where detailed information concerning them was readily available.[86] If the *De Excidio* was written for 'publication'[87] – rather than for some secret purpose – then that argument retains some credibility. There is certainly a contrast between Gildas's approach to the rulers of Britain in his preface (where he was justifying his decision to write, presumably to his immediate audience) – to whom he applied the polite terms *rectores* and *speculatores*[88] – and his scurrilous attacks on individual western kings. There may well be further, profound contrasts between his guarded and encoded criticism of policies pursued by influential men close to home and those of the tyrants in the west: contrast these last with his brief comment concerning the grandsons of Ambrosius Aurelianus, the

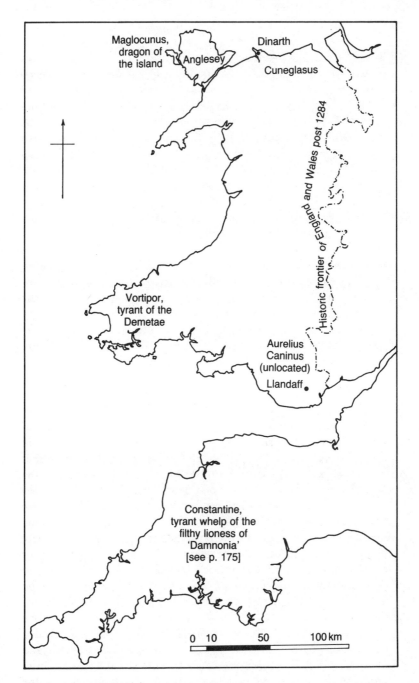

Maglocunus, dragon of the island

Anglesey

Dinarth

Cuneglasus

Historic frontier of England and Wales post 1284

Vortipor, tyrant of the Demetae

Aurelius Caninus (unlocated)

Llandaff

Constantine, tyrant whelp of the filthy lioness of 'Damnonia' [see p. 175]

0 10   50   100 km

Figure 3 The British tyrants of the *DEB*.

British authorities then apparently constructing dykes in southern Britain, or those anonymous British rulers who were in league with the Saxons.[89]

The order in which the several tyrants were discussed has a geographical rationale. The first was Constantine, king of Dumnonia (the south-west peninsula), the third was Vortipor of the Demetae (Pembrokeshire), the fourth, Cuneglasus, should be associated with Rhos, and Maglocunus with Anglesey (figure 3). The second, Aurelius Caninus, might be that Cunignos who was the subject of a memorial inscription of *c.* 500 in Carmarthenshire.[90] Whether or not, the sequence adopted depended either very largely, or entirely, on geographical location, the starting point being in the south west and the end point in the north west. It is arguable that this order has a relevance to Gildas's location when writing. It may be that the order selected began with the ruler nearest to Gildas (and the audience for whom he primarily wrote), and progressed steadily away from that point.

The accusations made against these rulers also vary in ways which may be significant. The crimes reputed to Aurelius Caninus, Vortipor and Cuneglasus are characterised by their generality: most concern sexual mores. Gildas offered more specific criticisms concerning Constantine, the first listed, and Maglocunus, the last. Concerning the latter – who attracted the longest diatribe of all – Gildas had specific knowledge of both his (apparently) Roman-style education and his flirtation with monasticism.[91] It may be that Maglocunus, the murderer and nephew of his predecessor, had been personally known to Gildas as an exile in his youth; alternatively, it is possible that he knew his teacher – such rhetoricians of renown cannot have been that common in Britain by the time that Gildas was writing. Whichever, there are identifiable avenues by which Gildas could have obtained the more specific ammunition for his attack on the distant but powerful Maglocunus.[92] For his more general accusations, at least, Gildas admitted his own dependence on rumours borne as if by the wind.[93] He was not, therefore, by any stretch of the imagination, writing close to the court of Maglocunus.

His attack on Constantine was far more specific in kind and dealt with a particular event which had occurred within the year of composition.[94] Indeed, the detail known to Gildas implies his acquaintance with some party to this tragedy, be it only the abbot, from whom he had heard of this very recent incident. Although Gildas used the term *cives* throughout the *De Excidio* with the general meaning 'countrymen', 'Christian Britons' or 'citizens',[95] it may be that here in chapter twenty-eight it carries a more specific meaning and that Gildas was referring more particularly to his own locality and his own community – fellow-members of his own *civitas* perhaps. Whether or not (and this is no more than a suggestion), the primary position given to Constantine, the geographical organisation of the several complaints and the differences in substance between them all imply that Gildas had a very specific knowledge of, and interest in, the ruler of the *Dumnonii*, such as one might expect from a member of a nearby, or neighbouring, community.

The locality of Gildas and his audience

These several elements within the 'historical' introduction collectively enable us to narrow down the likely locality in which the *De Excidio* was conceived, written and 'published'. The persistent town-focused viewpoint of Gildas surely derives from somewhere south of the Mersey and east of Long Mynd and his mistakes concerning the northern walls appear to confirm this. His awareness of the Channel crossings – to Belgic Gaul in particular but probably also to points further west – suggests a locality south of the Thames. So too does the confidence with which he corrected Orosius's error concerning the breadth of Britain. His attacks on named and contemporary rulers suggest that Dumnonian territory was not far distant from Gildas's own homeland. His comments on St Alban and SS Aaron and Julius imply that access to Verulamium and (probably) Caerleon was impeded by the presence of territory under direct Saxon control, such as is evidenced by archaeology from the mid-fifth century in the central to upper Thames basin. Individually, none of these factors are decisive. Taken together, all these various pointers offer a consistent impression of an author writing from a perspective derived from, and for an audience resident in, what is now the deep south of central England. In few other areas is it likely that a fifth-century author could have looked out through his window at 'stretched hills' on which agriculture was in progress even as he wrote. If we were to imagine Gildas as resident in, or in the general vicinity of,

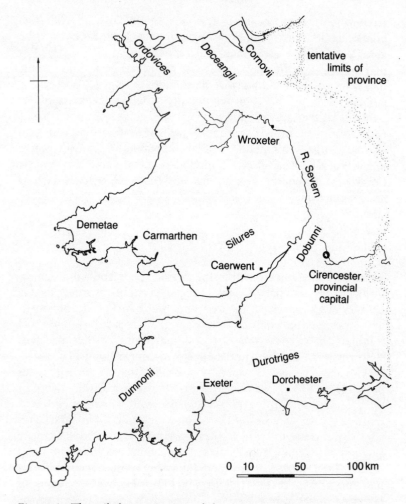

Figure 4 The tribal organisation of the province of Britannia Prima in the late Roman Period: tribal names in italics are not known to have been granted self-government as *civitates* but apparently remained under military jurisdiction throughout.

Wiltshire or Dorset, it would be improbable that we were very wide of the mark.[96]

If so, Gildas wrote within the lowland zone of the late Roman province of Britannia Prima, south of the Thames, probably in the territory of the Durotriges (figure 4). His comments on contemporary politics were almost exclusive to territory which had arguably belonged within that province. This fact may even imply that an ecclesiastical diocese specific to it remained intact to the time of writing, so providing a network for the transmission of political information throughout the region.

The late survival of a civilian, Romanised and Christian gentry with monkish sympathies in this corner of the erstwhile diocese would cause less surprise among archaeologists than most others. Parts of Britannia Prima now in England – particularly the Cotswolds – saw the furthest development of the villa as a stately home to be found anywhere in Roman Britain and comparatively late occupation can be attested at an important minority of them. Just how late such occupation might need to be to encompass Gildas and his audience depends on the dating of the year of composition, in the forty-fourth year after *mons Badonicus*, and it is to that that we must next turn.

Notes

1 A full list of options is offered by D. N. Dumville, 'The chronology of *De Excidio Britanniae* Book I', in *Gildas: New Approaches*, eds M. Lapidge and D. N. Dumville, Woodbridge, 1984, pp. 79–80.

2 *Vita Gildae*, by a monk of Ruys, in *Gildas: the Ruin of Britain, Fragments from Lost Letters, the Penitential, together with the Lorica*, ed. and trans. H. Williams, Cymmrodorion record series III, London, 1899, pp. 322–4, particularly p. 322, opening line.

3 M. Lapidge, 'Gildas's education and the Latin culture of sub-Roman Britain', in Lapidge and Dumville, *Gildas: New Approaches*, pp. 32–3.

4 As W. H. Davies, 'The church in Wales', in *Christianity in Britain 300–700*, eds M. W. Barley and R. P. C. Hanson, Leicester, 1968, p. 139; J. Morris, 'Historical introduction', in *Gildas: the Ruin of Britain and Other Documents*, ed. and trans. M. Winterbottom, Chichester, 1978, p. 3.

5 M. Miller, 'Bede's use of Gildas', *English Historical Review*, XC, 1975, pp. 241–61; Miller, 'Stilicho's Pictish war', *Britannia*, VI, 1975, pp. 141–5; E. A. Thompson, 'Gildas and the history of Britain', *Britannia*, X, 1979, pp. 203–26.

6 Thompson, 'Gildas', pp. 216–18.

7 P. Sims-Williams, 'Gildas and the Anglo-Saxons', *Cambridge Medieval Celtic Studies*, VI, 1983, p. 7, but note his caution in several respects; Dumville, 'Chronology', pp. 62–6.

8 Thompson, 'Gildas', p. 208.

9 *Ibid.*, p. 214.

10 *DEB*, XIV, 4.

11 Thompson, 'Gildas', p. 215.

12 *Ibid.*, pp. 216–19.

13 E.g. 'To think otherwise is to enter dreamland': *ibid.*, p. 217.

14 By C. E. Stevens, 'Gildas Sapiens', *English Historical Review*, LVI, 1941, p. 360. Thompson recognised as much: 'Gildas', p. 214.

15 Compare *omnem aquilonalem extremamque terrae partem* (*DEB*, XIX, 1) with *in extrema parte insulae* (*DEB*, XXI, 1). Note Dumville's doubts concerning Thompson's interpretation of this passage in 'Chronology', p. 64 and note 21.

16 For discussion, see N. Wright, 'Gildas's geographical perspective: some problems', in Lapidge and Dumville, *Gildas: New Approaches*, pp. 89–91.

17 *DEB*, XXIV, 1: see Thompson's attempts to reconcile this passage with his own thesis in 'Gildas', pp. 218–19.

18 Thompson, 'Gildas', pp. 206, 208.

19 See discussion of Gildas's purposes on pp. 7–29.

20 As Thompson himself argued, in my view incorrectly: 'Gildas', pp. 206–7.

21 N. J. Higham, 'Gildas, Roman walls, and British dykes', *Cambridge Medieval Celtic Studies*, XXII, 1991, p. 2, note 3.

22 *DEB*, XXVII, 1.

23 *DEB*, XXV, 1; V, 1.

24 Pomponius Mela, *De Chorographia*, ed. G. Ranstrand, Goteborg, 1971, II, v, 43; *Aeneid*, I, line 460; Orosius, *Histories*, I, ii, 12. See also Orosius for *regio*, I, i, 16.

25 *DEB*, XXII, 1: *a fine usque ad terminum regionem* – 'from one border even to the boundary of the region'. The translation of *regio* here as 'country', offered by M. Winterbottom, is therefore justified: *Gildas: the Ruin of Britain*, p. 25.

26 *DEB*, IV, XIV, XXVII.

27 That community was portrayed as God's *familia* in *DEB*, XXII, 1, and repeatedly characterised, through metaphor and analogy, as the Israelites or God's chosen people. Gildas's confusion between the island and the province, or diocese, arguably derives from the use of *Britannia* in both contexts in pre-existing Church histories.

28 *Contra* Dumville, 'Chronology', p. 62.

29 Zosimus, *New History*, trans. R. T. Ridley, Sydney, 1982, VI, 5; Gallic Chronicle of 452, 410.

30 Ammianus Marcellinus, *Historia*, ed. T. E. Page and trans. J. C. Rolfe, London, 1935, XXVII, 8.

31 Claudian, *On the Consulship of Stilicho, II*, in *Claudian*, II, trans.

M. Platnauer, London and New York, 1922, p. 20. This speech was delivered early in 400.

32   N. J. Higham, *Rome, Britain and the Anglo-Saxons*, London, 1992, p. 84.

33   Patrick, *Letter to Coroticus*, in *St. Patrick: His writings and Muirchu's Life*, ed. and trans. A. B. E. Hood, Chichester, 1978, II, XII.

34   Sims-Williams, 'Gildas', pp. 3–5.

35   As very tentatively suggested by Sims-Williams, 'Gildas', p. 5.

36   Following Sims-Williams, 'Gildas', p. 3.

37   *DEB*, I, 16, wherein Gildas anticipated the reception his work might receive.

38   *DEB*, XCII, 3 and see discussion on pp. 73–85 above.

39   *DEB*, XXVII: for his apparent interest in state exactions for the purpose of dyke construction, see discussion in Higham, 'Gildas', pp. 9–13.

40   As expressed in *DEB*, IV, 1.

41   Sims-Williams, 'Gildas', pp. 26–7.

42   *DEB*, XXVI, 2.

43   *DEB*, XCII, 3; X, 2.

44   *DEB*, XXXVI, 2.

45   Orosius, *Histories*, I, ii, 76–7. See discussion in N. J. Higham, 'Old light on the Dark Age landscape: the description of Britain in the *De Excidio Britanniae* of Gildas', *Journal of Historical Geography*, XVII, 1991, pp. 363–5.

46   Contrast the view of, for example, Thompson, 'Gildas', p. 210, with that of N. Wright, 'Did Gildas read Orosius?', *Cambridge Medieval Celtic Studies*, IX, 1985, pp. 31–42, which effectively supersedes earlier comment.

47   *DEB*, III, 1. Orosius used *promunturia* in his description of another island, Sicily, and this may have inspired Gildas's use of the term.

48   'Access for people crossing to its nearer shore is provided by a city called Richborough; from here it faces the Menapi and the Batavi': trans. A. L. F. Rivet and C. Smith, *The Place-Names of Roman Britain*, London, 1979, p. 77.

49   *DEB*, XXV, 1.

50   *DEB*, III, 1.

51   W. Davies, *Small Worlds: the Village Community in Early Medieval Brittany*, London, 1988, pp. 14–16.

52   As in *DEB*, XIV, XVI, XIX.

53   *Contra* Thompson, 'Gildas', p. 222.

54   *DEB*, VI, 2.

55   *DEB*, V, 1–2; VI, 2; XV, 2; XVII, 2, supposing only that he was mindful throughout of his own comments in III, 1.

56   *DEB*, XII, 3; XIII, 1.

57 *DEB*, XVIII, 3. The enemy was the Picts and Scots.

58 I assume that he was not using a lost written source, as suggested by Sims-Williams, 'Gildas', p. 5, since that would most likely be an insular document of the type which he expressly did not have: *DEB*, IV, 4. The Severn may have been navigable as far north as Wroxeter (although that was not a port), or even beyond: B. S. Trinder, *The Industrial Revolution in Shropshire*, London, 2nd edn, 1981, pp. 61–9. I am grateful to Dr Paul Stamper for drawing my attention to this work, and for his own comments on the subject.

59 *DEB*, XI, 1.

60 *DEB*, III, 3; Higham, 'Old light', p. 369.

61 *Ibid.*, p. 370.

62 *DEB*, XI, 1; XVII, 2.

63 *DEB*, III, 4.

64 That little beaches of pure white pebbles are a notable feature of the chalk streams of the Salisbury area was brought to my attention by Penelope Rundle of Wiltshire County Record Office, to whom my grateful thanks for this communication.

65 *DEB*, X, 2; G. R. Stephens, 'Caerleon and the martyrdom of SS Aaron and Julius', *Bulletin of the Board of Celtic Studies*, XXXII, 1985, pp. 326–35. Chester is a possible alternative to Caerleon, on the basis of its nomenclature in Welsh texts of the central Middle Ages.

66 I see no reason to separate the specific martyrs from Gildas's lament concerning these places, as argued by Sims-Williams, 'Gildas', p. 27, note 117.

67 As in the translation of M. Winterbottom, *Gildas*, p. 19. See comment of Dumville, 'Chronology', pp. 78, 82. In Classical literature, *divortium* can bear the meaning of a 'parting' or 'watershed'.

68 *DEB*, I, 5; *lugubre* in X, 2, has funereal connotations.

69 *DEB*, I, 14: *rectores*; the tyrants in XXVII; Tiberius in VIII, with whom contrast Diocletian in IX.

70 *DEB*, I, 5; perhaps also I, 14, if *speculatores* here refers to the bishops: see p. 87, note 51. *Britannia*, which Gildas regularly paralleled by Jerusalem, was portrayed as a bride in III, 3. Note that Jeremiah likewise makes widespread metaphorical use of 'bride', 'married woman' and 'widow' in reference to Jerusalem and the Israelites, and this was arguably Gildas's inspiration for favouring this metaphor.

71 As in *DEB*, XVII, 1.

72 Recall Gildas's reference to the Christian Britons as God's *familia*: *DEB*, XXII, 1.

73 See my more detailed comments in 'Gildas', pp. 1–14.

74 *DEB*, XVIII, 2.

75 *DEB*, III, 2, based on Orosius's description of Babylon: *Histories*, II, vi, 10.

76 *DEB*, IX: *platea* is the term used here and in XXIV, 3. It was originally Greek and perhaps reached Gildas via the Bible (e.g. Jeremiah, V, 1), rather than from indigenous traditions of urban terminology, which might be expected to have favoured *forum*.

77 *DEB*, XII, 2.

78 *DEB*, XXIV, 3–4.

79 *DEB*, XXVI.

80 *DEB*, VII.

81 *DEB*, XIV, XVI, XIX.

82 *DEB*, XXI, 1; see Wright, 'Geographical perspective', p. 92.

83 Higham, 'Gildas', p. 2, note, 3.

84 *DEB*, XVIII, 3. It would take very special pleading to argue that the Saxons were pertinent to Gildas's perspective in this context.

85 *DEB*, XXI, 1 and see discussion above.

86 E.g. Thompson, 'Gildas', p. 225, but note the caution of Sims-Williams, 'Gildas', pp. 5–6, and above.

87 See above, p. 97.

88 *DEB*, I, 14; XV, 3: 'governors' or 'rulers' and either 'guards' or 'bishops'. See below, pp. 151–9.

89 *DEB*, XXV, 3; XV, 3 and XVIII, 2 and XCII, 3, respectively. For the possibility that Gildas was criticising indigenous dyke construction, see Higham, 'Gildas'.

90 K. H. Jackson, '*Varia*: II: Gildas and the names of the British princes', *Cambridge Medieval Celtic Studies*, III, 1982, p. 31, but see pp. 177–9.

91 *DEB*, XXXVI, 1; XXXIV.

92 N. J. Higham, 'Medieval "overkingship" in Wales: the earliest evidence', *Welsh History Review*, XVI, 1992, pp. 154–9.

93 *DEB*, XXXIII, 3.

94 *DEB*, XXVIII, 1, 2. That year was then just one month old.

95 E.g. *DEB*, XV, 2.

96 Higham, 'Old light', p. 369. The view of A. W. Wade-Evans that Gildas lived at Glastonbury, although the product of reasoning with which I would prefer not to be identified, may not be so very far from the mark: *The Emergence of England and Wales*, Cambridge, 2nd edn, 1959, pp. 11–12, 159–60.

5

The chronology of the
De Excidio Britanniae

Despite his adoption of narrative history as the literary style
appropriate to his own 'historical' introduction, Gildas offered his
audience no dates according to any of the systems of calendaring
then in use. This need not indicate that he was unaware of dating,
nor imply that he lived in an age which made little or no use of
dates, since none were necessary to a text which answered to
providential and moral, as opposed to historical, imperatives.
There is no good reason to believe that the chronological fixing of
his own episodic narrative was high in his order of priorities. Only
the latter part, for which he had no literary sources, was provided
with a very basic chronology by reference to the present, by the
dating of *mons Badonicus* in years before that in which Gildas
composed the *DEB*, but it must be pertinent that that siege identified a year of importance not in history as such but in providential
history. It was this year in which Gildas believed that God had last
tested His people, to establish whether it loved Him or not (see
above, p. 50). The 'year of *mons Badonicus*' provides an anchor
point for the first half of the period during which the Britons had
been afflicted by the Saxons. It seems unlikely that he considered
that anything more elaborate was necessary.

Gildas was compiling a sequentially organised collection of
anecdotes not for historical purposes but as illustrations, or proofs,
of his own theory of causation. Since that theory was conceived
as of universal application, and was sustained as much by Old
Testament testimony as by recent insular example, his anecdotes
prior to mount Badon could be left joined together but floating
in a temporal soup without affecting their impact. That they
were apparently ordered chronologically probably owes much to

Gildas's knowledge of the Bible and Church histories, both of which were organised in a sequence obedient to time. His decision to begin the *DEB* by establishing his own theory of causation naturally led him to appropriate precedents, and to adapt to his own needs the narrative style in which those precedents which were available were already written.

There is nothing exceptional in a text written in late Antiquity and in an historical style which offers no dates: Constantius similarly included no dates in his *Life of Germanus*, despite its adoption of the same narrative idiom derived from history. This does not demonstrate that Gildas was unfamiliar with dating: indeed, his reading of Orosius, at least, had necessarily introduced him to dating by years since the foundation of Rome, albeit he need not have had any means of linking in a single sequence the recent past with more distant events known to him only from continental histories.[1] It does, however, cause substantial problems for those later generations for whom the *DEB* has long been almost the sole text on which to base a history of the fifth century.

The traditional dating of Gildas's life and work has rested on the thoughts – or guesswork – of some of the earliest of these generations, in particular on Irish and Welsh annalists several centuries later, whose assays cannot be tested, and so are best set aside.[2] More recent speculation has quite properly focused on the text itself,[3] or the relationship between figures named therein and other evidence for their lives.[4] The principal weakness of the latter approach lies in the non-contemporaneity of evidence regarding the chronology of such figures as King Maelgwyn, which rests on calculation over long periods of average generations. Such approximations offer only a very poor means of dating Gildas,[5] and these too are best set aside as potentially misleading.

The risk of circular arguments coming to dominate this issue is very high and it is currently a commonplace for historians or archaeologists intending to make reference to the *DEB* as an historical source to preface such discussion with a statement of the approximate date of composition which, to a large extent, begs the issue at stake. Attempts to establish a sequential chronology solely from a step-by-step approach to the 'historical' introduction have become so beset by value-judgements that any one set of results carries a probability of error greater than the range offered by many carbon-14 dates.[6]

119

This last approach rests also on the assumption that Gildas was attempting narrative history. That he was not is evident. Those few comparative indications of time passing – such as begin verses one and two of chapter twenty-five, respectively – are so vague as to be capable of bearing almost any interpretation. What is more, the phrase chosen in each instance arguably owed more to Gildas's assessment of his rhetorical needs than to any perception of actual time passing which he may (rightly or wrongly) have entertained. That a central section of the text appears to be fundamentally fictional is unlikely to imbue the modern scholar with much confidence in the accuracy, and regularity, with which Gildas marked the passage of time. The attempt to accumulate a chronology from Gildas's 'historical' sequence does not, therefore, offer much hope for an accurate dating of his authorship.

The latter part of the 'historical' introduction to the *DEB* is almost devoid of events which can be readily dated: after the death of Magnus Maximus in 388,[7] Gildas's immediate audience would have certainly been able to assign a date only to the year of the siege of Badon hill, which he obligingly informed them had ended forty-three years and one month before the date of composition.[8] Provided only that they had read, or heard, the *De Excidio* soon after it was written, and knew the present year, they could date *mons Badonicus* with ease. We, however, cannot, since the year of composition is now unknown.[9]

Between these two events, it has been claimed that Gildas knew of, and was making reference to, the 'Honorian Rescript',[10] of *c.* 410, but the evidence is far from convincing and, since it could encourage serious miscalculation, the association is best set aside.[11] With this gone, or at least in abeyance, only one event is generally recognised as offering an opportunity to assign a date to one of the later episodes within Gildas's sequence. That event was the sending of letters from the Britons to a named Roman leader on the Continent requesting aid against barbarian raids:[12]

Igitur rursum miserae mittentes epistolas reliquiae ad Agitium Romanae potestatis virum, hoc modo loquentes: 'Agitio ter consuli gemitus Britannorum;' et post pauca querentes: 'repellunt barbari ad mare, repellit mare ad barbaros; inter haec duo genera funerum aut iugulamur aut mergimur;' nec pro eis quicquam adiutorii habent. Thereupon once more the unhappy survivors sent letters to the warlike Agitius of Roman power, saying in this manner: 'to Agitius thrice consul, the groan(s) of the Britons;' and after a little lamenting; 'the barbarians push us back to the sea, the sea presses us to the barbarians; between these two types of deaths, we are either slain or drowned;' but they did not have any assistance from them [the Romans].

Although in every surviving recension Gildas addressed this appeal to 'Agitius',[13] opinion is now divided concerning the identity of the recipient, between Aëtius,[14] who could legitimately be described as thrice consul between January 446 and his death in September 454,[15] and Aegidius. The latter was a Roman general who was active in Gaul between the late 450s and the mid-460s, whose name is at least as close, and arguably closer, to 'Agitius' but who did not celebrate even one official consulship.[16]

The appeal to 'Agitius' has caused historians more problems than any other single episode in the *De Excidio*. Supposing Gildas's sequence to be correct,[17] a literal reading of his text places the invitation to the Saxons (in chapter twenty-three) several years, at least, later than 446. On the basis of archaeological finds, this is unacceptably late for the first settlements of Saxons in Britain,[18] yet it is an essential of Gildas's narrative that the Saxons to whom he refers were the first such settlers and that the impact of their rebellion was of general, not local, significance.

Such a mid-century date also contradicts the testimony of the Gallic Chronicle of 452 which refers in decisive terms to Saxon rule in much of Britain in the year 441.[19] Whatever the eventual outcome of the current debate surrounding the Gallic Chronicles,[20] it is accepted by all sides that the year 441 represents the date at which Saxon rule within a large part of *Britannia* became known to a southern Gaulish chronicler. His recognition of this fact is most unlikely to have predated the event. That Saxon rule was initially centred in East Anglia and the Thames Basin is implicit in the archaeological evidence.[21] If Saxons were already established in these parts of southern Britain in 441, their initial settlement as mercenaries in the 'east of the island' (as in *DEB*, chapter twenty-three, verse four) cannot be dated later than 446. Nor, given Gildas's insistent efforts to generalise concerning all Britain, is this an objection which can be set aside by placing Gildas in northern Britain,[22] without portraying him as a hopelessy myopic, upcountry recluse. That he clearly was not, and we reject the universality of Gildas's approach only at our peril.   Again supposing Gildas's sequence to be correct, a date as late as this for the appeal to 'Agitius' has the effect of forcing composition of the *De Excidio* towards, or into, the sixth century, and perhaps even into the second or third quarter of that century.[23] In many respects a date as late as this is implausible. Gildas had been educated in a manner which was archetypically Classical, rather than medieval,[24] he spoke Latin and knew it as a living language and he wrote in a Latin which has to be characterised as archaic if he was writing in the sixth century.[25] In its general cultural context, the *DEB* is a late Roman work, just as is that of Salvian, who was writing in Gaul in the mid-fifth century.[26] The close parallels between these two texts are easiest explained if Gildas was writing no more than a few decades after his Gallic counterpart. There have long been attempts to retrieve him from the sixth century and re-establish him closer to the Roman period.[27]

The chronological problems are at their most intense if 'Agitius' be identified with Aegidius,[28] giving a date for the appeal of 456×465, so pushing the invitation to the Saxons as mercenaries into the 450s or 460s and composition of the *DEB* towards the second quarter of the sixth century, or even beyond. The problem of reconciling such a date for the appeal with other evidence for the *adventus* is insurmountable. If the appeal was from Britain and to Aegidius, then the sequence as laid out in the *De Excidio* is unsustainable.[29]

Recognition of this objection has persuaded Aegidius's most recent advocate to propose that the appeal was not from Britain at all, but from Britons already established overseas in the Loire valley, who felt in need of protection from the Visigoths.[30] This suggestion has several advantages: it frees the appeal from the strait-jacket of a British chronology – although it also much reduces its value for the purposes of dating Gildas – and it is, at least superficially, a plausible interpretation. On close examination, however, it raises more problems than it solves. Not least of these is the need to explain the transmission of this document, or a copy of it, from the recipient, Aegidius, in Gaul, to Gildas in Britain in a form which was corrupt at least as regarding the spelling of the recipient's name, and divorced from any other information concerning its proper context. Gildas knew of emigration from Britain,[31] probably to Gaul, although this is disputed,[32] but his description of this event, like that of the

Channel crossings, is from a view-point which is quite consciously insular.[33] He knew of clergy returning from consecration abroad,[34] but remarked on them in such disparaging terms that it seems unlikely that he depended on them for the transmission of continental material. That Gildas, in chapter four of the *DEB*, denied having had access to material which had gone overseas with his fellow countrymen (and so had also come back via someone of them), surely rules out his use, whether knowing or unknowing, of a text written by a Briton in fifth-century Gaul.

If a continental context for the appeal be set aside on grounds of its ultimate implausibility, we are left with the inconsistencies outlined above. Supposing Gildas's sequence retains respect, the options are as follows:

1 The appeal should be dated to 446 or later, in which case Gildas was either misleading in his attempts to generalise concerning British history, or he was mistaken in the barbarians against whom it was aimed.[35]

Or:

2 The appeal lies in its correct position in Gildas's sequence but later interpretation has been mistaken in assigning it to the period beginning in 446. If the recipient was Aëtius, rather than Aegidius, it is important to recall that he was active in Gaul by the mid-420s. If it were possible to demonstrate that the appeal *could*, without damage to Gildas's text and its sequence, have long pre-dated 446, then the difficulties of chronology may disappear.

The first of these solutions has found little favour with recent historians because any departure from Gildas's sequence threatens it *in toto* and deprives the *De Excidio* of any independent value as a guide to the period. Since it is the only such guide to the 'English Settlement' and is in other respects at least internally consistent, historians have been loath to take that step. This may be false reasoning of the most subjective kind, but it finds some support in the sweeping generalisations which Gildas offered, wherein he was frequently discoursing on matters the fundamental veracity of which must have been public knowledge at the time of composition. Given that his text found sufficient favour with his audience to be copied and widely disseminated, it is difficult to dismiss the more recent, sequential material which prefaces and details the arrival of the Saxons as seriously flawed.

The second option has been explored in a recent essay by P. J. Casey and M. E. Jones.[36] They accepted that Gildas had sight of a badly garbled copy of an actual letter and that he quoted from the text: '*repellunt barbari ad mare, . . . aut iugulamur aut mergimur*'. Without discussion of the syntax behind what is a crucial editorial decision, however, they omitted the address (*Agitio ter consuli gemitus Britannorum*) from their use of quotation marks, so excluding the epithet 'thrice consul' from the original. By so doing the authors were able to explain this epithet as Gildas's own contribution, as opposed to being an original feature of the letter, included by him as a gloss designed to distinguish this Aëtius from another Roman official of the same name who was consul in 454,[37] with whom they felt that Gildas's audience might otherwise have confused him. This ingenious device allowed them to argue that the address was irrelevant to the status of Aëtius at the time of dispatch, but known to Gildas and his audience. They could therefore propose a date for the letter sufficiently early (e.g. *c*. 429, when an appeal to Rome from British churchmen first brought St Germanus to Britain)[38] to be reconciled with a Saxon rebellion which had already proved successful by 441.

This novel and important solution has at least two fundamental flaws: firstly, it sets up a tension in our perception of Gildas and his audience which is unsustainable. If Gildas felt that it was necessary to distinguish between one Aëtius and the other then he and his audience must be presumed to have known enough about them to be sure of the name. If not, then notice of which Aëtius was under discussion was utterly irrelevant and Gildas would have found it unnecessary to distinguish between them, even were he able; secondly, the required editorial changes are at odds with the conventions adopted in all modern editions of the *De Excidio*,[39] and of Bede's *Historia Ecclesiastica*,[40] which included this section from the *De Excidio* almost verbatim. In all these editions the address has been incorporated within the quotation marks. This has, of course, always been an editorial decision since such punctuation did not exist in the Latin original but, to be acceptable, any change must be justified syntactically. *Agitio ter consuli* is incontrovertibly in the dative and *gemitus* appears to be in the nominative. The entire phrase reads, 'to Agitius consul for the third time the groan(s) of the people of Britain'. The omission of a verb creates the impression that the whole is a form of address integral to what purports to be an extract from one of the letters following thereafter.

The entire section is introduced by the opening sentence of chapter twenty: 'So the miserable remnants sent off a letter.' This provides a context for all that follows, both the address and the extract. Use of the phrase *'hoc modo loquentes'* ('speaking in this manner') is a strong indication that a quotation is about to be introduced. The syntax demonstrates that Gildas intended to convey the impression that both the address and the extract following it were quotations from one or other of the letters. Subsequent editors have been right to punctuate it accordingly and attempts to alter this are unsustainable. If Gildas was quoting from actual documents then there is an equal case for attributing the address and the subsequent extract to those documents.

The solution proposed by Casey and Jones must, therefore, be rejected, however reluctantly, but their exploration of the chronological parameters of the appeal is worth further attention, if only because it is the only type of solution which enables us to retain the sequence of the appeal and *adventus* as offered by Gildas in the *DEB*.

The only indication that the appeal belongs later than 446 lies in the address. It has long been recognised that this is unlike that of other letters of the same period,[41] but these differences have been interpreted either as incompetence on the part of the isolated (even backwoods) Britons responsible for the appeal or as corruption in the text – particularly as regards the spelling of 'Agitius'.[42] These differences might, however, be considered so great that we are justified in considering whether they derive from an original document of any sort, however corrupt that might have been by the time Gildas had sight of it.[43]

Setting aside, temporarily, the problems surrounding the name 'Agitius', Gildas prefaced the appeal with a reference to the recipient as *Romanae potestatis virum*. *Vir* is a very general term which is wholly inappropriate in this context, meaning 'man', 'husband', at best 'warlike man'. It seems improbable that it could have been considered sufficiently laudatory to have been adopted by a British appellant for this purpose. That use of this term owed anything to an actual text, however corrupt, seems implausible.

125

Indeed, if this were all that Gildas knew or could contrive concerning 'Agitius', then the imprecision with which he prefaced his letter must imply that he had not had sight of the documents from which he purported to quote. His choice of words arguably owes more to a desire to parallel 'Agitius' with Ambrosius Aurelianus – that last of the Romans to succour Britain whom Gildas described in chapter twenty-five as *vir modestus*.

The address then opens with a reference to the *ter consuli* of 'Agitius'. It is this alone which consigns the appeal to the period 446–454, when Aëtius was, indeed, 'thrice consul'. Yet this, again, seems a less than appropriate form of address to one on whose military strength the Britons were hoping to draw. It was surely of more consequence to the Britons that Aëtius was *magister militum* in the west, with large forces of barbarian soldiers under his command, than that he had been honoured with a third consulship.

If these details did not derive from an authentic text it is legitimate to seek an alternative origin. Virgil's *Aeneid* is one work of classical literature which was certainly familiar to Gildas, and in which direct speech is very widely used. Given the specific nature of Gildas's address, the *Aeneid* cannot be expected to provide a precise parallel – most comparable passages in that work invoke the aid of gods, goddesses or kings. Yet it does offer several passages which are sufficiently similar to suggest that Gildas may have sought, and found, inspiration in this work when he was himself seeking to reconstruct a lost appeal.

Aeneas addressed his son in the following terms: *'nate, meae vires, mea magna potentia, solus'* ('O son, who alone are my strength, my great power').[44] To an audience familiar with the line, the *vir* of Gildas's preface might have been considered a clever play on *vires* ('force' or 'strength' but the terms are cognate), to which his use of *potestatis* may have served as a signpost.[45]

More significantly, Virgil made repeated use of *ter* in circumstances which directly parallel Gildas's address to 'Agitius'. Hence: *terque quatuorque beati* ('thrice and four-times blest'), with reference to the Trojan dead at Troy;[46] *ter comatus utramque viam, ter maxima Juno continuit iuvenemque animi miseratae repressit* ('thrice he essayed either way, thrice great Juno denied the young man and, from compassion, restrained him');[47] *terque quatuorque* ('thrice and four times').[48]

Virgil did use *ter* in direct address much as Gildas did but his usage was entirely conventional and should not be taken literally. If Gildas was attempting to reconstruct the appeal for his own rhetorical purposes, the *Aeneid* was an obvious and accessible source of inspiration. Supposing members of his audience to be familiar with it,[49] then the fabrication of his own address in conventions culled from it might have lent his reconstruction an (entirely bogus) aura of authenticity.

'Agitius' apart, therefore, the preface to, and address of, the appeal may be a reconstruction by Gildas influenced by the literature with which he, and parts of his anticipated audience, were familiar. If the address was his own creation, then there is a good case for arguing that the whole was composed by Gildas without sight of the original appeal, however corrupt. His use of *gemitus* – 'groans' – is certainly consistent with this interpretation, since he had already used the term in introducing the downfall of Britain following the spiritual and secular rebellions of Arianism and Magnus Maximus, respectively.[50] 'Britain', he then claimed, 'was rendered senseless and groaned for many years' under the attacks of the Scots and Picts. In this passage the term is fundamental to the creation of an image of Britain as a tragic heroine, albeit a divorcee – a role which is first established by Gildas's idealised portrayal of the Eden-like island of Britain in chapter three. The appeal to 'Agitius' could be interpreted as just the last of these groans, particularly given the Scottish and Pictish attacks which weld all between into a specific epoch in Gildas's portrayal of the past. His own undoubted responsibility for its use in this passage establishes a precedent which may imply that he was equally responsible for its use in the appeal to Agitius, which constituted a moment of similarly heightened tension.

Gemitus recurs in the complaints concerning Cuneglasus, whom Gildas depicted as threatened by the 'groans and sighs of holy men'.[51] Since the *DEB* was conceived, in part at least, as a 'lament', after the fashion of Jeremiah, Gildas was using such terms to reinforce his own general, and highly literary, portrayal of the funeral of *Britannia*, with attendant holy men as mourners. Significantly, it is as *querentes* – 'lamentations' – that Gildas described the contents of the appeal. Recurrence of this and similar terms plays an important role in bonding together into a single whole the comparatively detached episodes related in the 'historical' introduction.

Gemitus is, therefore, a word which Gildas used to good rhetorical effect in several passages. That it occurs in the 'appeal' makes Gildas's responsibility for that the more likely. Once more, a precedent is available in the *Aeneid*: in book one, line ninety-three, *ingemit* is juxtaposed with an appeal by Aeneas to the dead which opens: 'O thrice and four times blest'. The aptness of such parallels reinforce the possibility that the text of the appeal to 'Agitius' originated with Gildas. If his audience were familiar with such lines, they cannot fail to have been impressed by the erudition which Gildas was here displaying.

The remainder of the supposed quotation is no more convincing. A continental general would surely have expected more precise information concerning the Britons' enemies than that they were 'barbarians' and, however evocative the imagery adopted, the notion of Britons being pushed around by the sea, as well as the barbarians, is nonsensical. All that Gildas is really saying here is that the Britons found themselves 'between the devil (the Saxons) and the deep blue sea'. Reference to the sea invites comparison with Gildas's own characterisation of the great Saxon raid 'from sea to sea',[52] an event with which the putative author of a genuine appeal to Aëtius cannot have been familiar at the time of composition. Similarly, there is an unmistakable similarity of image between the appeal and the flight of some Britons across the sea and of others to refuges on the cliffs of the sea-coast.[53] Additionally, the text here invites contrast with the miraculous crossing of the Thames by St Alban, as already related.[54] In that instance, a virtuous man in accord with God was vouchsafed mastery over the waters of 'noble Thames'. In contrast, the iniquitous Britons responsible for the appeal were the playthings of the sea.

The plight of the Britons as revealed in the 'appeal' was, therefore, portrayed rhetorically as a consequence of their disobedience to God, in whose power it would have been to succour them had they been worthy. The imagery used is deeply embedded in Gildas's text and obedient to his purposes. It is most unlikely to have ever had an existence independent of his authorship.

A close parallel to the general context and purpose of the appeal is to be found in the Aeneid: '*miseri, quos improbus advena bello territat, invalidas ut aves, et litora vestra vi populat'.* ('O hapless people, whom, like frail birds, a shameless alien affrights with war, and rudely ravages your coasts.')[55] It could have been with this appeal by Saces to Turnus in mind that Gildas described the British suppliants as *miserae*, and this was a term which he used elsewhere in a very similar context.[56] Alternatively, the situation in which the Israelites found themselves having left Egypt and reaching the shores of the Red Sea is also comparable.[57] Had a prayer been included in the scene then it might well have been worded very similarly. Neither context provides a precise literary parallel but Gildas might have been mindful of images invoked by either, or both, when composing his own appeal. The assumption that that appeal was written by some earlier Briton must first surmount the similarity of its imagery, as well as its philosophy, to that deployed by Gildas in other sections of the text.

It is, however, widely accepted that significant differences of style exist between the appeal and the remainder of the *DEB*.[58] By comparison with the complex word-order and meter which characterises the *De Excidio*, the 'quotation' is a model of standard Latin. On this basis, it is generally held that Gildas is unlikely to have been responsible for the word order of the 'appeal'. If not, he necessarily derived it from an existing text.

This argument may be less compelling than is sometimes accepted, since it suffers from a fundamental flaw: it assumes that, just because Gildas adopted a particular style for the remainder of his work, he was incapable of writing in a simpler form and using the word order of older conventions, should he so wish. Since he was obviously well read in both Classical and biblical literature, Gildas was demonstrably familiar with very different styles of writing from that which he himself adopted in the *DEB*, and it seems most unsafe to imagine him to have been incapable of sustaining another style for a line or so. Additionally, we may have much longer texts of very different style in the *Letter Fragments* and *Penitentials* which have been assigned to his authorship,[59] the structure of which is far removed from that of the *De Excidio* in general, and somewhat closer to that of the appeal. The argument against his authorship is, therefore, an unimpressive one. It only requires that Gildas wanted this passage to pass as a quotation to be set aside.[60] If there is no overriding need to assume that Gildas had sight of a letter of any sort, then we are free to suppose that the fact of an appeal, the name of the recipient, and whatever information concerning that individual proves historical, reached him, like the remainder of his recent historical material, from one or more oral sources.

This suggestion is at odds with all discussion of the appeal to date but it does have certain advantages. Firstly, it offers an alternative to the propositions martialled by David Dumville in 1984 concerning the precise form of the appeal.[61] In his opinion the difficulties over the name 'Agitius' were a consequence of one of:

1 sixth- to tenth-century scribal error (i.e. post-dating Gildas);
2 error on the part of Gildas himself; or
3 error already present within the written material used by Gildas.

Although he considered the second the least likely, Dumville was clearly unenthusiastic concerning each of them. If Gildas's source for the appeal was oral, the situation is very different and the second option becomes far more attractive, since the spelling variant can be seen as phonetic. The shift from Aegidius to 'Agitius' is minimal in this context and that from Aëtius seems only marginally less plausible, particularly if the name had been somewhat corrupted in transmission by confusion with that of the later Aegidius, concerning whose exploits rumours perhaps circulated in Britain during the third quarter of the century.

In support of this argument, it should be emphasised that the appeal is the only document even putatively used by Gildas in writing that part of his introduction covering events later than 388.[62] That this document existed seems inconsistent with Gildas's own comments on his sources.[63]

Re-examination of the text reinforces this view. Gildas referred to more than one letter ('*epistolas*' in accusative plural) yet appears to quote from only one. Had that one been corrupt but others accurate, a more appropriate address would have been available to him. If he did not see several letters then Gildas presumably derived his knowledge that such existed from a verbal account. An oral tradition may, therefore, be necessitated.

Gildas introduced his 'quotations' with the word '*loquentes*' ('speaking'). We might infer from this that his source was the spoken rather than the written word. The entire *De Excidio* was described by its author as an '*epistola*' in the prologue, but its generally declamatory style implies that it was written as a formal speech or sermon. If Gildas understood an '*epistola*' to be something akin to the various *epistolae* in the New Testament, his use here of '*loquentes*' becomes more understandable, and a written text less necessary to the sense of his writing.

Although Gildas did not specifically state that the letters reached their destination, this is implicit (*nec pro eis quicquam adiutorii habent* – 'but they did not have any assistance from them'). On the basis of his own comments on his sources,[64] it seems that the letters were not thereafter returned to Britain from Gaul, although a reply may have been brought back, whether verbal or written. For Gildas to have had sight of these letters, therefore, it is necessary to postulate a series of prior stages. If we assume that the form 'Agitius' is not merely a late scribal error, [65] then these must be envisaged in the following order:

1 Copies were made before the originals were dispatched, then retained in an archive, presumably attached to the court or seat of government at which they had been written.
2 These were then badly copied at some date after 456–7 (when Aegidius was first active in Gaul), so causing the confusion over the name, but before the date of composition of the *DEB*.
3 These copies then reached Gildas isolated from other material which might have fixed them more firmly in time and sequence and were incorporated by him in the *DEB*.

Such an interpretation is overly complex and is implausible on two counts: firstly, it is necessary to consider the unique survival of this correspondence from an archive which might be expected to have contained material of general relevance to the *DEB*, yet there is no hint of further material derived from it; secondly, if the context in which Gildas placed the appeal be temporarily inviolate, this putative archive was arguably in eastern England, in the area to which Saxons were supposedly first invited to combat the same rumour of northern raids which 'Agitius' had been asked to deter.[66] The Saxon revolt occurred long before the date of composition and men of Gildas's status and inclinations were most unwilling to expose themselves to the risk of enslavement by entering territory under Saxon control.[67] If the name 'Agitius' was influenced by Aegidius, then the letters cannot have been copied at the court from which they had been sent. Such papers were of precisely the sort which Gildas had in mind when he referred to the burning of insular documents by the *hostes*.[68] On his own admission, none reached him.

In these circumstances the descent of any such documents to an author who wrote in another part of Britain a half century later and who denied sight of such documents becomes so problematical that it should be rejected as implausible. If a simpler interpretation is available it should be preferred. These difficulties disappear if we suppose that Gildas reconstructed an appeal known to him only from an oral source.

The search for such a source need take us no further than the *legati* – in this context, 'ambassadors' – who were elsewhere credited by Gildas with carrying such appeals to the Continent.[69] *Legati* who were active during the lifetime of Aëtius would have been either old or dead during Gildas's adult life, depending on the decade to which the appeal be assigned, but the appeal would have been a memorable event in their lives which they might often have described to acquaintances. Ambassadors would presumably have been selected from the civil elite of sub-Roman Britain, that is, the better-educated land-owning classes of the lowland zone such as had met with St Germanus on his two visits.[70] These men were still providing their sons with a Romanised education as late as the youths of Gildas and Maglocunus.[71] The *legati* were, therefore, likely to have been of the same class and generation as Gildas's own parents or, if not, his grandparents (depending on the date) and may well have been members of their broad circle of acquaintance.[72] Gildas may have met with one or more of them in his youth. Alternatively, he may have heard of their mission second-hand from those who had – and the latter option is far more probable if the appeal much pre-dated the 430s.

Such a source placed few constraints on Gildas and he seems to have reconstructed the appeal with an eye on the imagery used elsewhere in his work. It is unclear whether his reconstruction was influenced by what he proposed to write elsewhere, or other passages inspired by the appeal.[73] Whichever, the appeal does not stand in isolation. Such parallels illustrate the place of the letter in the complex web of cross-reference, repeating images and allusions which makes the *De Excidio* a single piece of literature.

In this respect at least, the letters bear the stamp of Gildas's authorship.

That Gildas chose to adopt a style which distinguished this passage from the remainder of the *DEB* is a matter which requires an explanation. The appeal performs an important function in the *DEB*. It brings to an unhappy conclusion that period of Britain's past which began with the end of Roman Britain,[74] an event which was interpreted by Gildas as a rebellion both against God and Rome. Without further reference to God, the entire period in between – with its attacks by the Scots and Picts, its inept British soldiers, its Roman expeditions and the northern walls – was characterised as one in which the Britons sought to restore relations with the Romans and so find protection from their enemies. The essential unity of this epoch is sustained within the text by repetition of key imagery and a repeating cycle of events, including the three appeals to Rome.[75] That this is, in detail at least, a period littered with unhistorical events only serves to emphasise the fact that Gildas was concerned not with history but with providence. His message here is comparatively simple: no amount of appeals to outsiders will solve the problems of the Britons so long as they continue in rebellion against God. With the appeal to 'Agitius' having failed, the Britons turned at last once more to God, and with his aid inflicted defeat upon their old enemies (chapter twenty, verses two to three).

With that victory, this, his penultimate epoch, was effectively over and with it the object lesson which it was designed to serve. He had further elaborated the fundamental importance of the contract between God and the Britons, explored the consequences of its breakdown against a backdrop of barbarian oppression and outlined the only effective method of resolving such a situation, by renewed obedience to God. More specifically, he had established that appeals were, alone, incapable of solving the problems of the Britons. By so doing, Gildas had enabled himself to attack in the most extreme terms the subsequent decision by Britons to appeal to the Saxons for help. The appeal to 'Agitius' has, therefore, a crucial role in the text, serving to associate a series of appeals to Rome *against* barbarians with an appeal *to* barbarians of an even more ferocious kind against the existing barbarian menaces, to devastating rhetorical effect. It is the effectiveness of this comparison which enabled Gildas to employ invective of unparalleled vigour in his denunciation of the 'proud tyrant', *et al.* (in chapters twenty-two, twenty-three). The providential imperatives of this account were the author's own.

The appeal signalled the end of Gildas's final opportunity to offer object lessons from situations which were in some respects analogous to the present. He moved from this past epoch to a rehearsal of the present, once more defining the epoch by moral and spiritual criteria. He made several references to 'our times' in the text (as in chapter one, verse five) but only once in circumstances which enable us to explore the length of time envisaged. At the end of chapter two, he stated his intention to say a little 'about the very last victory of our country that has been granted in our times by the will of God'. All the entries in chapter two are clearly assignable to later episodes in the 'historical' introduction, and this is necessarily a brief reference to that same *mons Badonicus* with which Gildas was to close his discussion of the 'War of the Saxon Federates'. 'Our times' were certainly perceived by Gildas, therefore, as stretching back to the year of his own birth, that is the forty-fourth year preceding the present. That this period had a unity of sorts was again spelled out by Gildas in his exordium, by reference to the particularly perfidious sins of 'our generation'.

How much longer was this epoch, which Gildas designated as 'in our times'? Since he construed the Saxons as a punishment on the Britons from God,[76] it was an essential feature of his text that the present should encompass not only the entirety of the period during which the Saxons were present, but also the earlier vices to which they were supposedly the antidote.[77] Once again, Gildas was thinking in periods defined by moral and spiritual factors, rather than historical ones. The present was, therefore, a period which stretched back at least one generation before Gildas's own.

Gildas's greater knowledge of this period, in contrast to the preceding epoch, and his fuller treatment of it, enabled him to adopt a far more subtle approach, sub-dividing it into periods characterised by a total breakdown of relations between the Britons and God (at its inception and conclusion), divided by a period when British successes required that God was 'testing His people'. This interlude was presumably forced on Gildas by knowledge of events but he used it to good effect, by establishing the virtues of Ambrosius Aurelianus as an exemplar against which the lesser leaders of his own generation might be measured.[78]

In contrast, Gildas's account of the period which opens with Magnus Maximus and closes with the appeal has little basis in historical fact and derives almost exclusively from his rhetorical purposes, which required the imposition on the past of a pattern derived from the present. That there is an escalation from each cycle to the next (as in the appeals themselves)[79] merely reinforces this imperative and serves to sustain Gildas's condemnation of the last appeal – that of the next epoch, which was directed to the Saxons. Indeed, this pattern was adopted by the author quite consciously, for rhetorical effect.[80] It was, therefore, to sustain the rising tension of his account that Gildas adopted direct speech for his third appeal, in a fashion with which he was familiar from classical literature, and particularly from the *Aeneid*. From the same source he may also have sought inspiration for his reconstruction of the augury taken by the Saxons prior to their journey to Britain,[81] the impact of which likewise offers a spurious air of authority.

The effect on his audience would have been much reduced had he retained his characteristic style. He therefore adopted a word order which he could pass off as authentic. If he relied on literary precedents for guidance in his reconstruction we can be confident that neither Gildas nor his intended audience had access to the original.

This does not mean that the appeal to Aëtius was a total fabrication. The name of the person to whom it was addressed (however corrupt) was not of the author's invention, so we can be reasonably confident that the fact of an appeal and the name 'Agitius' did reach Gildas from an authentic, albeit oral, source. It was the earliest element in a sequence of events which occurred during the lifetimes of his own parents and grandparents, and which led up to his own birth year, 'the year of the siege of Mount Badon'. That Gildas twice replicated that same sequence in his reconstruction of a more distant past suggests that he was reasonably confident of it in this, its last manifestation. In that respect the author's confidence in twice reconstructing a similar cycle confirms that the appeal to 'Agitius' should be considered as on a par, as regards its historicity, with 'Vortigern', the *adventus Saxonum* and Ambrosius Aurelianus.

The appeal of *DEB*, chapter twenty, is not, therefore, what it

135

purports to be. In some sense at least it was Gildas's own composition. Like other passages in his text it betrays influences which derive from his familiarity with classical literature. Gildas drew the idea from an oral source which may have provided no more than the fact of an appeal from Britain and the name of its intended recipient. That he departed from his normal style of writing implies that he intended his version of the appeal to be accepted as authentic, as indeed it has been. This effect was justified by his rhetorical purposes.

That it was Aëtius, not Aegidius, who was intended is necessitated by the sequence in which Gildas narrated these events, since an appeal to Aegidius which preceded the arrival and rebellion of the Saxons is insupportable when account is taken of other historical and archaeological information available to us. If Gildas's sequence is correct, the appeal necessarily occurred some years before 441 – the date at which a Gaulish chronicler recognised the Saxon take-over of some part of Britain. The possibility that Gildas's source for the appeal was oral offers a means of loosening this chronological garrotte. There are two alternative explanations available, each of which would enable the appeal to be dated far earlier than 446, when Aëtius was, at last, thrice consul:

1 Gildas borrowed the conventions adopted in his reconstruction of the appeal from the *Aeneid*. If Aëtius was 'thrice consul' only to the same extent that the Trojan dead at Troy were 'thrice and fourtimes blest' or Juno 'thrice great' then it is mere coincidence that Gildas described 'Agitius' as thrice consul.
2 If this coincidence be deemed too great, then we might surmise that Gildas knew of the appeal to 'Agitius' and knew that he had had the unusual distinction of having held three consulships but lacked any knowledge of the relative chronology of these events. In this case, in his reconstruction of the appeal we might suppose that Gildas marshalled all the meagre information at his disposal and in so doing accidentally linked the appeal to the third consulship of Aëtius, quite unaware that this might make for insurmountable problems of chronology.

In either instance, the appeal is liberated from the chronological constraints of 446–54 and can be redeployed in the later 420s or early 430s. By whichever route, it is the recognition that the appeal was of Gildas's composition in its entirety which frees us from the chronological problem implicit in his sequence.

An early date finds indirect support elsewhere. That St Germanus answered an appeal from Britain of a very different kind in 429 and then again, perhaps in the mid- to late 430s, demonstrates that British authorities were then still inclined to seek outside solutions to their problems. Such cannot be said of the 440s, by which time British government on the insular side of the Saxon Shore had apparently collapsed, taking with it direct contact between Roman authority in northern Gaul and prospective British appellants.

Since estimates of the date of composition of *DEB* have necessarily depended on the date of the appeal, a shift of the latter into the period *c.* 425–435 requires that the former be brought forward by a comparable time-scale. An attempt to improve on the chronology postulated by David Dumville, in 1984,[82] might take note of the Gallic Chronicle and use that as a guide to the absolute dating of events:[83] 'The Britains (i.e. the British provinces) even at this time have been reduced by various catastrophes and events over a wide area into the rule of the Saxons.'

If Gildas be recognised as writing in, and primarily of, southern Britain, he was necessarily concerned with the same problems as herein reported. Moreover, both recognised that the Saxons had triumphed and both attempted to generalise concerning (Roman) Britain as a whole, or at least some large part of it.[84] That Gildas and the Gallic Chronicle were referring to the same catastrophe is, therefore, quite plausible, in which case the following might be a more reliable guide to the chronology of these events:

388	Death of Magnus Maximus
388–425×435	The fictional events of *DEB*, XIV–XIX
425×435	The 'appeal' to 'Agitius'
428×438	The invitation to the Saxons, initial expedition, second expedition
430×440	The Saxon rebellion, 'War of the Saxon Federates', siege of *mons Badonicus*: 'various catastrophes and events' of Gallic Chronicle of 452
441	Saxon victory and conclusion of the war
479–484	Composition of *DEB*

This sequence does at least have the virtue that it renders Gildas's account and that of the Gallic Chronicle of 452 mutually consistent, so avoiding the necessity of imagining that Gildas could have been ignorant of such fundamentally important events as are retold in the latter.

Is there any reason why this model should necessarily be preferred to the popular attribution of Gildas to the next century? There is one further clue in the *DEB* which lends some direct support to this interpretation: as he approached the rhetorical climax of his 'historical' introduction, Gildas turned to the prophet Isaiah, whose words foretold the fall of Jerusalem to the Babylonians, to lend an appropriate sense of impending doom to his account of Britain's fall. He then abandoned this very obvious and apposite parallel in favour of one which was far more obscure, but which was concerned with relative dating:[85] 'For the time was approaching when their iniquity, as that of the Amorites, would be complete.' This allusion to Genesis requires some explanation. The full text of Abraham's dream reads:[86]

> Know of a surety that thy seed shall be a stranger in a land that is not theirs, and shall serve them; and they shall afflict them 400 years; and also that nation, whom they shall serve, will I judge: and afterward shall they come out with great substance. And thou shalt go to thy fathers in peace; thou shalt be buried in a good old age. But in the fourth generation they shall come hither again: for the iniquity of the Amorites is not yet full.

There are here two allusions to chronology. With reference to the period of 400 years, Gildas may have been attracted to this passage by his recognition that the period of his people's servitude – starting with that Roman conquest of AD 43 with which he began his 'historical' account[87] – was little short of this same period when Roman protection was supplanted by that of the Saxons. As Abraham had foreseen, those who had ruled – so the Romans – would themselves be judged, and Gildas may well have been aware of the collapse of Roman power in Gaul by the date of composition. If not, reference to that power was signally lacking in his text. If this is an appropriate interpretation, this passage would seem to confirm that the 'appeal' occurred during the second quarter of the fifth century, but before 443, which would have constituted the fourth centenary of the Claudian conquest, whether Gildas knew it or not. That the Gallic Chronicle noted the fall of Britain in 441, only two years adrift, may be apposite. The second allusion, to the fourth generation, might have seemed appropriate to the period separating the present from these events. Supposing (for simplicity's sake) the appeal to date from AD 425, Gildas was arguably writing around 480 and was himself of an age when he might expect to have seen his first grandchildren. Even if it be considered a trifle condensed, the timescale on offer is acceptable under this guise. If he was here offering contemporaries the message that the Saxons would be defeated and expelled after four generations, this would be consistent with the interpretation that the *DEB* constituted, albeit in the most reserved of terms, a call to arms.[88]

The peaceful intermission between the 400 years and four generations of Genesis may also be duplicated in the *DEB*, wherein Gildas was careful to identify a period of prosperous self-rule barely affected by barbarian raids prior to the arrival of the first Saxons.[89]

Gildas does, therefore, seem to confirm in this otherwise obscure allusion to the Amorites of Genesis that he was here interested in the chronology within which his 'historical' introduction had been conceived. He may have taken this opportunity to tie the downfall of Britain at the end of the 'War of the Saxon Federates' to the date at which Britain was first occupied by Rome. By so doing, he provides us with a hitherto neglected means of assessing the merits of different schemes for dating the later parts of his 'historical' sequence, and the moment of composition itself.[90]

There are some indications that Gildas's allusions here were noted and considered relevant by some later medieval writers. Despite also adopting Bede's dating of the *adventus* to 449, both the Laud and Parker versions of the *Anglo-Saxon Chronicle* included notice, under the year 443, of both the British appeal to Rome (i.e. 'Agitius') and an invitation to the Angles. Unless this derived from consideration of Gildas's somewhat obscure reference to the Amorites, it is difficult to imagine the basis of this calculation, which is certainly independent of Bede's *HE*. Again, Paul Grosjean's reconstruction of the now lost, earliest text of the *HB*, then at Chartres, noted that abbot Slebhine's visit to Ripon in 753 occurred 300 years after the Saxons came to Britain. The

significance of 300 years presumably rests on Gildas's reconstruction of the augury, in *DEB*, chapter twenty-three, verse three,
after which Celtic observers may have anticipated the collapse of
English control – in which case this abbot of Iona was presumably
on hand to reclaim his house's long-lost daughter monastery from
the English. Deduction of 300 from 753 produces a date for the
English arrival of 453, not 443, but this again is independent of
Bede,[91] and may have a bearing on the matter which is perhaps
obscured by some early numerical error. Similarly, the various
attempts by the author of the *Historia Brittonum* to date the
arrival of the Saxons likewise opt for early dates which are
independent of Bede, if not entirely consistent with one another.[92]
They may have resulted from recognition that Gildas's Saxons
necessarily reached Britain at a date earlier than that which Bede
deduced from the same source. These instances at least suggest
that early medieval intellectuals were prepared to explore Gildas's
text as a guide to the chronology of the fifth century, even where
the results were at odds with the authority of Bede's *HE*.

These later commentaries neither confirm nor deny the dating
of the *DEB* offered above, although they do suggest that the
arguments I have offered have a longer and more distinguished
history than may at first sight be apparent. They must ultimately,
however, stand on their own merits and these fall into two groups:
only an early date for the *DEB* enables the Saxon *adventus*
described therein as a phenomenon of almost universal interest
and impact across almost all of erstwhile Roman Britain to be
reconciled with other evidence for the chronology of the English
arrival, be that textual or archaeological; secondly, no other interpretation takes account of the southern bias of the text or of all
indicators of date within it.

These indicators are more numerous than has here been
elaborated so far, and consistently point to a date which is earlier,
rather than later, in the sub-Roman period: Gildas himself necessarily wrote in a coinless age, yet he clearly has a good grasp of
what coinage had been in Roman Britain;[93] his knowledge of
imports during the Roman period similarly implies an oral tradition
derived from no later than the early fifth century;[94] so too does his
apparently competent grasp of the technical meaning of various
terms concerning the employment and deployment of mercenary
soldiers as if by the Roman state;[95] if this is independent of

a written source, his knowledge that the eagle was peculiarly appropriate to a Roman army suggests strong links with the Roman world;[96] so too does his apparent assumption that the Scots were, throughout his narrative, heathen and barbarian;[97] that his parents should provide Gildas with an education in rhetoric seems increasingly unlikely if his birth occurred after the second quarter of the century; that he used terms such as *provinciae* and *rectores* accurately in the context of Roman Britain likewise suggests an early date.[98]

This list could be continued. In each instance it is possible that Gildas had available to him some written source which provided him with the necessary information, but in no case is that certain. The inference remains, therefore, that his familiarity with various aspects of Roman Britain favours a date for his composition of the *DEB* well within the fifth century. If Gildas wrote *c.* 479×484, then orally transmitted information concerning Aëtius might well have become confused, regarding, for example, the chronological relationship between his receipt of an appeal from Britain and his eventual, and very exceptional, consular status, or between him and the later, quite separate but equally dead, figure of Aegidius. It was Gildas's combination of a very small number of facts at his disposal, not the facts themselves, that have created the chronological conundrum which has so exercised later scholarship.

Notes

1   Constantius, *Life of St Germanus*, in *The Western Fathers*, ed. F. R. Hoare, London and New York, 1954, pp. 283–320; Orosius, *Histories*, *passim*.

2   E.g. *AC*, 516, 547, 565, 570.

3   E.g. D. N. Dumville, 'The chronology of *De Excidio Britanniae*, Book I', in *Gildas: New Approaches*, eds M. Lapidge and D. N. Dumville, Woodbridge, 1984, pp. 61–84.

4   D. N. Dumville, 'Gildas and Maelgwyn: problems of dating', in *Gildas: New Approaches*, pp. 51–9.

5   P. Sims-Williams, 'Gildas and the Anglo-Saxons', *Cambridge Medieval Celtic Studies*, VI, 1983, p. 5.

6   E.g. Dumville, 'Chronology', *passim*. Compare with E. A. Thompson, 'Gildas and the history of Britain', *Britannia*, X, 1979, p. 219.

7   *DEB*, XIII, 2, but which Gildas did not actually date and which it is possible that neither he nor his audience could date.

8   *DEB*, XXVI, 1.

9   See discussion in Dumville, 'Chronology', *passim*, for a full rehearsal of the imponderables facing attempts to establish time periods within the 'historical' account. For an alternative reading of the relationship between composition and *mons Badonicus*, see I. Woods, 'The end of Roman Britain: Continental evidence and parallels', in Lapidge and Dumville, *Gildas: New Approaches*, p. 23.

10   Thompson, 'Gildas', pp. 223–4, followed by Dumville, 'Chronology', p. 61.

11   Following Sims-Williams, 'Gildas', p. 17.

12   *DEB*, XX, 1.

13   See also *DEB*, II.

14   Aëtius has more often been given the benefit of the doubt: e.g. Thompson, 'Gildas', p. 214; P. Sims-Williams, 'The settlement of England in Bede and the *Chronicle*', *Anglo-Saxon England*, XII, 1983, pp. 6–9; Dumville, 'Chronology', pp. 67–8.

15   J. R. Martindale, *The Prosoprography of the Late Roman Empire, II, AD 395–527*, Cambridge, 1980, pp. 21–9.

16   L. Alcock, *Arthur's Britain: History and Archaeology AD 367–634*, London, 1971, p. 107; M. Miller, 'Bede's use of Gildas', *English Historical Review*, XC, 1975, p. 247; M. E. Jones, 'The appeal to Aetius in Gildas', *Nottingham Medieval Studies*, XXXII, 1988, pp. 145–8.

17   Dumville, 'Chronology', p. 62.

18   H. W. Böhme, 'Das Ende der Römerherrschaft in Britannien und die angelsachsische Besiedlung Englands im 5. Jaherundert', *Jahrbuch des Romisch-Germanischen Zentralmuseums*, XXXIII, 1986, pp. 469–574.

19   T. Mommsen, ed., *Chronica Minora*, I, Berlin, 1892, p. 660. For a translation, see below, p. 137.

20   M. E. Jones and P. J. Casey, 'The Gallic Chronicle restored: a chronology for the Anglo-Saxon invasions and the end of Roman Britain', *Britannia*, XIX, 1988, pp. 367–98; R. W. Burgess, 'The Dark Ages return to fifth century Britain: the "restored" Gallic Chronicle exploded', *Britannia*, XXI, 1990, pp. 185–96.

21   Böhme, 'Das Ende', Abb. 57, followed by S. C. Hawkes, 'The south-east after the Romans: the Saxon settlement', in V. Maxfield, ed., *The Saxon Shore: a Handbook*, Exeter, 1989, p. 89.

22   *Contra* Thompson, 'Gildas', pp. 214–15. See the doubts of Dumville, 'Chronology', pp. 66–7. For recent comment on Gildas's whereabouts, see N. J. Higham, 'Old light on the Dark Age landscape: the description of Britain in the *De Excidio Britanniae* of Gildas', *Journal of Historical Geography*, XVII, 1991, pp. 368–9, elaborated above, pp. 90–113.

23   Sims-Williams, 'Gildas', p. 5; Dumville, 'Chronology', p. 84. See

also F. Kerlouégan, *Le De Excidio Britanniae de Gildas: Les Destinées de la culture Latin dans l'ile de Bretagne au VI siecle*, Paris, 1987.

24 M. Lapidge, 'Gildas's education and the Latin culture of sub-Roman Britain', in *Gildas: New Approaches*, pp. 27–50.

25 Kerlouégan, *Le De Excidio Britanniae*, pp. 232–8.

26 Salvian, *De gubernatione Dei libri viii*, in *Salviani Presbyteri Massiliensis Opera Omnia*, ed. F. Pauly, Vindobonae, 1883, pp. 1–200, written 439×451.

27 T. D. O'Sullivan, *The De Excidio of Gildas, its Authenticity and Date*, Leiden, 1978, pp. 171–3; I. Wood, 'The end of Roman Britain', in *Gildas: New Approaches*, p. 23; M. W. Herren, 'Gildas and early British Monasticism', in A. Bammesberger and A. Wollmann, eds, *Britain 400–600: Language and History*, Heidelberg, 1990, p. 67; N. J. Higham, *Rome, Britain and the Anglo-Saxons*, London, 1992, pp. 56–7, which offers a précis of the arguments elaborated here.

28 See note 16, above.

29 C. E. Stevens, 'Gildas Sapiens', *English Historical Review*, LVI, 1941, pp. 360–3.

30 Jones, 'The appeal', pp. 149–51.

31 *DEB*, XXV, 1.

32 His preference for a northern context for the *DEB* encouraged Thompson to favour Ireland as a destination for the British emigrants: 'Gildas', pp. 217–20, but there is no other sanction for the theory and Gildas's virulent hostility to the Irish implies that they were in his opinion still heathen. For words of caution, Dumville, 'Chronology', pp. 74–5; also note 22, above, and p. 44.

33 Higham, 'Old light', and pp. 99–101, above.

34 *DEB*, LXVII, 5–6.

35 See note 29.

36 P. J. Casey and M. E. Jones, 'The date of the letter of the Britons to Aetius', *Bulletin of the Board of Celtic Studies*, XXXVII, 1990, pp. 281–90.

37 Martindale, *Prosoprography*, pp. 29–30.

38 R. A. Markus, 'Pelagianism: Britain and the Continent', *Journal of Ecclesiastical History*, XXXVII, 1986, pp. 191–204; Constantius, *Life of St Germanus*, pp. 283–320; Prosper Tironis, *Chronicon*, 429, in Mommsen, ed., *Chronica*, I, p. 427.

39 T. Mommsen, ed., *Gildas Sapientis De Excidio et Conquestu Britanniae*, in *Monumenta Germaniae Historica: Chronica Minora*, iv, Berlin, 1898; H. Williams, ed., *Gildae De Excidio Britanniae*, London, 1898; A. W. Wade-Evans, ed., *The Story of the Loss of Britain*, in *Nennius's 'History of the Britons'*, London, 1938, p. 151; M. Winter-bottom, ed., *Gildas: the Ruin of Britain and Other Works*, Chichester,

1978. The exception is the edition of J. A. Giles, *The Works of Gildas and Nennius*, London, 1841; see particularly p. 6.

40 J. A. Giles, ed., *The Venerable Bede's Ecclesiastical History of England*, London, 1887; C. Plummer, ed., *Venerabilis Baeadae Opera Historica*, I, Oxford, 1896; B. Colgrave and R. A. B. Mynors, eds, *The Ecclesiastical History of the English People*, Oxford, 1969. All references are to I, 13.

41 A useful collection of letter-headings was affixed to their essay by Casey and Jones, 'The date', appendix I, pp. 288–9.

42 Dumville, 'Chronology', pp. 67–8.

43 Higham, *Rome*, pp. 156–7.

44 *Aeneid*, I, line 664.

45 Such allusions to existing literature are characteristic of Gildas's style: N. Wright, 'Gildas's prose style and its origins', in Lapidge and Dumville, *Gildas: New Approaches* pp. 107–28, particularly pp. 113–14. See also Wright, 'Did Gildas read Orosius?', *Cambridge Medieval Celtic Studies*, IX, 1986, pp. 31–42; N. J. Higham, 'Old light', pp. 364–5.

46 *Aeneid*, I, line 94.

47 *Aeneid*, X, lines 685–6.

48 *Aeneid*, XII, line 155.

49 As is implicit in his several references to the text: Winterbottom, 'Preface', p. 287, and *Gildas: the Ruin of Britain and Other Documents*, p. 10, note 8; Lapidge, 'Education', pp. 39–40; Wright, 'Gildas's prose style', pp. 107–28.

50 *DEB*, XIV, 1.

51 *DEB*, XXXII, 2.

52 *DEB*, XXIV, 1.

53 *DEB*, XXV, 1.

54 *DEB*, XI, 1, alluding to Joshua, III and IV.

55 *Aeneid*, XII, lines 261 ff.

56 *DEB*, XVIII, 2; N. J. Higham, 'Gildas, Roman Walls and British Dykes', *Cambridge Medieval Celtic Studies*, XXII, 1991, pp. 1–14.

57 Exodus, XIV.

58 Winterbottom, *Gildas*, p. 8.

59 *Ibid.*, p. 10; R. Sharpe, 'Gildas as a father of the church', in Lapidge and Dumville, *Gildas: New Approaches*, pp. 201–2.

60 See below, p. 133.

61 Dumville, 'Chronology', pp. 67–8.

62 So later in the sequence than *DEB*, XIII. This is notwithstanding the suggestion of Dumville, 'Chronology', p. 73, note 60. See however, the suggestion that XXI, 4 and IV, 4 were inspired by Orosius, above, p. 21.

63 *DEB*, IV, 4.

64 *DEB*, IV, 4, and see above.
65 See above, note 42.
66 *DEB*, XXIII, *passim*.
67 Higham, 'Gildas', p. 12, note 37, but see also Dumville, 'Chronology', p. 82, note 98. See discussion, p. 104.
68 *DEB*, IV, 4.
69 *DEB*, XV, 1; XVII, 1.
70 Constantius, *Germanus*, XIV–XV; XXV–XXVII.
71 *DEB*, XXXVI, 1.
72 Lapidge, 'Education', p. 50.
73 E.g. *DEB*, XXIV, 1; XXV, 1.
74 *DEB*, XIV–XIX.
75 See above, pp. 73–6 but note the similarity of Gildas's second appeal to Lamentations, II, 10. The ultimate failure of outside aid is likewise a feature of Jeremiah's Judah (as Lamentations, I, 2) and Gildas's sequence of Roman interventions may well have been influenced thereby.
76 *DEB*, XXII.
77 *DEB*, XXI, the content of which bears comparison with XXVI onwards.
78 *DEB*, XXV, 2 and see p. 46.
79 *DEB*, XV, 1; XVII, 1; XX, 1.
80 See p. 24.
81 See p. 41.
82 Dumville, 'Chronology', pp. 83–4.
83 See above, p. 142, note 19.
84 See pp. 172–4.
85 *DEB*, XXII, 3.
86 Authorised Version: Genesis, XV, 13–16.
87 *DEB*, V.
88 See pp. 176–91.
89 *DEB*, XXI, 2.
90 But recall the problem of the ten-year period of waiting in the preface: Winterbottom, 'Preface', p. 282–3 and see p. 85, note 1, above.
91 K. Harrison, *The Framework of Anglo-Saxon History to* AD *900*, Cambridge, 1976, p. 99.
92 *HB*, XVI, XXXI.
93 *DEB*, VII but see reference to *denarius* in a contemporary context, in LXVI, 5.
94 *DEB*, III, which was presumably the source of similar comment in *HB*, IX.
95 Primarily, *DEB*, XXIII, 4–5. See discussion, pp. 40–2.
96 *DEB*, XVII, 2.
97 At latest in the sequence, *DEB*, XIX–XXII.
98 See pp. 151–5.

6

Gildas and his contemporaries

It is possible that Gildas wrote his *epistola* with a relatively small and specific audience in mind – to one of whom he made passing reference when he characterised a pre-existing text on the same general subject as written by 'one of us'.[1] If Gildas was located somewhere in the centre of the deep south of Britain, then so too was this audience. The political context in which he wrote was, however, universal: the 'damages and afflictions' of the 'fatherland' were not specific to one small British community but were consistently portrayed throughout his text as general, at least as regards Christian Britain. It was the entire people – the body of *cives*, the *patria* and *Britannia* herself – whose disastrous relationship with God conditioned, in his view at least, the catastrophe of the present. In practice, Gildas's knowledge of contemporary Britain does not seem to have extended beyond the Mersey so there is a northern horizon to the body politic to which he addressed himself. Nevertheless, even with this reservation, his 'letter' was conceived as an open sermon, which was, rhetorically at least, addressed to the entirety of the British people, the length and breadth of the erstwhile British provinces.

Taking his stance from the Bible and from Church histories, Gildas was of the opinion that it was primarily the moral and spiritual standing of the leaders of society – its secular rulers and its pastors – which determined the status at any one time of that perpetual contract which conditioned relations between God and His people. Just as the offences of King Zedekiah and his false prophets had incurred the wrath of God, and so enabled the Babylonians to sack Jerusalem, so too did Gildas direct the bulk of his own strictures towards the kings (both past and present) and clergy of the Britons. It was the blind and culpable stupidity of 'Vortigern' and his advisors which had initiated the disasters which characterised 'our times'. Only the moral and spiritual regeneration of Britain's shepherds would lead the entire flock to salvation.

Despite this emphasis, however, Gildas took care to condemn the morality of the total community: it was the abominable sins of 'our generation' which he believed conditioned the present;[2] their collective moral shortcomings were depicted as far exceeding those of the generation which had recently died, which God had once tested and to which he had even vouchsafed some success.[3] Only a very few were exempt from his condemnation – as Gildas made clear with specific reference to the present.[4] This desire to exclude certain individuals from his general moral condemnation of contemporaries posed a threat to his entire thesis, which he avoided by deploying an Old Testament precedent: their prayers supported Gildas but they were no more capable of averting the wrath of God upon a sinful people than would Noah, Daniel and Job have been in the stereotypically sinful land of Judah, prior to the Babylonian captivity. It was to the totality of that community that the prophet Ezekiel addressed himself and Gildas made copious use of his strictures. In parallel, 'holy mother church in a sense' did 'not see' their virtues.[5] Gildas variously elaborated on this theme: the true Christians of the present were few in number, so their collective virtue small by comparison with the vast pile of sin, and ingrained evil, built up over generations by the total community.

Gildas's message to this immoral majority took two forms: the lesser strand lay in the military domain, and he invoked the name of Rome to lend authority to his attempt to reinvigorate, and redirect, the military effectiveness of the Britons.[6] From the beginning, he was careful to exempt from his strictures those soldiers whom he considered to be courageous,[7] if indeed those to whom he here alluded were soldiers in the literal sense, as opposed to 'soldiers of Christ'.[8] Gildas recognised that good British *duces* – captains or military leaders – could be found,[9] but they were *'infaustus'* ('unlucky') because the sins of the five named (and more important) tyrants were so great that the virtues of other *duces* were insufficient to earn God's magnanimity.

Gildas was not entirely opposed to war but only to 'civil wars'.

It was exclusively wars against other Britons, or against Rome, for which he censured the five named tyrants and other, earlier British leaders.[10] His condemnation of these unjustifiable conflicts and rebellions contrasts with his approval of the use of force by both Romans and Britons against barbarians. This was the only category of warfare conducted by Britons which he invariably and explicitly interpreted as divinely aided.[11] Gildas was therefore extending a theory of justifiable warfare which was familiar to him with reference to the Israelites from the Old Testament, and likewise to the Romans from later Church histories, to encompass his own latter-day 'chosen people', the Britons.

Since barbarian oppression was the immediate cause of the present 'damages and afflictions' affecting his own people, Gildas was, by implication, justifying British warfare against the Saxons.[12] Indeed, his frequent references to the Lord in his guise of the Old Testament God of battles implies that this was a vital part of his message. For such warfare to be prosecuted to a successful conclusion, it was necessary that the Britons return to the Lord, *en masse*, as he depicted them having done in the past, and that they rally behind a leader whose virtues were such that divine support of their efforts would be assured, in contrast to the conditional support which God had given the generation now deceased.[13] Gildas's exploration of the character of each of the five British tyrants, and his successive rejection of each as morally flawed, demonstrates that he was actively seeking a British 'David', to pit against the Saxon 'Goliath', among the principal British war-leaders of the present. That divine aid would sustain a leader who was sufficiently virtuous was the message which Gildas drew from his treatment of Ambrosius Aurelianus and mount Badon. He anticipated, therefore, and sought to expedite, a divinely sanctioned and so universally triumphant campaign by the Britons which would blast away the Saxon oppression of the present.

One precondition of such a campaign was strength 'in beating off the weapons of the enemy', such as the Britons had displayed neither in the past nor the present.[14] The military virtues by which the Romans had sustained their empire and protected Britain in the past provided Gildas with an analogy appropriate to this rhetorical purpose.[15] His comments on the military activities of British contemporaries suggest that he expected his countrymen to overcome their disabilities in this area: there had been no lack of civil wars since the conclusion of the 'War of the Saxon Federates', even though peace had reigned between Briton and Saxon;[16] the military retainers of the various kings were depicted as having the appropriate soldierly skills.[17] The Britons did have soldiers, therefore, and not all of them were utter cowards.

The second, and far more central, strand of his advice to his 'countrymen' concerned the relationship between the Britons and God. It was his belief that the discomfiture of the Britons, in the present as in the past, was primarily a consequence of their repeated and recurring disobedience to the Lord. Reconciliation with God and the renewal of divine aid which that would engender were, in his opinion, essential prerequisites for a successful outcome of renewed warfare. It was the Britons' moral shortcomings and their disobedience to God that Gildas considered the crucial factors, and to which he directed the vast bulk of his attention, accusing, condemning and advising, like any Old Testament prophet, the people in general, but their kings and the priesthood in particular.

Gildas had much to say concerning his contemporaries. He was in some respects a realist, recognising that any hope of success in the immediate future depended on those Britons who already controlled the principal military resources at their collective disposal. These figures must necessarily be the five tyrants whom he so roundly condemned by name in his complaints, to whom we will return.

His individualised attacks on them were introduced by a passage – chapter twenty-seven – in which he sought to generalise concerning the errors currently characterising British kingship in general. Therein, in measured tones, without quotation but using the rhetorical device of thesis and antithesis to good effect, Gildas complained of their tyranny; of their impiety and partiality as judges;[18] of their polygamy;[19] of their oath-breaking;[20] of their civil and unjust wars;[21] of their hypocrisy concerning alms-giving, thieves and their military companions,[22] and of their unjustified imprisonment of innocent men.

It was clearly Gildas's intention that the qualities which he here attacked and characterised as tyrannous be compared unfavourably with the superior morality of that *vir modestus*, Ambrosius Aurelianus, and the generation who had formerly fought, albeit with only limited success, against the Saxons; but there is a fundamental problem of interpretation here: did Gildas intend his generalised condemnation to be specific to the five kings named and condemned thereafter, or was this passage intended to have a wider relevance than this, including other, anonymous rulers within his condemnation? Did other such anonymous, British kings even exist?

If Gildas is correctly located at some distance from the tribal kingdoms of the western tyrants whom he criticised, then it seems possible at first sight that he was using this preface to his more specific complaints against them to comment unfavourably, but anonymously, on kings whom he felt unable to attack by name, to whose power he perhaps felt himself to be vulnerable.[23] He did, after all, make some apparent effort to avoid his own identity becoming widely known,[24] and this might be considered a similar precaution.

The alternative to this hypothesis is the view that chapter twenty-seven was written solely with the five named tyrants in mind. These two options are equally sustainable in principle, but they are mutually incompatible and further attention to Gildas's text reveals several points which require that it is the latter which should be preferred:

1   Gildas provided a similar, ironically structured preface (chapter sixty-six) to his complaints concerning the clergy. In chapter two he offered a 'contents list' for his 'historical' introduction. Such introductory passages, which prefaced and structured the next part of his text, were, therefore, a consistent feature. That both the other two refer specifically to what would follow, without any more general relevance, implies that chapter twenty-seven was likely to perform the same function;

2   Each of his complaints concerning the individual tyrants (for which, see below) was confined to the same subject areas which were listed in this preface, selected in each instance as seemed appropriate to the ruler in question;

3   His deployment of biblical analogies thereafter, in chapters thirty-seven to sixty-five, were explicitly directed at those same five tyrants.[25] These were organised in a fashion which loosely mirrors the areas of criticism outlined in chapter twenty-seven.

4   Gildas had already made such general comments on the present as he felt necessary, both in his exordium (chapter one) and

in chapter twenty-six, with additional comments scattered through his 'historical' introduction.

It does, therefore, seem reasonably certain that he wrote chapter twenty-seven as an extended, ironically styled but judgemental 'subject list' relevant specifically to the five named tyrants, rather than to the wider, British community.

It was to the totality of that wider community that Gildas had already directed his attention: the '*reges, publici, privati, sacerdotes [et] ecclesiastici*', who had witnessed, and thereafter long remembered, 'the desperate destruction of the island' by the Saxons and 'the help beyond hope' of God which had brought victory at *mons Badonicus*, were now dead. 'But there succeeded [a generation] with their descendants which was ignorant of that storm and knowledgeable only concerning the present peace.'[26] These several orders were still, therefore, present in the Britain within which Gildas was writing. Concerning *reges* he would later have much to write,[27] and likewise the *sacerdotes* – the entirety of the priesthood[28] – but something can be learnt from the condemnation which he extended to other sectors of the body politic.

Publici is a generic term appropriate to all who were in public life – the entirety of officialdom – and might be translated as 'public officials' or 'magistrates'. *Privati* is appropriate to the remainder of secular society, encompassing those who hold no magistracies, and exclusive also of kings. It was probably also exclusive of the large underclass of the unfree, be they slaves or tied peasants, whose moral status was probably beneath Gildas's notice – but this is beyond proof within the text.

The only 'public officials' to whom Gildas otherwise referred were *rectores* – a term which literally means 'governors' but *could*, in principle, have been used here in a more general sense to denote 'rulers' or 'administrators' – a use which is standard in, for example, the writing of St Gregory a century later. That it was the more specific, and technically correct sense which Gildas had in mind seems probable from the contexts in which he used the term. *Rectores* were introduced at an early stage of the exordium as a rank worthy of exceptional comment.[29] Thereafter, it becomes clear that a *rector* would have been considered the normal person to organise any major public initiative in the civil sphere, such as the building of a great frontier wall.[30] In a fifth-century context the appropriate analogy may be the construction of an earthen or turf dyke.[31] Labour *corvées* had been a significant part of the obligations owed by provincials to the state in the late Roman period. If Gildas was here making passing reference to similar imposts in the present, then the entire area of taxation may have lain within the orbit of the *rector*. It was likewise the term appropriate to the individual responsible for the organisation of newly conquered Britain in Roman style.[32] That he had judicial functions[33] is confirmed by Gildas's use of 'the just governor' as an epithet appropriate to God.[34]

A signal feature of Gildas's use of *rector* is the consistency with which it refers to a 'civil governor'. In contrast to the various kings and tyrants, *rector* was never used with reference to any individual to whom Gildas attributed a military role. The British kings could be styled *duces* but were never *rectores*. This is not just a matter of negative evidence: in reference to the administrators of early Roman Britain, Gildas was led into the error of assuming them to have been entirely without soldiers, the armies of the initial conquest having all returned to Rome.[35] His mistake is easiest ascribed to his assumption, applied to this period retrospectively, of their exclusively civilian responsibilities.

This occurrence has two other important facets: it is the only circumstance where we can be absolutely confident that Gildas used the term in the traditional Roman sense, for the governor of a province. Other instances are consistent with this interpretation but do not require it; secondly, the occurrence of *rectores* – in the plural – in this context implies that Gildas assumed there to have been several governors. Indeed, *rectores* always occurs in this text in the plural, excepting only when applied to the Lord. This implies that the provincial geography with which Gildas was familiar was that of the several provinces of the British diocese, which had come into existence either under Diocletian or shortly thereafter. He did not, admittedly, correct the allusion to Britain as a single province which he derived from St Jerome,[36] but his own literary sources were not consistent in this respect, reflecting as they did the changes which had occurred over several centuries. When composing freely, as opposed to quoting, his use of *rectores* as a plural – as in the context of the Boudiccan rebellion – would seem to refute any possibility that Gildas was aware that Britain had originated as a single province, under a single governor. He certainly considered Christian Britain to have been more than one province prior to its suffering 'damages and afflictions' at the hands of the Saxons.[37]

The second point is this: his general assumption that *rectores* had never had any military responsibilities – which was, of course, patently untrue of early Roman Britain – suggests that Gildas's familiarity with the Roman system of government was limited to the epoch of separate civil and military jurisdiction, which does not pre-date the fourth century. Just as we might expect of a writer of the 470s or 480s, Gildas's perception of *rectores* and the specifically civilian sphere of activity appropriate to them was very much that of late Antiquity.

The *rectores* of the present were not, therefore, kings, yet his passing reference to *rectores* in the introduction without any gloss concerning their function presupposes that they were still active, and well known so to be, in the present. If they were then literally 'governors' in the late Roman sense (as seems likely from the several contexts discussed above) then the small provinces of late Roman Britain retained some effective administrative reality down to the date of composition.

That the late Roman provinces still had some meaning as late as 441 is implicit in the reference under that year to the 'Britains' in the Gallic Chronicle of 452,[38] but, in isolation, this could be dismissed as a Gaulish anachronism of no relevance as such to contemporary Britain. Similarly, that Constantius also made passing reference to a 'province' in a British context could likewise be set aside as the comment of a poorly informed, continental author.[39] It is Gildas's use of *rectores* and *provinciae* which confirms that these continental references to the British provinces had some reality.

This point finds further support in Gildas's ordering of the Britons in a contemporary context. If we return to his list of five 'orders' or categories (as noted above), it is obvious that they can be usefully subdivided: the first three, of 'kings', 'public officials' (or 'magistrates') and 'private persons' refer to the three principal subdivisions of the secular community – or at least the less servile sections of it; the 'priests' and 'congregations' pertain to the Christian community – the Church. Gildas conceived of society, therefore, much as did other fifth-century Christian writers, in terms of an interlocking pair of hierarchies – the secular order and the religious one.[40] The greater complexity of the secular hierarchy is due to a fundamental division between kings, whose role was in origin imperial and encompassed military leadership, and officials, whose role was exclusively civil. Gildas's categorisation also reflects, therefore, the division of military and civil government which was a fundamental characteristic of late Roman Britain. That it was still considered valid as a means of subdividing British society after *mons Badonicus* confirms that the basic, civil structure of Roman Britain had remained intact even to that date and beyond.

What was the role of these 'officials' in the present? Gildas did not spell this out but he did make it clear that the *rectores* – whom he presumably counted among them – were then 'bowed down by such a great burden' that he envisaged them without the time necessary to formulate or effect their own solution to the problems of the 'fatherland'.[41] They were clearly busy men. He introduced them to his text at a stage which immediately followed, and was dependent on, passages which established the nature of the 'damages and afflictions' then facing Britain, then sketched out his own solution to those problems.[42] Given that the only administrative task which is implicit therein is the organisation of the tribute of the British, Christian community, we might be forgiven for supposing that it was this onerous and surely unwelcome task which so weighed down upon the *rectores* and their partners, the *speculatores*, in the present.[43]

There seems, in addition, to be a geographical division between the kings and the public officials to whose morals Gildas variously directed attention. If the former also made use of magistrates this was of little interest to him since their moral standing was inseperable from that of their patrons: Gildas dismissed their associates and servants in chapter twenty-seven as 'thieves'. The kings – or tyrants – of the present exercised the twin roles of civil rule and military protection over one and the same community; it was in part their judicial and custodial activities to which he objected, due to their ignorance of 'the rules of right judgement'. If this last phrase has a clear meaning it presumably pertains to Roman law, since the philo-Roman and arch-conservative Gildas is most unlikely to have conceded such an aura of rectitude to any law code which originated in sub-Roman Britain. If the kings of chapter twenty-seven had perverted this area of government then his *rec-*

tores – whose origins were Roman and whose functions included civil jurisdiction – were not active in areas currently ruled by kings. At the time of writing, *rectores* and tyrants therefore had functions which were incompatible with one another and cannot have overlapped.

This reading of the text is sustained by reconsideration of the moral values attached to kings and *rectores* on the one hand and tyrants and their agents on the other. Kingship over Britain had in the distant past been exercised by Roman emperors,[44] who governed Britain through *rectores*. The agents of the tyrant Diocletian were not so termed:[45] in contrast to the high moral value implicit in the term *rector* – and its associations with rectitude and benignity – the Roman tyrant had ruled Britain through antithetical *persecutores* and dispatched St Alban via a *carnifex*. With Magnus Maximus, Gildas identified the beginning of a unified and specifically British kingship of comparable kind, but he referred to it as a tyranny not because of its constitutional shortcomings but on account of his sinful rebellion,[46] a crime which had already been characterised (in chapter four) as one of the fundamental evils inherent in the British national character. Gildas's Magnus Maximus was, first and foremost, a military leader, and this seems to be a fundamental component of his perception of kingship (or tyranny) throughout, but he was more than a mere general – a *dux* – being the equivalent of a Roman emperor or king. Gildas's kings (and his antithetical tyrants) were, therefore, men who exercised authority of a kind which was equivalent to that of Roman emperors.

This single British kingship continued thereafter via a sequence of anonymous kings, each of whom had unjustifiably usurped the authority of his predecessor.[47] Although Gildas forebore to make this explicit, their moral inadequacies are implicit in the text, with each worse than his predecessor. As already noted (p. 21), it is far from improbable that Gildas was here inspired by Orosius's far more detailed comments regarding the sequence of British tyrants whose morality he contrasted unfavourably with that of both Honorius and Constantius.[48]

In reality (although Gildas may have been entirely unaware of it) the sequence of tyrants noted by Orosius reaches to 410 or slightly beyond – that is, to within, and perhaps well within, two decades of 'Vortigern's' invitation to the Saxons. He may, therefore, have been the immediate successor to those tyrants referred to by Orosius, and specifically to Constantine III whose death at Arles left authority over Britain in abeyance. That the activities of 'Vortigern' were placed by Gildas in the moral context of all Britain is clearly established by his comments on the *familia* of God, the threat of barbarian settlement 'from the frontier even to the boundary of the *regio*' (so 'Britain') and the 'foolish people' in chapter twenty-two. The political unity of Britain as apparent under Magnus Maximus was therefore, in Gildas's opinion, still a reality when 'Vortigern' met with his council to devise a means of protecting the 'homeland' (*patria*).

Gildas emphasised this unity by contrast with the splinters of British kingship of his own day, when he described (in chapter thirty-seven) the five tyrants of the present as if 'the five aforesaid wanton and mad horses of Pharaoh's retinue' by whom his army had been lured to destruction in the Red Sea. He had already established Pharaoh as a metaphor for 'Vortigern' in chapter twenty-three, so his retinue (*satellites*) were the councillors of that same passage. Gildas is not suggesting that the tyrants of the present had themselves been among those councillors a half-century ago, for they are represented as the steeds rather than the horsemen themselves, but he does seem to be establishing close linkages between the two groups which may imply that they were kin. His allegorical method of delivery is of itself interesting, recalling as it does the role of the sea in the appeal to 'Agitius', as much as the red fire of the great Saxon raid, but the crucial message must be that the tyrants of the present were equivalent to the councillors of 'Vortigern's' day.

'Vortigern' convened his council to obtain advice on military matters. Just as Magnus Maximus had disposed of armies, so too was 'Vortigern' here quite explicitly taking responsibility for matters of defence. To the extent that Gildas's message enables us to judge, he was acting as if an insular emperor with authority across all of erstwhile Roman Britain. In practice, his administration may have utilised *rectores* but Gildas's business was not with them but with the 'proud tyrant' himself and his errant councillors. It was their moral condition – their blindness – which resulted in the invitation to the Saxons, and so conditioned the present.

'Vortigern' was the last British figure to whom Gildas referred as if the ruler of Britain. Those who rallied around Ambrosius

Aurelianus were not all the Britons, or even representative of them. On the contrary, the fundamental unity of the British community was apparently shattered by the Saxon rebellion, with some dead, others in perpetual slavery to the barbarians and others again migrating overseas. Only some of them – the survivors – were tested by God. Likewise, their only named war leader during the 'War of the Saxon Federates' was not termed a 'king', or even a *dux*, despite his reputed imperial and Roman descent. He was, therefore, probably a *privatus* – a private citizen.

The tyrants of the present of whom Gildas complained differed as regards the extent of their power from 'Vortigern'. Although they each clearly exercised the same mixture of civil and military functions as any emperor, they did so only within specific communities, each within a distinct geographical location. The sequence of universal British kingships was, therefore, portrayed by Gildas as destroyed in the Saxon rebellion. Thereafter the surviving fragments of that insular *regnum* were ruled by the sort of men from whom 'Vortigern' had recruited his council, each governing what amounts to a *civitas* or tribal community. At the date of composition, it was the rulers of these splintered remnants in the west whom Gildas described as tyrants, and who he felt bore a considerable responsibility for the continuing failure of God to succour His people. Elsewhere, British kingship was now dead. With no Christian or British rulers present above the rank of *rectores*, Gildas made passing reference to them as regards their responsibilities for the civil administration of the provinces.

Gildas's imagery had long since predicted the current diversity of British tyranny: when dealing with the end of Roman authority in Britain, he referred to 'growing thickets of tyrants' which threatened to become a 'monstrous wood'. Magnus Maximus was depicted as the first 'seed' of this development. Gildas's metaphor bears comparison with one of the many which he applied to the Saxons.[49] Although set in the past tense it was presumably formulated with the present situation in mind, when the British tyranny had indeed fragmented into sufficient parallel lineages to be termed (with a little poetic licence) a 'thicket' or 'wood'.

The text requires, therefore, that the Britain with which Gildas was familiar was in part ruled by British kings who had usurped to themselves all the functions of an emperor, both military and civil, but in part by *rectores*, independent of British kings, whose functions were limited to civil jurisdiction and organisation. Even if the lesser, and more virtuous, *duces* to whom he later referred should be placed in the same areas as the *rectores*, they did not enjoy such authority or freedom that he was prepared to accord them the title of king.[50] *Rectores* were specifically associated by Gildas solely with *speculatores* – literally, 'watchmen', so possibly men of a military stamp, but there is a degree of ambiguity in the term which makes it impossible to be sure of its meaning in this context.[51] The juxtapostion of *rectores* and *speculatores* probably refers either to the governmental partnership of civil governor and military captain, or to civil authority and ecclesiastical authority. The latter would parallel the importance of bishops in controlling provinces in early fifth-century Gaul.[52] That it was the *ecclesia* – the 'Christian community' or 'Church' – which Gildas portrayed as responsible for paying tribute might support the view that Church and State had, by the date of writing, become virtually inseparable as organs of civil government but it may alternatively be merely a Bible-inspired term for 'the British people', as it was therein for the Israelites.

Gildas's own education in grammar and rhetoric may imply that the law courts and magistracies, which had provided the normal career path of the aristocracy in the Roman provinces, were still functioning, or at least expected to resume functioning, when his parents were considering his educational needs, some thirty years before the date of composition. The only alternative would be to postulate that the educational system used by the civil elite in fifth-century Britain exhibited substantial inertia, but such is unlikely to have sustained an entirely inappropriate system over generations. Gildas's prominent interest in, and comments on, the derelict towns of Roman Britain,[53] where such courts would presumably have functioned alongside the principal church congregations, may also be relevant: perhaps it was his own generation which was the first to witness the final separation of civil government and jurisdiction from its traditional urban setting. Gildas's acerbic comments on the lack of interest of contemporary kings concerning the 'rules of right judgement' implies the recent collapse of Roman law under the British tyrants – and this he apparently prophesied by his association in chapter thirteen of British tyranny with the collapse of Roman laws and customs. If so, Gildas may be offering his audience a contrast between Roman civil law and administration which was still in being under *rectores* (who were answerable ultimately to the Saxons), at the very time when it was falling away under the upcountry British kingships of the west.

One other text supports the notion that Roman law survived some way into the fifth century: Constantius implied that British courts remained respectful of imperial law when Germanus visited lowland Britain,[54] some years before Gildas was born. That *rectores* were still in post and bowed down by their responsibilities when he wrote certainly gives substance to that inference.

The clergy and the Saxons

Gildas's most clear-cut complaint concerning the oppression of the present was in respect of tribute payment: he implied, in chapter one, verses five and six, that the once wealthy British 'sons of Sion' were impoverished thereby. If the church still offered a tax haven, or merely new sources of income, then a flow of otherwise poorly motivated candidates into it certainly makes sense. That inadequate candidates were finding preferment within it was one of Gildas's principal complaints concerning the clergy of his own day.[55]

The general character of that Church emerges from his text: it appears morally lax, certainly, but in other respects it was apparently well established: it had monks, some at least of whom Gildas approved,[56] and some of whom were organised in monasteries presided over by abbots;[57] it had buildings – presumably churches;[58] it clearly had access to the Testaments and some other literature; it had a territorial basis in the *parochia* – here perhaps the diocese;[59] it had a hierarchical organisation headed by bishops and a numerous priesthood,[60] and the wealth to support this edifice.[61] Indeed, Gildas's charge of simony implies that many offices were lucrative,[62] presumably controlling both alms-giving and landed wealth.[63]

The contemporary churchmen against whom Gildas initiated his attacks were in his eyes deeply flawed: he opened his complaints by declaring them to be incompetent, shameless and greedy men who provided an inadequate example to the laity and were insufficiently diligent in their offices and priestly duties.[64] Exploiting the rhetorical instrument of thesis and antithesis to an extent equalled in this work only in the preface to those complaints which were specific to the tyrants,[65] Gildas let loose a torrent of ironic denunciation: they were *'raptores'* ('plunderers'), *'lupi'* ('wolves'), *'ventres'* ('stomachs') and 'usurpers' (*'usurpantes'*), who teach 'bad customs' (*'mali mores'*), hating 'the truth as if *inimicus'* ('hostile') and favouring 'lies as if dear brothers' (*fratres*); 'they react to the just poor as if seeing wild snakes while shamelessly venerating the profane rich as if heavenly angels', giving no charity, and ignore 'the abominable profanity of the people'.[66]

Not only does the juxtaposition of thesis and antithesis govern the structure of this passage but it is also reflected in its imagery. Gildas deployed numerous images redolent of the Saxons,[67] obtaining greater impact from the inappropriateness of their use in the context of British clergy whom one might otherwise expect to be the very antithesis of the heathen and described by imagery indicative of their Christian virtues. He made a point of using terms in this passage in an evil context which are associated elsewhere in the text with virtuous Christians: *frater* is one such, which was used of holy men in the exordium and thereafter in numerous circumstances where the Christianity of the individual concerned was blameless – so of St Alban's 'confessor' and of St James, brother of St John.[68] Its most recent use at this point was in chapter sixty-four, verse two, again in a benign context, in a quotation from St Paul's Epistle to the Romans.[69] That same passage, which was ostensibly designed to conclude Gildas's comments on the tyrants, also spelled out the moral status of snakes in his dialectic, whom he likened on biblical authority to lions.[70]

Gildas therefore penned a complex and ironic denunciation of the priesthood, a salient feature of which was his moral equation of them, via metaphor and allegory, with the heathen Saxons. This was no accident: he clearly perceived the contemporary British church as hopelessly flawed by its association with, and respect for, the pagans. Its priests were 'in the lowest depths of hell',[71] so subject to devils (Saxons), and many had purchased 'the office of bishop or presbyter for a worldly price'.[72]

The error which he considered commonest was this:[73] 'they buy counterfeit and unprofitable priesthoods not from the apostles or their successors but from the tyrants and from their father the devil (*pater diabolus*).'

Given the content of chapters twenty-seven to sixty-five, there can be no doubt that the tyrants whom he had in mind were the five British kings whom he had just castigated. No other contemporary tyrants are even implicit in his text: indeed, his various comments on the named British tyrants (particularly in chapter thirty-seven, verse two) require that these were the only independent British rulers then remaining in (southern) Britain.

The association of *pater* and *diabolus* is the example, *par excellence*, of antithetical imagery as discussed above, the 'father' otherwise, in this quintessentially Christian text, being God. The antithesis is Satan or the antichrist but the context necessitates that Gildas was here using the term as a metaphor for a human being: only thus can the juxtaposition of the British tyrants and this 'diabolical father' as patrons of churchmen be sustained.[74] Gildas had in mind, therefore, some human agent of the devil. Given the clarity of the association between hell, hell-fire, devils and the Saxons which Gildas had already gone to great pains to establish, this 'father-devil' can only have been a Saxon king.

That this reference is singular implies the existence of one supreme figure, at the time of writing, with ultimate authority over all that part of Britain which was under Saxon domination. This interpretation is sustained by the singular of the '*diabolus* (devil)' to whom so many of the Britons were depicted as 'slaves', at the end of chapter twenty-six, but it is this reference to the tyrants and a single demonic figure which necessitates the existence, at the time of writing, of a single Saxon ruler dominating lowland Britain. Gildas lived in a world, therefore, that answered either to one of five British kings in the far west or to a single Saxon ruler of the remainder of (southern) Britain.

Gildas considered that it was a matter worthy of lament that the Britons outside of those same five tyrannies paid tribute to that pagan Saxon ruler. That he additionally exercised patronage in the Church, even over clerical appointments, was, in Gildas's view, a form of pollution, so perhaps relevant to his comments on that subject, through Old Testament exemplars, in his introduction.[75]

Even those of the priesthood whom he exempted from his more scathing comments were tarnished in his eyes with one great defect: he considered them far too politic in their behaviour towards immoral men around them – by whom he meant both the barbarians and those who were their moral equals:[76] 'Which (of them) hated the counsel of malignant men and refused to sit down with the impious?' Both the *malignantes* and *impii* of this passage have strong associations with the Saxons and the ills that derive from them.[77] Similarly:[78] 'Which of them refused admission into the ark of salvation (now the church) to anyone who was God's adversary?' The devil here is surely a metaphor for a pagan, so a Saxon, who was hated by both God and man. He continued:[79]

> Which [of them], in order to lay low thousands of gentiles, adversaries of the people of God, sacrificed his only daughter (by which is understood his own pleasure) . . . ?

> Which of them went forth filled with faith, as did Gideon, to confound, put to flight and lay low the camps of proud gentiles with men symbolising (as above) the mystery of the Trinity, fine pitchers and resonant trumpets in their hands (that is, the sentiments of the prophets and apostles) . . . ?

> Which of them, being ready to die to the world and live in Christ, laid low, as did Sampson, so many wanton guests of the gentiles praising their gods . . . ?

If his audience were expected to identify the Israelites of these quotations with the Britons of their own day, the '*gentes*' can only be the Saxons: indeed, Gildas had already established this useage as a pseudonym for the Saxons when referring to the 'War of the Saxon Federates'.[80] He was, therefore, denouncing contemporary priests for their failure to provide that core of anti-Saxon sentiment and moral leadership which he considered essential to any move to expel these 'enemies of God' from Britain. He used these passages metaphorically, certainly, but the repeated selection of biblical texts which make reference to the triumphs of Israel over her enemies is too clear-cut to set aside. Gildas stressed that Diocletian had, in the past, been successfully resisted by the fervour of a massed Church. In the present, he considered the clergy far less resolute than their forebears and excessively pliant towards another, heathen and transmarine oppressor.

It was certainly not invariably Saxons who were the villains of these passages: his reference to Melchisedek is clearly intended as a criticism of those priests who failed to withstand the iniquities perpretrated by the British tyrants, whose influence over Church appointments was considered by Gildas to be on a moral par with that of the Saxons.[81] Even the Christian tyrants were characterised herein as oppressors of the Church and unworthy to act as its protectors, for were they not as if 'the princes of Sodom, whose vile crimes had led the Lord God to sweep them away?'[82] Greater space however, so greater weight, was attached to his condemnation of the complacency of priests towards the 'enemies of God's people'.

By directing attention to the martyrs of the early Church, Gildas sought to highlight what he interpreted as the pusillanimous conduct of contemporary priests. His use of the benign *'princeps'* – literally 'prince' – would suggest that it was Roman authority which he had in mind when referring to the execution of James,[83] but his next example implies that it was the barbarians whom he principally had in mind: 'Which [priest], like the first deacon and martyr of the gospels, was stoned by abominable hands for the mere crime of having seen God when the faithless could not see him?'[84] Saint Stephen was offered up repeatedly by Gildas as an exemplar of Christian – or more specifically, of priestly – behaviour, which he considered particularly appropriate to the present.[85] It was with St Stephen that his audience had been invited to equate the primary insular martyr – St Alban.[86] These twin pillars of Christian faith were portrayed as suffering in the fight against the heathen. Their example was sustained and augmented by reference to various other martyrs of the early Church,[87] for the collective purpose of underwriting Gildas's criticisms of his own generation's supine attitudes to heathen rule.

There were, therefore, two strands to this condemnation which can be separated according to the authority under which particular priests were living: on the one hand, Gildas was urging the priesthood to correct the lives of the British community, and most particularly those kings to whom he necessarily looked for the military leadership and resources by which the Saxons were to be expelled. It was to the priests in this context that he addressed his concluding words in this section:[88] 'Which of you under the shock of the tyrants kept rigidly to the rule given by the words of the apostle: "One must obey God rather than men"?' It was to this quarter that Gildas looked for a divinely sanctioned attack upon the Saxons; but other members of the priesthood – and presumably the majority – were living under the ultimate authority of the 'father-devil' – so the king of the heathen Saxons – from whom many had even received preferment within the Church. Such priests should repent and reject such pollution. Like SS Stephen, Alban,

Ignatius, *et al.*, they should defy the heathen, even at the risk of martyrdom at their hands.

That there was an active interface between British priests and congregations, on the one hand, and Saxons on the other, is a fundamental of Gildas's perception of contemporary society. His criticisms of their behaviour should be placed beside further indications of Saxon-British interaction which occur throughout the text. His repeated and insistent identification of himself with Jeremiah, and contemporary Britain with Jerusalem after its capture by Nebuchadnezzar, requires that the Saxon domination of his own times approximated to the Babylonian captivity of Israel. This allegory was introduced early in the exordium, then repeatedly reintroduced throughout the text, even by the subtlest of allusions – such as the use of Orosius's description of Babylon as the basis for comment on Britain's towns in chapter three. To this Gildas added a second fundamental allegory for the present – that of hell under the rule of devils – which was juxtaposed with his truncated account of the 'War of the Saxon Federates' as a method of describing the world in which Gildas and his contemporaries lived. It is these allegories which condition our own interpretation of Gildas's text as a historical source.

The continuing Saxon domination which these biblical allegories characterise are sustained by several points of detail: Gildas knew at least one Saxon word (*cyules* – 'keels'); he was aware of the Saxon use of prophecy when making major decisions (if not perhaps the actual wording of this instance),[89] and he was familiar with British tribute-payment. With his comments on the British clergy, this Saxon-British interface begins to grow in shape.

Recurring references in a recent context to a *foedus* implies that the 'War of the Saxon Federates' was concluded by a treaty. It may be possible to establish some, at least, of the terms of that agreement: it involved the payment of tribute by some Britons;[90] likewise some Christian British communities lay outside the fatherly protection and lordship of their natural 'friends and protectors' – the British kings – and subject to a *foedus* with their 'enemies' – the Saxons.[91] It seems likely, therefore, that it was these communities who paid tribute to the Saxons. It was also presumably these same communities who were governed by the *rectores* (and *speculatores*) of Gildas's introduction, whose role appears independent of the British tyrants. The civilian character of their authority has already been established. In the communities over which they presided, military power and ultimate authority apparently lay with the barbarians – a common pattern found over much of the western Empire during the later fifth century.

If Gildas was himself responsible for the wording of the Saxon augury of chapter twenty-three, then he and his contemporaries necessarily lived within the 150-year period during which they were destined to 'repeatedly lay waste the British fatherland'. That fate was averted at the present by tribute payment regulated by treaty but the general context was likened by Gildas to the Babylonian sack of the temple at Jerusalem, so he clearly considered the flow of British wealth to the Saxons to be as serious an evil as Saxon raiding. Despite the pagan, so disreputable, nature of this putative augury, it still serves to sustain this interpretation of the political situation at the time of composition – that Saxon domination extended across the bulk of Britain. For those already in its grip, that domination was reflected in tribute payments by the Britons. For those who still remained outside, in the British west, that domination posed a threat of further military aggression which might at any moment sweep away those kingships, steeped as they were in moral turpitude and unprotected by the Lord.

The British abandonment of walled towns could represent a further condition of the treaty by which the war was concluded. As already noted, Gildas gave considerable attention to the fate of the towns, which he depicted as overthrown by the barbarians in siege warfare. Whether this is strictly true is debatable,[92] but Gildas may be echoing oral traditions which recall the use of towns, even when already in a comparatively derelict condition, as havens to which many may have fled for safety when the Saxons were raiding in the countryside. Behind the safety of their well-constructed walls, civilians might have remained relatively safe from raiders at least as long as supplies lasted. Certainly, continental towns sheltered a cross-section of civilian society – including bishops and their congregations – from barbarian attacks during the same period, and some stood siege, or were blockaded, – as did Rome and Arles, both in 410, and Clermont Ferrand later in the century. The walls of Roman Britain's numerous defended towns and forts *may* have seriously inconvenienced the Saxons in their struggle for control: we should remember that the only actual conflict known to us by name from the *DEB* was a siege and this is at least as likely to have been of a Roman walled settlement as a hillfort (or similar). Indeed, Roman Bath has long been advocated as one possibility,[93] even if the reasoning behind this case remains entirely unconvincing.[94] If it was a condition of the peace that the towns be abandoned and thereafter remain unoccupied, then this might at least explain the sweeping generalities which Gildas offers concerning their condition across the entire British fatherland, since many presumably lay in regions which were beyond his knowledge at first hand, and perhaps even at second. If he was right to generalise as freely as this, Gildas's juxtaposition of their universally abandoned and ruinous state and the ending of external wars may at least imply that these two facets of contemporary life were linked in some way. He had already, in chapter three, reminded his audience of their existence, perhaps in anticipation that they could be reused against the Saxons, and he clearly lamented their passing.

Gildas offers a vision of a contemporary Britain which was unevenly divided between the five British tyrants in the west and a powerful, but shadowy, Saxon king ruling the remainder. The Saxons were, therefore, the military arbiters and political masters of most of Britain. British communities, their officialdom and many of their clergy, had found it necessary to deal with, and court, Saxon influence.

Beneath this contrasting hierarchy of Saxon warriors and British aristocrats, contemporary Britain does not appear deserted, despite Gildas's repeated references to destruction and the survival of just a few Britons.[95] It was no virgin land, ready for the onset of waves of incoming Germanic peasants. It was Gildas's view that the Romans departed once their conquest was achieved because there was insufficient land for them, so his vision of a fully occupied countryside stretches back even to the first century. That image was, however, conceived in the present and only transposed into the past – since it is inconceivable that Gildas had any specific knowledge of the size of population in the era of the conquest.

A substantial rural population is implicit in his references to the widely cultivated landscape of the present day in chapter three,[96] wherein transhumance was also practised. The evocation of bees round a hive as a simile for the Britons gathering round Ambrosius Aurelianus is likewise suggestive of a well-peopled world,[97] as is the 'so great multitude' of those whom Gildas considered lost to hell (so to Saxon control), in the present and recent past.[98] Such a work of rhetoric and providential history cannot be used as a census of the Britons, but it does seem clear that Gildas thought the British population a large one. He was clearly most concerned that so many of his countrymen should have fallen into perpetual slavery to the barbarians,[99] and this may have coloured his whole perception of Britain's history.[100] It is implicit, in chapter ten, that any attempt to reach the sites of particular martyrdoms might result in enslavement by the Saxons. Gildas was aware, therefore, of the widespread existence of British communities enslaved by the Saxons, and these were apparently additional to those paying tribute to them, who were under subordinate British administration. On seventh-century precedents, it would be understandable if it were considered that even tributary status were to have 'enslaved' those subject to it.

The Britain in which Gildas lived seems capable of division into three, as regards relations between Briton and Saxon:

1 The least affected by the Saxon presence were the British kings of the west.
2 Other British communities had their own civil government and clergy but no independent military resources, and paid tribute to the Saxons. Such may have been seen by Gildas as a mark of slavery. It was perhaps in a community of this sort that he himself resided.
3 Other British communities were 'occupied' (*habitatus*) by the barbarians, and so thoroughly and totally enslaved, but there need be no clear-cut geographical separation of these from those paying tribute.

Gildas made some remarks which may reflect on this last condition of enslavement. His vision of the Saxon menace was certainly not a static one. The imagery he used was that of the horticulturalist:[101] the Saxons were 'the seed of iniquity, the root of bitterness, the virulent plant . . . sprouting in our soil with savage shoots and tendrils'. Such imagery was nothing new in the *DEB*: Gildas had used it already to characterise both the rebellion of Britain against Rome and God, and the age of luxury and sin which, in his view, heralded the Saxon arrival.[102] This was, however, by far his most comprehensive use of it. The Saxons were, therefore, being portrayed as a great plague of weeds which had grown from a single seed, putting down roots in that land of Britain into which, using the imagery of wild beasts, they had earlier affixed their claws.[103]

This sense of vigorous growth is an important aspect of Gildas's perception of the Saxon menace which is, perhaps, sufficiently clearly defined to bear some interpretation. There is already within his text explicit reference to an increase in the number of Saxons present in Britain, the first small contingent having been reinforced by a larger one even before the Saxon revolt,[104] but his horticultural analogy would seem to imply continuing growth thereafter. If so, it may be that Gildas was conscious of a rapid increase in the number of Saxon warriors present. This may have been in part a consequence of the polygamous liaisons of what was presumably an affluent warrior elite: if a comparatively small group had achieved victory over the Britons and had become dominant as a consequence of the resulting peace, one might envisage that they could afford the luxury of reproducing at a rate far above that of replacement – and the first generation of their children would have been adult by the date of composition.

An alternative explanation, but one which need not be exclusive of the above, is that the supremacy of Saxon warlords in Britain brought with it such wealth and opportunities that other members of the same (or similar) tribal groupings in northern Germany may have sought the patronage of their *nouveau riche* cousins in Britain in expectation of a share of the bonanza which they had gained by the sheer audacity of a successful rebellion. One might envisage the passage in both directions of exiles, young men seeking generous lords, diplomatic missions and brides, any of whom may have carried with them either ideas or prototypes for new styles in metal-work or similar, or the artificers responsible for them.

Tribute-enriched Saxons in Britain could presumably afford the bride-prices necessary to entice socially respectable women from the Germanic homeland to join them. Archaeological evidence certainly supports the view that women adorned with conspicuous items of Germanic personal jewellery were among the first Anglo-Saxons to be buried with traditional rites in Britain. That they were brought over after rebellion had broken out – or after victory in that rebellion – by a newly enriched warrior class must be preferred to the possibility that they had accompanied the primary or secondary bodies of mercenaries which Gildas described.

Archaeology certainly suggests that regular contacts with the Baltic region were maintained over the early centuries of Anglo-Saxon England, and the movement backwards and forwards of such individuals and their retinues could easily explain much of this evidence.[105] Although the horticultural metaphor may be easier interpreted in the context of the first of these explanations, it certainly does not exclude the second, and it may well be appropriate to envisage both in operation in tandem.

But Gildas has further pointers to Saxon activity, even in peace time. When looking back to the actions of the Picts and Scots, he commented on: 'the imminent arrival of the old enemy, bent on total destruction and (as was their wont) on settlement from the border even to the end of the region.'[106] Although there is some evidence for Irish settlement in western Britain,[107] they do not seem to have settled east of Wroxeter and nothing in the *DEB* suggests that Gildas was aware of their activities even in the far west.[108] On the contrary, he portrayed the rulers of the west of Britain – even the Demetae – as if both Britons and Christians. There is no evidence that Pictish 'settlement' ever occurred inside the bounds of what had been Roman Britain. It seems most unlikely, therefore, that either he or his audience were well informed concerning settlements habitually established by Picts and Scots across the length and breadth of Britain more than forty-four years before. He could, however, count on their awareness of barbarian settlements of a later date – being the archaeologically well-attested settlements of Anglo-Saxons founded around and after the mid-century. His comment on the settlements habitually established by the northern barbarians may, therefore, reflect his retrospective assumption that the Picts and Scots had, in the past, behaved in ways which were familiar from the Saxons of his own times. Similarly, his familiarity with their appearance *might* reflect nothing more than an awareness of the personal appearance of the Saxons of his own day, which could be similarly reassigned to the northern barbarians.

If the Saxon population inside Britain was increasing – as Gildas's horticultural metaphors seem to suggest – then the Saxon leadership was presumably under some pressure to reward their followers with the estates that were necessary to enable them to marry and establish households of free status. Just such a pattern of aristocratic households supported by estates valued in hides – so in terms relevant to renders – is what emerges into history in the seventh and eighth centuries. The Saxons are likely, therefore, to have been competing with other landowners – primarily the British aristocracy and the church – for the surplus from Britain's wide acres. That competition did not occur on a level playing field: if the Saxons had won the war and effectively disarmed their opponents, their leaders were constrained by nothing more than self-interest – primarily the expectation of tribute – from redistributing British-controlled estates on a wholesale basis. In this respect, the collapse of so much of sub-Roman Britain may have had closer parallels with the Norman conquest than has hitherto been acknowledged. Whether or not, it was most certainly a conquest.

Archaeological evidence does confirm that there was a comparatively rapid increase in the number of Anglo-Saxon settlements over the first century or so of England's history, with new settlements being founded successively in areas which had previously shown no sign of their presence. There can be little doubt that British control of land, and the revenues deriving from it, gave way to Saxon control during this period, even if the geography of this process appears erratic. This was not a steady process, by which a frontier was gradually pushed back on a wide front. On the contrary, the appearance of Germanic communities in each of the old Roman provinces within Gildas's own lifetime may indicate that the Saxons considered it necessary to establish at least some presence in each.

Even so, there are large tracts of what would ultimately become England which display either no pagan English burials of any sort,[109] or very few and of very late date.[110] It has often been suggested that these several areas – such as the Chilterns or Shropshire – retained sufficient military resources to sustain their independence vis à vis the Saxons well into the sixth century,[111] yet such is extremely unlikely. The north-west Midlands – to take a single example – had been a political and economic backwater in late prehistory and would remain such throughout the Roman period, exhibiting low levels of investment in Romanisation in all its many forms. The area was generally characterised by an embedded economy and levels of population and output incapable of sustaining the density of urbanisation or market penetration present in the deep south and the east of southern Britain. The region was perhaps already subordinate to more powerful neighbours even before the Roman conquest and would be marginal to the organisation of Britain throughout the occupation, whatever the configuration of her provinces. During the fourth century, the territory of the Cornovii, administered from Wroxeter, formed a peripheral part of Britannia Prima, the core of which – and its capital – lay far to the south, in Gloucestershire. Such peripheral territories with a long tradition of dependence are unlikely to have offered greater resistance to the Saxons than they had the Romans, four centuries before. Such marginal parts of the old Roman organisation may have survived for generations under British control. That such peoples were ultimately dependent on Germanic warlords, or kings, even from an early date is far from implausible.[112] There is, therefore, plentiful scope in the later fifth century for British-controlled territory inside what would eventually become England, the leadership of which was subordinate to and dependent on the Saxons. Such a relationship would certainly be consistent with Gildas's reference to tribute paid by a humbled, impoverished and reduced Christian community.

Gildas's comments on the northern walls may suggest that he was familiar with, and critical of, the construction by some British authority of a turf (or earthen) wall – probably a dyke.[113] If so, one at least of these peripheral British societies was capable of showing some initiative vis à vis the Saxon menace, and its leaders may have even been considering defiance. If so, that defiance has no history and was not ultimately succesful. The great divide which would eventually distinguish Celtic Britain from Anglo-Saxon England was already in place when Gildas wrote and it recognised nothing outside English control excepting only those kingships to which he referred in his complaints, in the south-west peninsula and Wales. Both areas would lose territory to English kings through the mid- to late Anglo-Saxon period, but both proved far more resistant to anglicisation, in both its political and cultural modes, than any part of central Britain. That tribute payment to the Saxons was established in these areas, but not in the far west, may be one facet of the difference.

Gildas and the Gallic Chronicles

Only the Gallic Chronicles provide a second perspective on the realities underlying Gildas's perception of the Britain in which he lived. The earlier of two anonymous authors abandoned his chronicle of recent events with an entry for the year 452, so probably wrote in, or only very shortly after, that date. He was, therefore, a contemporary but distant observer of the events in Britain to which he referred under the year 441, his account spilling over due to its unusual length into the line reserved for 442. His comments have commanded little recent respect,[114] yet the organisation of his chronicle has stood up to the most rigorous re-examination.[115] It should, therefore, be considered as an historical source which may have something to contribute to our understanding of Gildas's text, and to our exploration of the British-Saxon interface.[116] It was written by a Romanised Gallic cleric, who could be forgiven for exhibiting some interest in the fate of the island diocese which had for so long been an important component of the Gallic Prefecture, and an integral part of its defences.[117] That Churchmen from Gaul had been active in Britain in 429, and even later, might encourage us in the expectation that he had sources which were both reliable and up to date to support his comments concerning the state of Britain in 441. It may even be that his sources included men of the ilk of the psalm-singing Christian emigrants from Britain to whom Gildas referred in the context of the Saxon revolt,[118] for whom Gaul was always going to be the obvious landfall.

What the chronicler wrote was this:[119] 'The Britains even at this time have been handed over across a wide area through various catastrophes and events to the rule of the Saxons.' A second Gallic Chronicle, closing in the year 551, offered a variant on this text: 'The Britains, lost by the Romans, fell under the control of the Saxons', but claims that this entry is independent of the earlier one are not particularly convincing, and it is clearly not a contemporary account, at least in the guise in which it survives.

Let us therefore concentrate on the earlier account. The 'Britains' are clearly the British provinces, suggesting that the chronicler thought it appropriate to generalise about what had been Roman Britain, and its four or five provinces, as of the early fifth century. As noted above, his useage implies that these provinces were still meaningful in 452, although it requires Gildas's later references to *rectores* and provinces to confirm that the chronicler was not, in this respect, being anachronistic. Taken together, these two quite independent texts suggest that the provincial structure of the late Roman diocese – if not the diocese itself – survived the collapse of Roman authority and remained the fundamental scheme of government even during the 'War of the Saxon Federates'.

What the 'catastrophes and events' had been, the chronicler neglected to inform us: whether or not he knew, he was constrained by considerations of space. It is implicit in his text, however, that he was referring here to reversals in war with the Saxons, since there is a sense of causation: it was owing to the catastrophes and events that the handing over of rule took place, else there was no reason for him to refer to them. To that issue we must return. Suffice it here to make two points: there is a marked similarity between the useage of the Gallic Chronicler concerning these unspecified disasters, and the 'damages and afflictions' to which Gildas referred in his opening passage of the *DEB*. Although the latter have a current relevance, it seems most unlikely that they differ much in kind, since both authors were interested here primarily in the rise to dominance of the Saxons; secondly, it is a striking fact of this contemporary annal that the author makes no reference to a Saxon invasion of, immigration into, or colonisation of, Britain – events which might be thought worth his attention had they occurred. On the contrary, he asserted that the Saxons established *dicio* of large parts of the British provinces. This term was elsewhere used of Roman imperial rule over subject peoples and provinces,[120] much as was the *ius* – 'law' or 'authority' – of the enemy, to which Salvian noted with bitterness that his miserable countrymen had become subject.[121]

The very similar useages of Salvian and Gildas both imply a degree of legality, or at least of legal form. That the right to rule over various parts of Gaul was granted to particular barbarian leaders by Roman authority is a matter of fact, recorded by several continental writers.[122] If the Gallic Chronicler was correct in envisaging that something similar occurred in Britain, that could only have been achieved by agreement between British authorities, who were, in the chronicler's eyes at least, legitimate rulers, and the Saxons. It was the leaders of the Britons, therefore, who had ruled Britain outside of the Empire for thirty years, who

173

now transferred *dicio* to the Saxons, albeit under duress, over a large part of the British provinces. One might infer that this was achieved in the form of a treaty, in 441, which closed the sorry chapter of 'catastrophes and events'.

The brief entry in the Gallic Chronicle is, therefore, consistent with the reinterpretation of the *DEB* offered above: both refer to the discomfiture of the Britons; both imply the existence of a treaty between Britons and Saxons which recognised Saxon domination; both convey hints that that domination extended not to the whole of Britain but to a very large part of the old Roman provinces. The *dicio* of the Saxons in the chronicle is consistent with Gildas's favourite analogy for the state of Britain – the Babylonian sack of Jerusalem and its temple and subsequent Babylonian rule over Judah – and with his assertion that the British Christians were, in his own day, both tributory and subject to the devil. Gildas's much longer work provides us with far more information concerning the ensuing peace, but the chronicle provides the all-important date at which this humiliating treaty was made. Given a year or two, the Saxon domination of much of Britain was a fact established by treaty in the year 441.[123] Re-examination of Gildas's text confirms that the 'War of the Saxon Federates' was lost by the Britons at about that date.[124] Perhaps most important of all, the reinterpretation offered above of the British 'appeal to Agitius', of *mons Badonicus* and of the outcome of the war enables us to recognise that the chronicler and Gildas were both referring to the same sequence of military disasters.[125]

These disasters and the peace settlement which ensued led to the establishment of a Saxon protectorate, in the wide lowlands of what had been Roman, then sub-Roman Britain. From that developed Anglo-Saxon England. Only in the far west (and perhaps the north) did British rule survive outside of Saxon control and only Gildas, through his complaints, provides us with the capacity to explore the second generation of the history of a separate Wales.

The British kings

Reconciliation of the entry for 441 in the Gallic Chronicle of 452 with Gildas's *DEB* enables us to make considerable progress in the task of defining those 'large parts of the British provinces' over

which the Saxon *dicio* was then established.[126] This is best approached via those parts which remained outside Saxon 'rule'. The
Gallic Chronicler made no effort to define them, and may have
been incapable of so doing, but the five British kingships to which
Gildas referred by name in the west clearly had military resources
of their own and were necessarily exclusive of Saxon control. His
use of horticultural metaphors makes it clear that Gildas saw these
as the ultimate descendants of the British kingship (or tyranny)
founded by Magnus Maximus but his perception of them in the
present becomes explicit only through his condemnation of their
patronage within the Church: in chapter sixty-seven it was the
interference of these tyrants and the 'father-devil' (so the Saxon
king) to which he objected. This context implies that there were
no other authorities of comparable stature exercising patronage
within the church to his knowledge, so in southern Britain. Had
Gildas been aware of further British kings, he would surely have
tested them too as potential saviours of his people. That he did
not so do likewise implies that such did not exist, at least within
his ken.

There were, therefore, one Saxon king – or perhaps 'overking' –
and five British kings. The frontier separating them would eventually be one of enormous cultural and linguistic importance,
dividing Celtic Britain from Anglo-Saxon England. In Gildas's lifetime it was already of political significance, dividing the patronal
and military influence of the British kings from the Saxons. It may
have been clearly marked, but not necessarily in a form which can
be distinguished today.

It is possible to speculate concerning this frontier: if the Roman
provinces had been conditioned by existing tribal boundaries, it is
tempting to imagine that the treaty that ended the 'War of the
Saxon Federates' utilised similar *civitas* frontiers to distinguish
those peoples obliged to pay tribute to the Saxons from those who
did not. If so (and this is no more than speculation since the
boundaries of Roman *civitates* and provinces are rarely known),
the frontier may have followed ancient boundaries. That Gildas
could describe the kingdom of Constantine by a pejorative pun
which recalled its Romano-British *civitas* name – *Damnonia* (for
Dumnonia) – implies that the frontier of 'free Britain' and 'Saxon-
dominated Britain' here followed the eastern boundary of that
tribal unit.[127] The province of Britannia Prima was apparently

split between Saxon and British kings (figure 4). Whatever the precise line adopted for this frontier, the special cultural status of medieval Wales and Dumnonia derives in large part from implementation of the terms of the treaty by which the war which had begun with the Saxon rebellion was concluded, *c.* 441.

In chapters twenty-eight to thirty-six of the *DEB*, Gildas accused the five contemporary British kings ruling west of this frontier of gross immorality. He was apparently writing in or about AD 480 from the comparative safety (in this context) of a British community between the Thames and the Channel which was under indigenous rule but subject to the ultimate protection of the Saxons.[128]

Gildas arguably began with the nearest of the kings to himself when he turned to Constantine of Dumnonia (figures 3 and 4),[129] whose best publicised crime had occurred in the very year of composition.[130] Like the British rebels against Rome,[131] but more particularly like the Saxons,[132] extended leonine metaphors were used of this tyrant,[133] who bears comparison, therefore, with the enemies of God, so the Saxons, who were to be described via numerous allegories of this type, as, for example, the lions who had beset St Ignatius.[134]

The terrible deed with which Gildas opened was the sacrilegious murder of two royal youths and their guardians, despite Constantine's oath not to do so, and their being in sanctuary within a monastic church. His tearing, with sword and spear, at their tender sides, their outstretched arms and reference to their blood at the altar are all images reminiscent of the passion of Christ. He was, therefore, portraying these unnamed youths as if martyrs. He may have had some very personal interest in them, and in their murder but, if so, this is beyond reconstruction. His treatment of Constantine, in contrast, recalls that accorded Diocletian and his henchmen,[135] and other heathen persecutors of the Church, so the British people, including the Saxons and northern barbarians. Under his diabolical rule, Dumnonia was as if *Damnonia* – a 'place of ruin'. Gildas's wit, at least, had not abandoned him.

Gildas went on to accuse Constantine of past crimes of adultery, what he interpreted as bigamy, and sodomy, on which he discoursed via a series of horticultural metaphors which necessarily recall those he had used of the Saxons,[136] before concluding with an impassioned plea that he return to obedience to the Lord. That plea was empowered by the use of a battery of biblical quotation and concluded with the parable of the prodigal son.[137] Constantine, was, therefore, in Gildas's eyes, a Christian king so given over to wickedness that he was destined to hell.[138] As such, he was an entirely inappropriate leader of a British *jihad* against the Saxons, success in which required the command of a virtuous man in obedience to God.[139] Indeed, he was portrayed as no better than the moral equal of the enemies of God.

The imminence implicit in Gildas's threat of divine vengeance suggests that he envisaged that the Lord might soon lose patience with Constantine and let loose on him his own diabolical agents of correction – the Saxons. That he apparently shared a frontier with Saxon-dominated Britain implies that the threat was a very real one. The devil that was Constantine might, therefore, be gobbled up by the great 'father-devil' that was the Saxon king, should he not repent.[140]

Having established the tenor of his complaints, and his threats, in this example, Gildas proceeded in similar vein to vilify Aurelius Caninus, introducing him with another leonine metaphor as well as deriding him by comparison with a dog.[141] Concerning this king, Gildas offered a list of highly generalised accusations – parricides, fornications, adulteries, civil wars and plundering – rather than specific accusations – so once again perhaps betraying the influence of Jeremiah.

He did not indicate the locality of this kingship. Inscriptional evidence might suggest Aurelius Caninus be located in Carmarthenshire in the heartland of the Roman Demetae, near their tribal capital of *Civitas Demetarum* – Carmarthen,[142] but the case is far from compelling: there is no distinguishing feature which necessitates that this tombstone should be associated with this king and the name – or variations thereon – may have been common at this date. Given Gildas's subsequent passage from east to west across northern Wales, it seems more probable that Aurelius Caninus should be identified with the south east of the principality. That he described King Vortipor, in chapter thirty-one, verse one, as if ruler of all the Demetae (so both Carmarthenshire and Pembrokeshire) certainly seems to exclude him from the south west.

Where these kings are certainly identified, their kingdoms seem to have been based on Roman *civitates* or tribes. The only other tribe in southern Wales is the Silures, a people with a long and

distinguished history, and initially a powerful opponent of the
Roman conquest – which was governed during the later Roman
period from Caerwent, with a territory stretching at least throughout Gwent and at least the more easterly of the several modern
Glamorgans. That this community eventually emerged as an early
medieval kingship is implicit in the Llandaff charters, the geographical context of which lay east of the Gower.[143] Circum-
stantial evidence would therefore suggest the Silures as a context
appropriate to Aurelius Caninus. In support of this, it was arguably
here at the tribal capital that the shrines of SS Julian and Aaron
lay, concerning which Gildas recorded his regrets that his own
fellow citizens were unable to reach them.

Aurelius Caninus was necessarily sufficiently notorious in the
locality in which Gildas wrote for comment on his locality to
be unnecessary. It may be worth recalling in this context that
Constantine's whereabouts were noted only as an accidental by-
product of Gildas's pejorative pun on the tribal name, so his
locality was likewise apparently a matter of public knowledge
among Gildas's associates. By contrast, Vortipor was located as if
his sphere of influence was less well-known. Constantine and
Aurelius Caninus were, therefore, likely to be the nearest to Gildas
at the time of writing. The Silures look the most promising candidate for his kingship but the location of Aurelius Caninus is
ultimately beyond proof.

As with Constantine, it was clearly Gildas's intention that
Aurelius be portrayed as a war leader who was so deeply flawed
as regards his morals as to be hell bound, likewise an inappropriate
figurehead for a British war of liberation against the Saxons –
unless of course he could be prevailed upon to repent. Gildas
threatened that God might strike him down for his sins: one
interpretation of this Bible-inspired text would have the Saxons as
God's weapon in so doing. Given that the Lord had already
attempted to 'doctor' his family (the Britons) with the rumour of
barbarian attacks, such a view is entirely consistent with Gildas's
own perspective. Aurelius Caninus was depicted, therefore, as
morally equivalent to the Saxons, or of other enemies of God. His
current wife was no better: she was described as *furcifer germana*
– 'gallows-bird of the same parentage' (as his previous spouse):
furcifer had already been used of the Scots and Picts and the
Saxons, while the possibility that the latter constituted a pun on

'German' must be borne in mind.[144] Gildas's condemnation of this royal couple was forthright, therefore, but it also utilised the weapons of irony and humour, and these more subtle aspects of his attack may have proved at least as damaging to the king's reputation among Gildas's immediate audience.

Gildas referred to the 'fathers and brothers' of Aurelius Caninus, so placing him in a known lineage. They were not, however, portrayed as royal, but merely as men who had a 'spreading imagination', and who were ambitious – which may imply that his royalty was comparatively new at the time of writing, having been founded within his own lifetime.

Aurelius Caninus was clearly considered by Gildas to be at risk of God's vengeance. If the Saxons be assumed to be the weapon of the Lord that Gildas had in mind, this too suggests that Aurelius ruled in the east of Wales, in an area vulnerable to the Saxons.

Gildas turned next to Vortipor, 'tyrant of the Demetae', for whom he adopted the parallel of a leopard, rather than his customary lion.[145] Like the grandchildren of Ambrosius Aurelianus, he was depicted as a moral degenerate by comparison with his forebear – in this instance his father – and was accused of a specific crime, rape, as well as the by now customary and very generalised litany of murders and adulteries. Once more, Vortipor is destined for hell should he fail to repent, as Gildas urged, but this tyrant is depicted less in the guise of a warrior than his contemporaries, perhaps because he was an older man with greying hair, whose life was gradually drawing to an end.[146] Mention of his royal father suggests that the kingship of the Demetae had already been in being at least one generation but this need not project it back before the 'War of the Saxon Federates'.

Cuneglasus of *Dineirth* (Dinarth) was portrayed as a far more vigorous king, whom Gildas used every contrivance to besmirch.[147] In Cuneglasus, the twin crimes of the Britons – conflict with fellow-citizens and rebellion against God – were personified,[148] but Gildas offers his audience little beyond a generalised comment concerning his 'civil' wars and a stereotypical condemnation concerning his divorce and marriage to his erstwhile sister-in-law – one sworn to chaste widowhood.[149] Again, he offered an image of a king reminiscent of the heathen enemies of God, whose sins resembled those of the Israelites prior to the Babylonian sack of Jerusalem. The Church – depicted once more as a flock (of sheep)[150] – had called him to repentance and threatened him with hell. Once more, there is the threat of divine vengeance 'even in this life': his analogy between the 'groans and sighs of holy men' at Cuneglasus's crimes,[151] and the 'teeth of an appalling lioness that will one day break your bones' suggests that it was the Saxons, again, whose intervention he had in mind. His court at Dinarth identifies Cuneglasus with Rhos but the parallel of the tribal kingdoms of Constantine or Vortipor, for example, implies that his rule extended over a far wider area. All north-east Wales was probably in the hands of the Deceangli during the Roman period and that unit eventually re-emerged as the shadowy kingdom of Powys, ruled in the early ninth century at least from Deganwy – which is just a stone's throw from Dinarth. If, as Gildas seems to have assumed, his power approximated to that of the other kings named, then he was probably ruler of a large part, at least – probably all – of north-east Wales. Whether or not, he was, like Aurelius Caninus, more exposed than Vortipor or Maglocunus, both in the far west, to the threat of Saxon attack and this is reflected in Gildas's text.

It was with Maglocunus, 'dragon of the isle', that Gildas completed his inventory of the kings and their evils,[152] and he spent far more time and energy on the arraignment of this ruler than on any other. To take length first, in the most recent edition of the text,[153] Gildas treated of Constantine in two chapters totalling thirty-nine lines, Aurelius Caninus in one chapter of eighteen lines, Vortipor in one of nineteen and Cuneglasus in one of twenty-six – a total of 102 lines. In contrast, he dealt with Maglocunus in four chapters totalling 122 lines, considerably in excess of all the others combined.

His complaints concerning the first four tyrants were presented according to a very regular pattern: first, Gildas identified the individual and his alleged crimes, then beseeched him to reform, quoting from the Bible for support, and threatening him with dire consequences. The two sections are in each case approximately equal in length. His treatment of Maglocunus involves a far more extended and chronologically organised review of his life, identifying and condemning alleged wrong-doing in greater detail and over a long period. Although Gildas adopted the same division between crime and exhortation (the divide occurs at *DEB*, chapter thirty-five, verse four) the latter section is far more clearly personalised than earlier examples, with several allusions to the archetypal judicious king of the Old Testament, Solomon, and references which pick up themes in the earlier section, such as temporal riches, justice and military competence. Maglocunus was not threatened at the close with a violent end, although he was considered by Gildas to be destined to hell. Instead the threat of divinely inspired retribution in this world for his brutal crimes came early in the first section, juxtaposed for causal effect (in chapter thirty-three, verses four to five) with Maglocunus's murder of his own uncle.

Gildas's criticisms of Maglocunus are closer in kind to his strictures concerning Constantine than to his far more generalised condemnations of the intervening three tyrants, but this similarity may be entirely superficial. His special attention to Constantine centres on the immediacy of his knowledge and, arguably, his propinquity to the author's own locality and social contacts. In other respects – as, for example, regarding Constantine's other, earlier crimes and the puns and bestial imagery which Gildas used in reference to him – his comments on this tyrant differ little from those regarding the three who follow. Despite deep-rooted criticisms, Gildas's treatment of Maglocunus was more deferential than that which he accorded any of the other tyrants. He addressed him in terms which acknowledged his greatness, however grudgingly:[154]

> What of you, dragon of the isle, destroyer of many tyrants in their lives even more than their rule, latest in my speech, first in evil, greater than many in power as well as malice, more generous in conferring gifts, more extravagant in sinning, strong in weapons, but stronger in the annihilation of the soul, Maglocunus.

The use of thesis and antithesis recalls the introduction to the complaints, in chapter twenty-seven, which are here brought to fruition by reference to the greatest of the British kings then living. Unlike his pun-ridden and pejorative address to the other tyrants, Gildas steered clear of references to dogs, lions, bears or panthers, referring to Maglocunus instead as a 'dragon' – a term which, later at least, would come to symbolise Welshness and Welsh power.[155] The isle was clearly Anglesey, so the terms used by Gildas to define the kingship of Gwynedd were apparently identical to those used by Bede over two centuries later.[156] Maglocunus was not portrayed as a sacrilegious murderer (like Constantine) – although he certainly was said to have committed murders. Nor was he a perpetrator of civil wars (as Aurelius Caninus or Cuneglasus) but he was a 'usurping king' of a kind familiar from the actions of 'overkings' in England in the seventh century,[157] driving out lesser kings, depriving them of their realms and suppressing their kingships for his own benefit.

Concerning Maglocunus, Gildas resorted wholesale to the use of comparatives, superlatives and other literary devices indicative of the exceptional rank of his subject: he was *primus* ('first') in evil, *novissimus* ('latest' or 'at the extreme') in Gildas's list, *maior* ('mightier') in power and malice, *largior* ('more generous') in his conferring of gifts. If he had deprived other tyrants of their kingdoms, he had clearly proved himself more powerful than them. Those who had lost their lands are obviously not the other tyrants named excepting only his own uncle, yet Gildas's recognition of Maglocunus's military superiority must imply a political supremacy of some sort over the kings he had already listed.

This impression is reinforced by further comments by Gildas: Maglocunus had a *regia cervix* ('royal neck').[158] Such a recognition of regality, as opposed to tyranny, is unique to this king: despite their being introduced as 'kings' at the opening of chapter twenty-seven, it was exclusively by the antithetical term 'tyrants' that Gildas had hitherto addressed them. In the next sentence God is portrayed as *rex omnes reges* – 'king (of) all kings' – in a context which invites interpretation as a subtle metaphor inserted in recognition of the special status of Maglocunus, vis à vis the other kings already named. Gildas had already recalled that the king was 'mightier than many' and he returned to this theme to claim that he was 'higher than the *duces* (military leaders) of almost all Britain' in both royalty and physique.[159] His kingship was uniquely associated with precious metals,[160] and with court eulogists or poets.[161] Gildas reinforced his earlier metaphor by writing of Maglocunus's tutor as 'the [most] elegant teacher of the teachers of almost all Britain'.[162] He used *rex* of Maglocunus's predecessor as king, who was his uncle,[163] and *regnum* ('kingship' or 'kingdom') occurs in chapter thirty-four, verse one, wherein he described the usurpation of Maglocunus, and again in thirty-four, verse two. Through the contrivance of his own imagery, Gildas even sought to link Maglocunus with the great, if iniquitous, Magnus Maximus: both, for example, were associated with 'nets' (*retia*); both were tyrants who had been raised up against more legitimate

182

authority by force; both attached other lands to their own realms; both were perjured and liars; bird imagery was used of both.[164]

When he came to describe the soldiers of Maglocunus's uncle, Gildas returned to the leonine metaphor which he had used of Constantine and Aurelius Caninus.[165] By so doing, it is arguable that he was conscious that a similar relationship existed between Maglocunus and the other named tyrants to that which had existed between his uncle and his household warriors. The implication is again one of a British 'overkingship' operative in the west, centred on Anglesey but stretching across all Wales and Dumnonia, wielded by the exceptionally royal Maglocunus, as successor to his uncle.

Since Gildas's attention in these passages is focused on Maglocunus's moral inadequacies rather than his political status, it follows that his mirror image of the latter – be it explicit or implicit – was at the time of writing a matter of common knowledge. Indeed, he referred in *DEB*, chapter thirty-three, verse three, to 'crimes that have been published on the wind far and wide', and again when commenting on Maglocunus's brush with monasticism. Gildas was, therefore, in this respect, merely recognising current realities and general knowledge, access to which he shared with his intended audience. That such information was subsidiary to his purposes in writing the *DEB* renders it far more convincing than it might otherwise have been. We can, therefore, rely on Gildas's portrayal of Maglocunus as the most powerful, and also the most famous (or notorious), of the British kings: he was the king responsible for suppressing other kingships; his royalty was of a higher order than those other, named tyrants; his court was richer and better served and he was himself better educated. There can be little doubt that Maglocunus was the superior king – the 'overking' – of the Britons west of Saxon-dominated Britain at the time of writing.

If Maglocunus was of such exceptional status, Gildas's reservations concerning the uniqueness of his power must be significant. He was termed not mightier than all, but 'mightier than many (*multis*)'; he was not the most powerful *dux* in Britain, but 'almost' (*paene*) the most powerful. Since none of the kings already mentioned by name were his equal in power, these reservations must imply that Gildas knew of the existence of at least one more powerful ruler at the time of writing. His delicacy in withholding further details concerning at least one even greater king requires that his person and status was a matter of public knowledge. A British king in northern England or southern Scotland *could* be intended here but Gildas's purposes would surely have required that he test the morality of such a man as a candidate for the task of leadership against the Saxons. That he did not strongly implies that he had a very different figure in mind: this reading of the text is sustained by Gildas's apparent lack of interest in contemporary Britain north of Wales. Although arguments *ex silencio* are necessarily weak, this is just one more indication that Gildas had a powerful Saxon ruler in mind. This is, therefore, another reference to the anonymous 'father-devil' (Saxon king) whom he had already introduced (as *diabolus*: 'devil') in chapter twenty-six, and to whom he would again make reference in chapter sixty-seven. Maglocunus's military inferiority to this unnamed Saxon king is, therefore, a matter of reasonable inference and the most plausible interpretation of Gildas's comments on the greatest of the British kings.

Gildas does provide a unique insight into the political system then operative in western Britain. He identified five kingships beyond the regions dominated by the Saxons and made it clear that they were not all of equal status. Four were subordinate to the fifth, the great Maglocunus of Anglesey. Reference to precious metals in the context of his kingship is reminiscent of Roman coins in (so taxation of) Britain, as well as current tribute payments by the British *ecclesia*.[166] His military and political superiority was reinforced by a portfolio of literary imagery. It seems clear that he was, in some sense or other, 'overking' of the British west, the object of respect for, and perhaps even in receipt of tribute from, the other British kings. As such, his career was of exceptional interest to other Britons, even those who, like Gildas, were separated from his court by many weary miles of mountain and moorland. Hence the latter felt able to comment only on 'those of your crimes that have been published on the wind far and wide'. Maglocunus's court was the political focus of the entirety of that part of southern Britain ruled by British kings. As such, it was the principal, but unequal, counterweight to the courts of the Saxon rulers of the remainder of southern Britain, wherever those might then be.

Gildas may well have imagined that a British campaign against the Saxons led by Maglocunus could expect to be sustained by the military resources of all free Britain but it was obvious to him that even these were inadequate to the task – hence the *paene* of his text. To Gildas, the prospects of success depended on the relationship between the putative leader of that campaign and God: with divine aid, biblical precedents suggested to him that the prospects were excellent; without such aid, the imbalance in material resources meant that the entire enterprise was doomed. Maglocunus's repentance was, therefore, for Gildas a greater prize than that of any of the other kings – hence his far fuller and more honorific treatment by this self-appointed prophet of the Britons. To challenge the Saxons, Maglocunus would require the aid of God in his Old Testament guise of arbiter of the fortunes of His people.[167]

Gildas arraigned Maglocunus on the charge that he had reached the throne only by killing his own uncle and his men,[168] but was more interested in his subsequent sortie into the religious life, when he was publicly believed to have become a monk.[169] That phase of repentance might have made of Maglocunus the virtuous leader whom Gildas sought, but it was not to be. Gildas portrayed the failure of this initiative as the responsibility of the Devil, resorting to a mass of imagery reminiscent of that which he had already used concerning the various enemies of God. He made particular play on the same popular, Bible-derived juxtaposition of Christian lamb and diabolical wolf as he had adopted in his references to past interaction between various heathen peoples and the Britons.[170] Into this context he injected a range of pejorative vocabulary, such as *nefandus* ('abominable'), *vomitus* ('vomit'),[171] yet drew back from overly personal slander: instead of referring to Maglocunus as *canis* ('a dog') as he had the lesser tyrants and the Saxons,[172] he was portrayed as a *molossus aegrus* ('sick hunting dog'). This far more honorific term presumably reached him from classical literature and conveys an image of a valuable beast of far higher status, which would probably have been obscure to any but the best-read contemporary. The difference may be subtle but it is as relevant to Gildas's differential treatment of his several royal victims as it is to our perception of the audience for which he primarily wrote.

Gildas was vitally interested in the potential of Maglocunus as a virtuous war leader and lamented what he perceived as the king's betrayal of the righteous, British cause:[173] 'After you reneged, your limbs are exhibited to sin and the devil as the weapons of iniquity when they should properly have been exhibited to God as the weapons of justice.'

Maglocunus should have been (figuratively) a spear wielded by God. Virtuous Israelite kings of the Old Testament were regularly portrayed as instruments of divine policy used to attack and drive out heathen enemies. It was apparently in Gildas's mind that Maglocunus *could*, had he not fallen into the traps of the devil, have been the means by which the Lord would have expunged the Saxons. Once more, the ambiguity which is inherent elsewhere in the text between 'Saxons' and 'devils' is present. Should we infer that the Saxons themselves had played some part in Maglocunus's rejection of his monastic vocation? Gildas's comments might (but certainly need not) imply that Maglocunus had come to some accommodation with the Saxons and was, at the time of writing, in league with them. In purely practical terms, it is difficult to see how the 'overking' of all the west could be utterly oblivious to the opinions and policies of more powerful neighbours to the east, be they Saxons or not. His predecessor was presumably a party to that 'treaty' by which the 'War of the Saxon Federates' had been concluded and it was the continuing adhesion to that treaty by all parties that gave Maglocunus his current freedom from Saxon intervention.

Gildas went on to contrast the priests and monks whom Maglocunus had rejected, with the eulogists of the king's court, for whom he had nothing but contempt. The next object of his ire was Maglocunus's complex marital relations, concerning which he made the king out to be a double murderer and husband of his nephew's widow,[174] before reverting in familiar style to biblical quotation in support of his condemnations,[175] and prophesying that doom was not far off.

If Maglocunus had authority of some sort over all Britain west of Saxon domination, then it was Gildas's view that the wickedness of this man, alone, placed all at risk:[176] 'if a ruler listen to unjust words, all his subjects are wicked'. It is in the context of a moral advisor that Gildas then introduces the 'refined (*elegans*) master of almost all Britain', who has quite properly been interpreted as a rhetorician,[177] but who was perhaps envisaged here as a profoundly Christian teacher, who Gildas anticipated (or even knew) shared his own interpretation of the woes afflicting the

Britons. Gildas juxtaposed that 'refined master' with biblical warnings concerning the present, using most aptly as his first reference one taken from Solomon, before turning once more to Jeremiah, the prophet with whom he most clearly identified himself throughout this work. Maglocunus and the polity which he ruled were seen by Gildas as directly analogous to Jerusalem, the Israelites and the 'house of Jacob'.[178] Gildas used 'Jerusalem' elsewhere as an analogy for the entire *patria* of Christian Britain, or for its (collective) souls, as a sort of heavenly city.[179] There is therefore a sense in which Maglocunus was here recognised as uniquely responsible for the Britons, whether this be in this context 'free Britain' or all Christian Britain.

Alluding once more to the same events which had so influenced his exordium, Gildas borrowed Jeremiah's prophesies of doom wholesale, in four references given in order so implying that he was reading Jeremiah in parallel with writing his own text.[180] The first two quotations were connected by a passage which emphasises Gildas's own perception of himself as a latter-day prophet to be compared directly with Jeremiah, and a similar passage links the last pair, after which Gildas lent this section symmetry by returning once more to Solomon's proverbs. Gildas had referred to Jeremiah in his exposition concerning Cuneglasus,[181] which was his last biblical allusion prior to commenting on Maglocunus, so perhaps written with the latter already in mind. Otherwise such references do not occur in the context of the other tyrants. Again, Maglocunus's unique status is apparent, even as his inadequacies were being exposed and censored.

Gildas described all that he had written to this point as this *querula historia* ('plaintive history') of the 'evils of the age' – so referring back once more to the 'mournful complaint' and 'evils' with which he had opened the preface.[182] He then passed directly from the treatment of this, the last king to be attacked by name, to what he interpreted as oracular utterances in the Old Testament concerning all five. Nothing more clearly demonstrates Gildas's perception of the present as an extension of the Bible. In his view, the British situation was linked to that past by a powerful web of prophecy and divine causation, albeit with the added dimension that immorality post-dating Christ be considered more heinous than that occurring in the Old Testament.[183]

Gildas turned first to Samuel's condemnation of Saul, concerning one of whose crimes (which were minimal compared with those of Gildas's kings) he had already made brief reference in his preface.[184] For Gildas, Samuel's words clearly had a message appropriate to the present:[185] 'God has torn the kingdom of Israel from you today, and given it to a neighbour of yours, who is better than you. The victor over Israel will not hold back, he will not be turned by remorse, for he is not a man, that he should repent.'

The Philistines of Samuel's prophesy were, in the view of Gildas, analogous to the Saxons of the present, who, as non-Christians, were similarly immune to remorse and were depicted as brute-beasts and plants, less than men. The relevance of this passage to his own circumstance was then highlighted by Gildas: by equating, with Samuel, the sin of idolatry with disobedience to God, he was able to justify accusing the British kings, who were Christians and not idolators in the literal sense, of one of the crimes imputed to Saul. The reasoning is circuitous, but it brought the results which Gildas required.

The moral of just kingship under the rigorous eye of God was examined by Gildas thereafter, through further biblical exegesis. He extolled the virtuous shepherd which was King David, who personified the unique and pivotal relationship between God and a virtuous Christian king when that was working well, offering (the otherwise generally praiseworthy) Solomon as the antithesis, whose kingdom God would therefore 'rend and tear'.[186] That the sins of the individual king would prove disastrous to his entire dynasty was illustrated,[187] and reliance on false priests castigated.[188] Gildas insisted on the contractual nature of kingship: Asa killed 100,000 Ethiopians but the divine aid which enabled him to achieve this depended on his own obedience to God; all must detest evil and refuse succour to those who are evil; those who do evil (particularly those who slay their own kin) will be struck down.[189] 'You have abandoned the Lord, and He will abandon you' is a fundamental message on which Gildas developed:[190] 'If you are willing and hear me, you shall eat the good things of the earth. But if you are unwilling and provoke me to anger, the sword will devour you.' Once again, he anticipated the British kings meeting their ends in battle, perhaps against the heathen.

Gildas devoted all chapter forty-three to an extended condemnation of the kings as judges, which recalls his comments in chapter twenty-seven. That 'the people has been led captive ...

their nobles have perished of hunger, and their multitude has dried up with thirst',[191] additionally invites comparison with his introductory remarks in the preface.[192] The petty and flawed judgements of the kings were contrasted with devastating effect with Gildas's own expectation of an imminent Day of Judgement,[193] when he anticipated that a just but vengeful God, now thoroughly out of patience, would strike down those who had reneged on the fundamental contract between the Lord and His people. It is in the nature of the biblical extracts which he used that his vision of this day is once again profoundly urban in context, and this may also have influenced his own reconstruction of the fall of the towns of Roman Britain.[194] Again, quotations from Isaiah in chapter forty-six recall precisely those indictments of the present and recent past which Gildas had already voiced.[195]

In chapters forty-seven to forty-nine, Gildas used unusually long extracts from his favourite Old Testament prophet – Jeremiah, exploiting the ultimate veracity of Jeremiah's prophesies concerning Jerusalem's fall to good rhetorical effect, adding, in a present context, 'Let us hope you escape what follows.' Thereafter, in chapter fifty, he briefly abandoned quotation to address the five British kings, to point out the consequences of their failure to repent for those few virtuous captains (*duces*) who still existed, whose prayers were rendered useless by God's anger with the greater *duces* in the west. Gildas probably intended this reference to military leaders to be taken literally (and *dux* was only otherwise used herein in a literal context) but it is characteristic of the ambivalence of so much of his imagery that this could be read as another metaphor for the small corps of virtuous clergy, or monks, who can be identified as *milites* – 'soldiers', or similar, elsewhere in the text.[196]

Returning to biblical authority once more, Gildas asks the fundamental question:[197] 'Why have these *mala* ("bad things") occurred?' It seems safe to assume that he was here referring once more to the 'heaping up of *mala*', which were the 'damages and afflictions of the fatherland' with which he opened his exordium, and to which he referred once again at the close of chapter twenty-six. The question is rhetorical and the answer predictable: 'Because of the magnitude of your iniquity'. Gildas then resumed his commentary on the theme of a fundamental contract between God and His people, which the latter had broken, accompanied by warnings of dire consequences:[198] 'in the fire of His displeasure will be covered the whole land, and the Lord will bring ruin and devastation to all dwellers in the land'.

There are further references to the captivity of the Britons and their death in warfare at the hands of their enemies:[199] 'all the nations will know that it was because of their sins that the house of Israel were led captive, because they forsook me. I turned my face from them, and handed them over to their enemies and they all fell by the sword'.

This too is surely a matter of contemporary relevance. Gildas was necessarily referring here, through a biblical analogy, to the Saxons as enslavers and conquerors, as the wielders of the sword by which his people had been slain, and would be so again should the British kings not repent. It must be significant that it is with this message that he brought his collection of Old Testament prophecies and complaints to a close.

Gildas rounded off this section of his work with a series of more positive pieces of advice to the kings, then introduced his next theme, in which he proposed to accuse those priests who had raised 'great mountains of wickedness against God.'[200] Such men included not only bishops and other priests but even clerks in his own order – whatever that may have been, although his later comments in this same chapter suggest that he was as yet no more than an aspirant monk. The wrong-doers were to be 'stoned with word-rocks' – an allusion to the unjust ending of St Stephen, the first martyr and one of Gildas's most persistant examplars of righteous behaviour, which he proposed that contemporary clerics should seek to emulate. To one of their sins, he had already alluded: the false advice given to kings by immoral priests was one cause of their inadequacies.[201]

Conclusion

Gildas's treatment of his own generation was, therefore, consistent over a long and many-faceted text. It was his view that it was primarily, but not exclusively, their sins and their disobedience to God's commandments that had caused Him to withhold His protection and active assistance from them. He detailed those sins – specifically sexual offences, judicial failings, civil wars, murders and false oaths – then offered a mass of biblical prophecy and condemnatory passages which he felt to be appropriate. The fundamental context – of a *foedus* – 'treaty' – between man and God is rarely lost from sight but Gildas contrasts it with a different type of *foedus*, which the Britons have made with 'death' and 'hell',[202] so with the Saxon. Through his image of a divinely ordained *foedus*, and its present antithesis, as in so many others, Gildas developed through his complaints many of the issues and ideas which he had introduced in his exordium. In particular, his own close association with the prophets linked to the 'Babylonian Captivity' (Isaiah, Ezekiel and Jeremiah) and his repeated return to the *mala* ('bad things', or 'evils') afflicting the Britons, serve to enhance our understanding of earlier sections of the *DEB*, and of the intricate trails of image, metaphor and repetitive use of specific vocabulary which both confirm the fundamental unity of this work and emphasise its claims as a minor literary masterpiece.

At the same time, Gildas reinforced his own message: that the Saxon oppression of the present could only be thrown off by Britons in obedience to God and led by a virtuous king – and Gildas looked outside of Saxon-dominated Britain for such a leader. Until such a time as these conditions might be realised, the bulk of the Britons would remain slaves of the Saxons, or tributory to them. Even those living in 'free Britain', in the far west, would be vulnerable to Saxon attack, so long as God's anger at His chosen people should encourage Him to use the swords of the barbarians to chastise them: Gildas deployed the threat of such attacks as a spur to encourage the more vulnerable kings (particularly those bordering 'England') to repent.

Behind Gildas's own purposes, and his rhetorical style of delivery, there lies the picture of a political system in which Celtic Wales and the south west were already sundered from a nascent Saxon realm which, although still peopled largely by Britons, had begun to develop into England (figure 5). That system apparently stemmed from the destruction of the British *regnum* as a consequence of the 'War of the Saxon Federates', one generation before. The bulk of that *regnum*, or tyranny, had fallen to the Saxons, just as the Gallic Chronicler reported. By *c.* 480, it lay under the control of a single Saxon king, whom Gildas forbore to name but to whom he referred metaphorically as 'the devil' and most graphically as *'pater diabolus'* – 'father-devil', a term which recognises both his authority and protective role,[203] on the one hand,

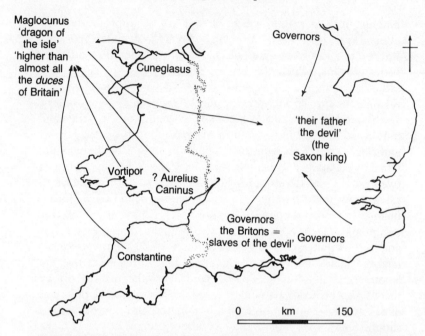

Figure 5 The political structure of Gildas's Britain: a very tentative reconstruction of the hierarchy of Anglo-British political and military superiority *c.* 480, based exclusively on the text of the *DEB* (arrows point towards the superior figure in each case).

and his paganism on the other. On Gildas's lips, the term is little short of blasphemy and it was probably intended to shock those clergy who regularly had closer, and more fraternal, contacts with the Saxons than that self-appointed, latter-day prophet would have liked.

The British kingships of the west presumably owed their inception to the same period of warfare as resulted elsewhere in Saxon domination. They were, therefore, at the time of writing probably less than a half century old, although the families who had secured control had probably been influential in these areas over a much longer period – as Gildas's association of them with 'Vortigern's councillors would seem to indicate. Around 480, most were held by the second generation, at least, of these newly royal families, and were becoming progressively less 'Roman' and more 'Welsh' in their laws and customs. This western system was interlocking, hinging on the superiority of Maglocunus as an 'overking', but even he was less powerful militarily than the Saxon ruler of the British lowlands. Perhaps the latter, too, was an 'overking', as his better documented successors would be in the years around 600. He certainly ruled over British communities as well as Saxon, with *rectores* and bishops still in place and continuing still some semblance of a Roman-style civil and ecclesiastical administration.

Why Wales and the south west remained aloof from his authority is not entirely clear. Gildas's reference to the Saxon raid which devastated 'almost' all the island (of Britain: chapter twenty-four) may imply that they did not even then penetrate the far west. I have elsewhere attempted to justify the separate development of these upland parts of Britain on grounds of a different social structure which was less Romanised than the remainder, and more capable of its own defence.[204] Combined with such factors was the difficult nature of the local topography – and the Saxons were probably quite unfamiliar with mountainous country, the difficulty of living off the land when campaigning, the long distance from their eastern bases and a low expectation of rewards should those areas be conquered. Wales had long withstood Roman conquest and had operated its own political systems in late pre-Roman Britain which were distinct from its neighbours. The north, at least, was treated very differently by the Romans, and its leaders may have retained some notion of separateness, and the clannishness to sustain that separation. Several factors may, therefore, have combined to encourage the Saxons to accept limits to their rule, and control of the southern lowlands arguably gave them more than enough problems, as well as rewards, in the short term. By Gildas's own lifetime, a British 'overkingship' in the west was in existence which perhaps offered some guarantee of effective opposition to new Saxon expansion, since such could expect to be resisted by a combination of kings who were, perhaps, anxious to avoid being picked off one by one and destroyed.

The chronology is such that Gildas's 'father-devil' is unlikely to have been the Saxon leader who won the war and dictated a *foedus* to the Britons that gave him authority – *dicio* – over the bulk of Britain. Later generations of Anglo-Saxons would recall this founding father, rightly or wrongly, as Hengist.[205] It was he, whether correctly named or not, who was responsible for the English conquest.

Notes

1 *DEB*, XCII, 3.
2 *DEB*, I, 13.
3 *DEB*, XXVI, 3, contrasting with XXVI, 1–2.
4 *DEB*, XXVI, 3–4.
5 Specifically *DEB*, LXI, 2, quoting Ezekiel XIV, 12–16, but see also LXI, 1, 4; XC–XCI: the quotation is from XXVI, 3.
6 *DEB*, XVIII, 1: see p. 23.
7 *DEB*, I, 2.
8 See pp. 75, 158.
9 *DEB*, L, 1, supposing this to be a literal use of the term *dux*. See p. 189.
10 So, for example, Constantine, *DEB*, XXVIII, 2; XXIX, 1. See also IV, 4; VI, 1; XIII.
11 E.g. *DEB*, XX, 3; XXV, 2–3; XXVI, 1.
12 Cf. P. Sims-Williams, 'Gildas and the Anglo-Saxons', *Cambridge Medieval Celtic Studies*, VI, 1983, pp. 29–30.
13 *DEB*, XX, 3; XXV, 2 to XXVI, 1, when the Britons had 'burdened heaven with unnumbered prayers'.
14 *DEB*, XXI, 1.
15 *DEB*, V, VI, XIV, XVII, XVIII, XXV, 3.
16 *DEB*, XXVI, 2; XXX, 1; XXXII, 1, although these may have been less wars, *per se*, than usurpations.
17 Particularly those of Maglocunus's uncle: *DEB*, XXXIII, 4, for whom see p. 183.
18 Impiety is also a quality imputed to the Saxons, but not through this specific term: *DEB*, XXIV, 1, 2. *Impius* is a pejorative term normally used in the *DEB* of Britons, particularly of kings. Their role as judges is twice attacked in this passage.
19 F. Kerlouégan, *Le De Excidio Britanniae de Gildas*, Paris, 1987, pp. 534–6.
20 The accusation occurs twice in this passage and recurs in XXVIII, 1.
21 Carrying the implication that external wars, which were necessarily against the Saxons, would be just.
22 There is here a recurring and antithetical theme of injustice towards the worthy and reward for the wicked.
23 See p. 97.
24 See above, p. 97. I had not yet discarded this hypothesis when I wrote *Rome, Britain and the Anglo-Saxons*, London, 1992.
25 As numbered once more in *DEB*, XXXVII, 2. That they were just five is reinforced in LXIX, 3.
26 *DEB*, XXVI, 2–3. The Book of Jeremiah contains a very similar list (II, 26) which may have inspired Gildas to incorporate his own.

27 *DEB*, XXVII–LXV; see pp. 174–90.
28 *DEB*, LXVI–CX; see pp. 159–64.
29 *DEB*, I, 14 and see below.
30 *DEB*, XV, 3.
31 N. J. Higham, 'Gildas, Roman Walls and British Dykes', *Cambridge Medieval Celtic Studies*, XXII, 1991, pp. 10–12.
32 *DEB*, VI, 1.
33 *DEB*, VI, 1: '*enuntianda vel confirmanda Romani regni*'.
34 *DEB*, XI, 2.
35 *DEB*, VI, 1.
36 *DEB*, IV, 3, incorrectly attributed to Porphyry: see M. Winterbottom, *Gildas: The Ruin of Britain and Other Documents*, Chichester, 1978, p. 148.
37 When the British *ecclesia* could be represented as a 'prince over provinces': *DEB*, I, 5. For *ecclesia*, see Lamentations, I, 10.
38 See above, p. 137.
39 As E. A. Thompson, *St Germanus and the fall of Roman Britain*, Woodbridge, 1984, p. 9, commenting on Constantius, *Life of St Germanus*, XXVI. Note also Constantius's use of *regio* in the same passage.
40 Compare, for example, St Augustine, *The City of God*, written 413×427, which conceived of human society as consisting of the two parallel hierarchies of state and priesthood.
41 *DEB*, I, 14.
42 *DEB*, I, 3–7 and 7–12, respectively.
43 For comment on the latter, see above, p. 75.
44 As in *DEB*, V, 1. For *regnum* and *imperium*, see XIII, 2.
45 *DEB*, IX–XI.
46 *DEB*, XIII, 2.
47 *DEB*, XXI, 4. If Gildas had actual historical figures in mind, the successive usurpations of Marcus, Gratian and Constantine III provide an appropriate precedent, some of whom he *may* have been aware of from Orosius's *Histories*, VII, xxxvi.
48 Contrast *DEB*, IV, 4 and *Histories*, V, xxii, 7; *DEB*, XIII; XXI, 4 and *Histories* VII, xi, 4–7; xlii, 1–6, 15.
49 *DEB*, XXIII, 4, and see discussion above, p. 53.
50 *DEB*, L, 1.
51 See p. 87, note 51. Note also that *defensores* were a rank of administrators in sixth-century Italy and this term might be comparable in meaning.
52 D. Frye, 'Bishops as pawns in early fifth-century Gaul', *Journal of Ecclesiastical History*, XLII, 1991, pp. 349–61.
53 *DEB*, XXIV, 3, 4; XXVI, 2, wherein opens his category of laments.
54 Constantius, *Life of St Germanus*, XIV, in *The Western Fathers*,

ed. F. R. Hoare, London and New York, 1954; and see comments of Thompson, *St Germanus*, pp. 28–9.

55 *DEB*, LXVI, 1.

56 Gildas pays tribute to his 'brethren' and 'noble soldiers of Christ' in *DEB*, I, 16, and may be referring to nuns in XXXII, 2 and LXVI, 3.

57 *DEB*, XXVIII, 1.

58 *DEB*, LXVI, 1: the use of *domus* suggests a church, but see *domus Juda* in Jeremiah, III, 18.

59 *DEB*, LXVII, 5.

60 *DEB*, LXVI, 7; LXVII, 1.

61 *DEB*, LXVI, 5.

62 *DEB*, LXVI, 6; LXVII, 1, 2.

63 *DEB*, LXVI, 3.

64 *DEB*, LXVI, 1.

65 So in *DEB*, XXVII.

66 *DEB*, LXVI, 1–2. Note the recurrence of *nefandus* at this juncture, for which see p. 53.

67 As concentrated in *DEB*, XXIII–XXIV, and see discussion, pp. 53–6, above.

68 *DEB*, I, 16; XI, 1 and LXXIII, 3.

69 Romans, IX, 3.

70 On which see p. 55. The serpent's role in the Garden of Eden must be relevant to this imagery.

71 *DEB*, LXVI, 5. This is another image which is inseparable from the Saxons: cf. XXIV, 1; XXVI, 4.

72 *DEB*, LXVII, 1.

73 *DEB*, LXVII, 2. The phrase recurs in CVII, 3.

74 But see *DEB*, XXXIV, 4, where God the Father is juxtaposed with Satan, 'father of all the damned'. A *double entendre* is probably intended here.

75 Particularly as regards his quotations from Leviticus, X, 1–2, and Joshua, III–VI, in *DEB*, I, 4. See pp. 68, 77.

76 *DEB*, LXIX, 2, quoting from Psalms, XXV, 5.

77 *Malignantes*: see *maligna* in *DEB*, LXXXVI, 1; *mala*: I, 1; XXVI, 4. The association is strengthened by the use of *malignitate* in XCVII, 3, where Gildas diverted St Paul's message to the heathen, in I, Corinthians, XI, 1, to the British priests. Note the use of *malitia*, in Jeremiah, I, 16; II, 19. For their 'impiety', see p. 53.

78 *DEB*, LXIX, 3.

79 As set out in *DEB*, XXVI, 1; LXX, 2 to LXXI, 1.

80 *DEB*, XXVI, 1. For discussion of such pseudonyms, see p. 53.

81 *DEB*, LXIX, 3, making reference to Genesis, XIV, 18, *et al.*

82 *DEB*, XLII, 3; note the contrast with the moral characterisation expressed by Gildas's source in *DEB*, XCII, 3.

83   *DEB*, LXXIII, 3; *princeps* was used of the Church in I, 5, so would be entirely inappropriate for a Saxon chieftain.

84   *DEB*, LXXIII, 3: 'faithless' implies non-Christian; *nefandus* had already been used to characterise the name 'Saxon' in XXIII, 1, although it occurs elsewhere (in XXVIII, 2; LVI, 3) to carry the strongest possible censure of a Briton.

85   See also *DEB*, I, 11; LXVII, 4.

86   *DEB*, X; XI.

87   *DEB*, LXXIV; LXXV. See particularly the extended reference to St Ignatius and the lions, drawing on Jeremiah's regular use of 'lions' for the Babylonians' wasting of Judah.

88   *DEB*, LXXV, 3.

89   See p. 41.

90   *DEB*, I, 5.

91   *DEB*, XCII, 3, but note Gildas's far less politic attitudes towards these same kings.

92   Sims-Williams, 'Gildas and the Anglo-Saxons'; N. J. Higham, *Rome, Britain and the Anglo-Saxons*, London, 1992, pp. 82–3.

93   L. Alcock, *Arthur's Britain: History and Archaeology*, AD 367–634, London, 1971, pp. 70–1, 359.

94   Based on the assumption that the location of the 'Badon' of the *AC*, 665, should be equated with the Bath which reputedly fell to the Saxons in *ASC(A)*, 577. Neither episode need be historical.

95   Compare the handful who survived the Roman suppression of rebellion recounted in *DEB*, VII, at the opening of what is generally accepted as being a period of very high population levels, with the British survivors of the Saxon revolt of XXV, 1. This imagery of desolation is based ultimately on Jeremiah, e.g. II, 1, 6, and particularly IV, 7, which Gildas paraphrased in *DEB*, XXVI, 2.

96   N. J. Higham, 'Old light on the Dark Age landscape: the description of Britain in the *De Excidio Britanniae* of Gildas', *Journal of Historical Geography*, XVII, 1991, pp. 363–72, and p. 102 above.

97   *DEB*, XXV, 2.

98   *DEB*, XXVI, 3.

99   Implicit in *DEB*, IX, 2; explicit in XV, 2; XXV, 1. The image once more invokes Jeremiah's comments: Jeremiah, II, 14.

100   Note Gildas's characterisation of the Britons as slaves in *DEB*, VII; XXII, 2, in which his moral judgements are necessarily retrospective.

101   *DEB*, XII; XIII.

102   *DEB*, XXI, 2.

103   *DEB*, XXIII, 4.

104   *DEB*, XXIII, 4.

105   E.g. J. Hines, *The Scandinavian Character of Anglian England in the pre-Viking Period*, Oxford, 1984, British Archaeological Reports,

British series, 124. See also the same author's 'Philology, archaeology and the *adventus Saxonum vel Anglorum*', in *Britain 400–600: Language and History*, eds A. Bammesberger and A. Wollmann, Heidelberg, 1990, pp. 17–36.

106   *DEB*, XXII, 1. The 'border' (*finis*) may be the northern wall. The image is certainly universal as regards Britian.

107   E.g. Higham, *Rome*, pp. 88–9.

108   But see p. 95.

109   A. Meaney, *A Gazetteer of Early Anglo-Saxon Burial Sites*, London, 1964; N. J. Higham, *Origins of Cheshire*, Manchester, 1993, pp. 77–80.

110   E.g. for Derbyshire, A. Ozanne, 'The Peak dwellers', *Medieval Archaeology*, VI–VII, 1962–3, pp. 15–52.

111   E.g. J. Morris, *The Age of Arthur*, Chichester, 1973, *passim*; K. Rutherford Davis, *Britons and Saxons: the Chiltern Region, 400–700*, Chichester, 1982; G. Webster, *The Cornovii*, Stroud, 1991, pp. 137–40.

112   Higham, *Origins*, pp. 68–77.

113   N. J. Higham, 'Gildas, Roman Walls, and British Dykes', *Cambridge Medieval Celtic Studies*, XXII, 1991.

114   E.g. M. Miller, 'The last British entry in the Gallic Chronicle', *Britannia*, IX, 1978, pp. 315–18; P. Bartholomew, 'Fifth century facts', *Britannia*, XIII, 1982, pp. 261–70.

115   R. W. Burgess, 'The Dark Ages return to fifth-century Britain: the restored Gallic Chronicle exploded', *Britannia*, XXI, 1990, pp. 185–95.

116   As argued by M. E. Jones and J. Casey, 'The Gallic Chronicle restored: a chronology for the Anglo-Saxon invasions and the end of Roman Britain', *Britannia*, XIX, 1988, pp. 367–98.

117   Despite E. A. Thompson, 'Ammianus Marcellinus and Britain', *Nottingham Medieval Studies*, XXXIV, 1990, pp. 12–13. Recall the use of 'watchtower' for Britain in Orosius, *Histories*, I, ii, 70.

118   *DEB*, XXV, 1.

119   Translated from *Chronica Minora*, I, Berlin, 1892, ed. T. Mommsen, p. 660.

120   See, for example, Bede, *HE*, I, 3, using the term as an alternative to *imperium*; compare Orosius, *Seven Histories Against the Pagans*, VII, vi, 10 (quoting Suetonius): 'without any battle he [Claudius] received into *deditio* ('surrender') within a very few days the greater part of the island [Britain]'.

121   Salvian, *De Gubernatione Dei Libri VIII*, in *Salviani Presbyteri Massiliensis Opera Omnia*, ed. F. Pauly, Vindobona, 1883, IV, 54, xii.

122   See discussion in H. Sivan, 'On *Foederati*, *Hospitalitas* and the settlement of the Goths in AD 418', *American Journal of Philology*, CVIII, 1987, pp. 759–72.

123   See above, p. 172.

124 See above, p. 137.

125 See above, pp. 120–38.

126 See above, p. 172; for a parallel see 'the greater part of the island' which reputedly surrendered to Emperor Claudius in AD 43: Orosius, *Histories*, VII, vi, 10.

127 *DEB*, XXVIII, 1, alluding to *damnatio* (condemnation) or *damnum* (ruin or injury); see also Higham, *Origins of Cheshire*, pp. 68–77 for some discussion of the northern end of this frontier.

128 See pp. 128, 167, and *DEB*, XCII, 3.

129 *DEB*, XXVIII–XXIX: see Higham, 'Old light', p. 369, and p. 110 above.

130 *DEB*, XXVIII, 1.

131 *DEB*, VI, 1. For comment, K. H. Jackson, '*Varia*: II. Gildas and the names of the British princes', *Cambridge Medieval Celtic Studies*, III, 1982, p. 30, note 2.

132 *DEB*, XXIII, 3; see also p. 55. Note the use of *nefandus* – 'abominable' – of his sins in XXVIII, 1, which may also imply that Gildas wished here to draw an analogy with the Saxons.

133 Extended to his use of sword and spear rather than teeth: *DEB*, XXVIII, 2.

134 *DEB*, LXXIV, 1–3; see p. 55 for an analogy with the Saxons, as suggested by use of this term in Jeremiah for the oppressors of Judah.

135 *DEB*, IX–XI.

136 *DEB*, XXVIII, 4; compare XXIII, 4, and recall also Gildas's various references to Sodom and Gomorah: see p. 61, note, 48. This and later very general imputations of marital impropriety were probably inspired by Gildas's reading of Jeremiah, III, 1–9.

137 Luke, XV, 11–32, specifically 22–3. Note that Gildas depicted the problem in terms of the Old Testament but offered a solution couched in New Testament imagery, as already proposed in the exordium, for which see p. 79.

138 *DEB*, XIX, 1, 3; note the analogy of hell and hell-fire with Saxon dominion of Britain, as proposed on p. 56.

139 As Ambrosius Aurelianus, *DEB*, XXV, 3; see p. 45.

140 If Tintagel was a favoured royal residence at this date, its situation on the coast may imply that the Dumnonian kings recognised that Saxon invasion might necessitate prompt flight to other Celtic realms overseas – but this is entirely speculative.

141 Jackson, '*Varia*: II', p. 31.

142 V. E. Nash-Williams, *The Early Christian Monuments of Wales*, Cardiff, 1950, no. 142.

143 W. Davies, *The Llandaff Charters*, Aberystwyth, 1979, particularly p. 96.

144 For God as 'doctor', *DEB*, XXII, 1; for *furcifer germana*, *DEB*,

XXXII, 2; compare the use of *furcifer* in XIX, 1 and XXVI, 1.

145 *DEB*, XXXI, 1. For discussion of Vortipor, see Jackson, '*Varia*: II', pp. 31–2. Jeremiah similarly used leopard as an occasional alternative to lion: Jeremiah, V, 6.

146 Gildas stressed the brevity of his life expectation in several passages, although there is something not dissimilar concerning Aurelius Caninus in *DEB*, XXX, 2.

147 *DEB*, XXXII; Jackson, '*Varia*: II', pp. 32–3.

148 Compare most forcefully, *DEB*, XII, 3; XIII.

149 *DEB*, XXXII, 2; compare Aurelius Caninus, above, and Patrick, *Confession*, XLI, XLII, in *St Patrick, His Writings and Muirchu's Life*, ed. A. B. E. Hood, Chichester, 1978, p. 31. For Gildas's views on marriage, see F. Kerlouégan, *Le De Excidio Britanniae De Gildas*, Paris, 1987, pp. 529–36, but see also note 136, above.

150 *Grex*: Gildas usually used this term figuratively in biblical fashion as the 'flock' of the faithful, but it occurs also (in the plural) to denote the war bands of the bestial Picts and Scots (*DEB*, XIX, 1) and Saxons (XXIII, 3).

151 Note recurrence of *gemitus*: cf. the groans of Britain under barbarian attack, and the 'appeal to Agitius': *DEB*, XIV and XX, 1, respectively.

152 *DEB*, XXXIII–XXXVI: note Jeremiah's use of 'dragon' for the desolation wrought by Nebuchadnezzar: L, 33.

153 M. Winterbottom, *Gildas: the Ruin of Britain*, pp. 99–106. The following paragaphs are based on N. J. Higham, 'Medieval "overkingship" in Wales: the earliest evidence', *Welsh History Review*, XVI, 1992, pp. 145–59, with special reference to pp. 154–8.

154 *DEB*, XXXIII, 1.

155 At least by the early ninth century, when the 'Tale of Emrys' was included in the *Historia Brittonum*, XLII: J. Morris, ed., *British History and the Welsh Annals*, Chichester, 1980, pp. 71–2, but recall note 152, above. It may be that it was Gildas's useage that rendered it benign in later, Gwynedd-centric circles.

156 *HE*, II, 9.

157 As Æthelfrith of Northumbria, *HE*, I, 34.

158 *DEB*, XXXIII, 2.

159 *DEB*, XXXIII, 2.

160 *DEB*, XXXIV, 2.

161 *DEB*, XXXV, 3; XXXVI, 6.

162 *DEB*, XXXVI, 1.

163 *DEB*, XXXIII, 4.

164 Compare the language and imagery of *DEB*, XIII with XXXIII–XXXVI.

165 *DEB*, XXXIII, 4.

166 *DEB*, XXXIV, 2; VII; I, 5. For the sense of *ecclesia* here, see Lamentations, I, 10.

167 E.g. *DEB*, XXXVIII, 4, quoting Samuel XV, 28−9: 'God has torn the kingdom of Israel from you today and given it to a neighbour of yours'.

168 *DEB*, XXXIII, 4−5.

169 *DEB*, XXXIV, 1−2.

170 E.g. the executioners of St Alban: *DEB*, XI, 1; Scots and Picts: XVI; XIX, 3; Saxons: XXIII, 1.

171 For other occurrences of *nefandus*, see p. 53 above and note 132, this chapter.

172 *DEB*, XXIII, 4, 5; XXX, 1; XXXII, 1. See pp. 54−5 for discussion.

173 *DEB*, XXXIV, 5.

174 *DEB*, XXXV, 2−3. Recall Jeremiah, III, 1, 8, 9.

175 *DEB*, XXXV, 4−6.

176 *DEB*, XXXV, 6. Parallel the analogy of the fall of Jerusalem in the preface and see p. 73.

177 M. Lapidge, 'Gildas's education and the Latin culture of sub-Roman Britain', in *Gildas: New Approaches*, eds M. Lapidge and D. N. Dumville, Woodbridge, 1984, p. 50.

178 *DEB*, XXXVI, 1, quoting Jeremiah, IV, 14; XXXVI, 4. See also references to Jeremiah XXIII, 9, in *DEB*, XXXIII, 1.

179 See above, p. 53.

180 *DEB*, XXXVI, 2, quoting Jeremiah, XVIII, 7.

181 *DEB*, XXXII, 5, quoting from Jeremiah, II, 19.

182 *DEB*, XXXVII, 1; compare I, 1. Note also reference to *mala* and *bona* in XXXVI, 3.

183 *DEB*, XXXVII, 4, quoting from St Paul's letter to the Hebrews, X, 28−9.

184 *DEB*, I, 4; see pp. 68 ff.

185 *DEB*, XXXVIII, 4, quoting I Samuel, XV, 28−9. The translation is by M. Winterbottom, *Gildas, the Ruin of Britain*, p. 37. Contrast the moral superiority of the sub-human barbarian here with his lack of a moral identity.

186 *DEB*, XXXIX, 3−4. Their moral relationship mirrors that of Vortipor and his father, above, or Ambrosius Aurelianus and his grandsons. The threat of Saxon 'rending and tearing' is implicit.

187 *DEB*, XL, 1, by reference to Jeroboam and Baasha. Note the appearance of dogs here and in XL, 2, in a pejorative sense.

188 *DEB*, XL, 3−4.

189 *DEB*, XLI, *passim*.

190   *DEB*, XLII, 5. Cf. Lamentations, III, 42: 'We have transgressed and have rebelled: thou hast not pardoned.'

191   *DEB*, XLIII, 3. Cf. *'transmigrationem Jerusalem* – the carrying away of Jerusalem, captive', in Jeremiah, I, 3.

192   Particularly *DEB*, I, 5–6.

193   *DEB*, XLIV–XLV.

194   *DEB*, XLV, 1, quoting Isaiah, XXIV, 7–13. Compare IX, 3; XXIV, 3–4. The ultimate source of this image may be Jeremiah, I, 15.

195   Cf. *DEB*, XXI; XXVI.

196   So referring back to the point he had made in *DEB*, XLI, 2. See also p. 87, note 51 and also *DEB*, XII, 1: *Christi tirones* – 'newly recruited soldiers of Christ', but a literal interpretation is sustainable, particularly given the use of *milites* for the Saxons – 'as if soldiers' – in XXIII, 5. *Speculatores* is similarly ambiguous but may likewise refer to non-royal British captains outside the authority of the western tyrants.

197   *DEB*, L, 2.

198   *DEB*, LV, quoting from Zephaniah, I, 18.

199   *DEB*, LXI, 4, quoting Ezekiel, XXXIX, 23–4.

200   *DEB*, LXV, 1. Note the repetition and strengthening of the image found in I, 1: 'a heaping up of bad things'.

201   *DEB*, XL, 3–4.

202   *DEB*, LXXIX, 1.

203   Although it was more normally used of God, *fæder* does occur as a term of secular lordship in Anglo-Saxon England (e.g. *ASC(A)*, 924), so Gildas may have been offering a literal translation of part, at least, of the title by which this man was known, which he combined with 'devil' in order to sustain his allegory of hell for contemporary, Saxon-dominated Britain. See also use of *pater* in *DEB*, XCII, 3.

204   Higham, *Rome*, 86–97.

205   *HE*, I, 15.

7

Postcript: Gildas and the 'Age of Arthur'

It would be facile to imagine that we were now in a position to offer a full and detailed reconstruction either of the war between the Saxon *foederati* and their erstwhile employers, or of that 'peace in our times' which has come to be associated with the name of the mythical Arthur: the historical evidence is thin in the extreme, excessively generalised and largely anonymous. Even so, the outline of events can be discerned through careful examination of Gildas's text.

The principal challenge facing the historian today in approaching this text as a source lies in the difficulty of distinguishing image from reality. That the *De Excidio* was conceived as an allegory is obvious, if only from Gildas's identification of himself, in the exordium, with Balaam's ass – an image which he drew from Numbers (chapter twenty-two) but the allegorical and metaphorical content is far greater than this: indeed, it is all encompassing.

In the exordium, Gildas briefly characterised the present, as part of his justification for proceeding, through a series of extracts from the Old Testament, the most prominent of which was an extended reference to the Babylonian captivity of the Israelites following Nebuchadnezzar's sack of Jerusalem. It was this allegory which Gildas offered to his audience as that which he considered the most appropriate to the 'damages and afflictions' of contemporary Britain, using it as a vehicle by which to register his opposition to current tribute-payments. By implication, those went to the metaphorical Babylonians of the present – so the Saxons. As a consequence, the Christian Britons – the *ecclesia* – were both humbled and impoverished. Gildas's assumption that the Britons were a divinely 'chosen people' justifies, and renders comprehensible to a like-minded audience, his development and recurring use of this biblical allegory throughout his text. It is this device which enabled him to refer repeatedly to the Britons by reference to the Israelites: they were characterised by this means either as a race presently undergoing torment – so under Saxon rule – or in danger of it, in the case of the western kingships which yet lay outside Saxon control.

The enemies of the Britons are referred to by name but also – and far more frequently – through biblical analogy. Since they were heathen barbarians, Gildas was free to deploy for this purpose every savage enemy of the Jews to be found in the Old Testament, be they diabolical, human or animal. The present oppressors of the Britons were necessarily and indubitably the Saxons, and Gildas's lament requires that it was to them, in recognition of their political domination, that the Britons owed tribute. For that domination, Gildas developed his second major allegory of hell for contemporary Britain, using it primarily with reference to the larger part which was actually subject to a Saxon king (the 'father-devil') but also using it to stigmatise that part which lay under British kings, whose moral lapses he considered so severe that they were as the 'princes of Sodom' or the very Saxons themselves.

Gildas contextualised the present problem by constructing a providentially conceived, anecdotal review of British history, the principal purpose of which was to sustain his own explanation of the present. That 'historical' introduction has, for centuries, been extensively mined for 'facts' concerning the fifth century, but it has no value to the historian if divorced from his very contemporary purposes. Only his comments on 'our times' – so probably from the invitation to the Saxons forwards – have any real claim to be historical, excepting only the fact of a British appeal to Aëtius at some marginally earlier date. No modern scholar would consider Gildas a primary source for Roman Britain: neither does the *DEB* offer the basis for a narrative history of the first quarter of the fifth century. Pictish and Saxon raids at this juncture are very probable and offer a credible reason why a British ruler should employ Saxon mercenaries – the general context is therefore sustainable – but the sequence of specific events which Gildas offered to fill these years was conceived for dialectical rather than historical purposes. Even the sinful peace of the period immediately prior to the invitation to the Saxons was, in this providential framework of history, a necessary precursor of God's punishment of the Britons – so of the arrival of the Saxons.[1] Its characteristics arguably owe more to Jeremiah's castigation of Jerusalem on the eve of its fall than to historical reality. Other features of these years seem to have been imagined by the author either in order to sustain the rising tension of his account or to offer varied but opportune case studies pertinent to the interaction of God and the British people in the present. Such of the latter as Gildas deployed from existing literary sources denied him the opportunity to develop the logic of his providential perspective in a context sufficiently close to the present. To achieve this necessitated barbarian attacks and he therefore offered a generally spurious reconstruction of such, and responses to them, in disarming detail.

Gildas's account of the employment of Saxon mercenaries is internally consistent, logically presented and sufficiently empowered by the technical vocabulary of late Antiquity to be accepted as factual, if the rhetorical – even at times hysterical – content be set aside. It seems clear that, by this point, Gildas's 'history' was conditioned by the fact that his audience knew at least as much about it as he did. The Saxons came, therefore, in two separate groups, the second of which was uninvited, and larger than the first. Their rebellion began the war in which Roman Britain finally perished.

To this point, Gildas seems to have imagined that the fundamental unity of Roman Britain had survived, with its several provinces, under a single, insular king. Given his (entirely conventional) use of the term *rex* for Roman emperors, we might even be justified in describing these figures as insular emperors. Although we might now prefer an alternative starting point, Gildas introduced them by reference to Magnus Maximus, the Spanish-born emperor who was easily the most successful of them in the late fourth century, having established himself throughout the Gallic Prefecture before his death in civil war in 388. Thereafter Gildas named no names but he was conscious of a succession of such kings and his near-ubiquitous habit of generalising about Britain (i.e. Roman Britain) as a whole requires that he viewed them all as rulers of the entire diocese. The last of these was that *superbus tyrannus* – 'proud tyrant' – who invited in the Saxons and whom Bede was arguably right to name Vortigern. That his was a universal kingship within the old diocese is implicit in Gildas's account – and particularly in his linking of the tyrants of the present with his council. That British *regnum* is only represented, therefore, as ending in 'our times', so it was arguably the 'War of the Saxon Federates' which brought it low. Under the terms of peace by which that war was concluded, the *dicio* – 'rule' – of much of Britain passed to the Saxons. Gildas does not, therefore, provide any justification for the use of such terms in the present as 'sub-Roman Britain' by which to define a period of time between Roman Britain and Anglo-Saxon England. As far as he was concerned, a Roman type of kingship (or its antithesis, 'tyranny') survived up to the war in which England began.

That the Britain that these kings ruled over was both poorly defended and vulnerable to raids by the Picts and Scots seems likely and a poorly remembered appeal to Aëtius for Roman forces to prevent such attacks makes excellent sense at any date between *c.* 425 and 454. In practice, it seems probable, from internal evidence as much as comparison with other sources, that the Britons sought the aid of Aëtius soon after he began to establish himself in Gaul, between *c.* 425 and 430.

It is only Gildas's retrospective reconstruction of this appeal, which he is not likely to have ever seen, which led to its association with the period in which Aëtius was thrice consul, from January 446 until his death.[2] Far from being an original document, these letters seem to have been as much Gildas's own product as was his account of the second appeal, key features of which he borrowed from Jeremiah,[3] but the retrospective telescoping of Aëtius's career which it accidentally achieves has created major problems for dating the text, as well as the more recent events described therein. With the appeal freed from the strait-jacket of Aëtius's third consulship, we are at liberty to recast it two decades or so earlier, thereby bringing Gildas's Saxons into line with those of the Gallic Chronicle of 452. The 'War of the Saxon Federates' therefore began in, or soon after, *c.* 430 and ended *c.* 441.

This reconciliation of our two most significant historical sources is essential if we dismiss the hitherto influential view that Gildas wrote in the sixth century, about, and in, the north of Roman Britain.[4] Detailed attention to his text suggests that the theory of a 'northern Gildas' should be abandoned in favour of a central, southern British context for the *DEB*,[5] written in the decade centred on *c.* 480.[6]

From the viewpoint of the historian, the crucial point at issue is, however, the end result of the 'War of the Saxon Federates'. That this began with the rebellion of the Saxon mercenaries is not in dispute, although there have been many attempts to deny the war the near universal context which Gildas demanded; that the war passed into a phase which witnessed both British and Saxon successes – the former of which began with an unnamed victory won by Ambrosius Aurelianus – is likewise common ground. It is the end result of the war which alone is in dispute, and specifically the relationship between British victory at *mons Badonicus* and the ensuing peace of 'our times'. It is that which is central to the history of this period and which conditions our perspective on the next half century or so of British history.

If British success at 'mount Badon' terminated the war, then it was British victory over the Saxons which conditioned the ensuing peace. If so, there is some justification in hailing that as an 'Arthurian Age' – a final period of heroic British victory which stemmed for half a century or so the tide of Germanic invasion and conquest. Translation of the term used to condition this victory in chapter two – *postrema* – as 'final' has encouraged (although it never required) this view. So too has the juxtapostion of British victory at mount Badon, in the year of Gildas's own birth, and his characterisation of the already lengthy peace of the present. So too has Gildas's subsequent and quite specific reference to these events and their ultimate consequences:[7] 'And truly mention of such a hopeless destruction of the island and of un-looked for aid remained fast in the memories of those who had witnessed both wonders.' The 'hopeless destruction' was the Saxon raid which followed immediately on their rebellion, and their subsequent activities. The 'unlooked for aid' was that of God when he vouchsafed the Britons their victories – most specifically at *mons Badonicus*. We can be reasonably confident of these attributions.

That mount Badon terminated the war is, however, a later interpretation, not a feature of the text. Gildas neither stated nor even implied that this was the result he had in mind. If the *postrema* of chapter two be translated 'very last', rather than 'final', as is entirely proper, then this brief notice of the only named British victory loses the aura of decisiveness which has posthumously become attached to it. Gildas himself is our witness that it was not actually the last victory won by the Britons –

through his use of *novissimaeque ferme* – 'almost the most recent'.[8] Several factors, apart, that is, from its military impact, apparently conditioned his choice of this siege as the sole conflict named, and he used it primarily as an indicator by which to identify the year in which he believed that God's testing of His people had ceased. It is quite unnecessary to suppose that that period of testing had brought the war to its end. Indeed, the contrary is necessitated by the text itself.

In his later comment, Gildas recalled those two events – the Saxon devastation and God's aid to the Britons – which he considered most pertinent to his own providential explanation of the present. He did this in a typically erudite fashion, using two contrasting terms which shared the same root (*desperatus*: *insperatus*), one qualifying the deeds of the Saxons and the other those of God, so with recourse to his oft-favoured juxtaposition of good and evil, in thesis and antithesis. He did not, however, even imply thereby that the aid of God had been such as to entirely counter the deeds of the Saxons. Rather, he offered this construct as encouragement to his own generation to seek the far greater aid which was necessary to undo the Saxon domination of the present.

Many of these interpretational problems derive from later observers reading specific sections of Gildas's text – primarily the latter part of the 'historical' introduction – without reference to the work as a whole. That *mons Badonicus* was not a decisive British victory is necessitated by the several allegories by which Gildas characterised the present, and from the tenor of the complaints. Although the latter do postulate the threat of new Saxon warfare, that is only in the context of the five western kings. It was Gildas's view that the sins of the British tyrants were such that they warranted new divine vengeance and he deployed this threat with some circumspection, apparently in the hope that the kings might be frightened into contrition. He therefore threatened the collapse of the last bastions of southern Britain which were free of Saxon authority. If the Saxons were in a position to threaten eastern Wales and Devon, what of the fate of England?

Otherwise, the ruin of God's people was in the present – not just a risk but an actuality. Since Britain's ruin was conceived in moral terms, it had to be paid for through God's wrath. The ultimate penalty was anticipated – and Gildas expended much energy on his threats of divine vengeance, but the precise nature of the shortcomings of the British priests illustrate the present: they were attacked for buying Church office not just from those British tyrants in the west but from the 'father-devil',[9] who can be no other than the Saxon king;[10] they protested too faintly when Saxons entered churches and made little effort to avoid contact with the heathen. Repeated references to a *foedus* with the 'barbarians', the 'devil', 'death' and 'hell' reflect Gildas's hostility to the peace treaty by which the war was ended, and he quoted the comments of another 'one of us' – so a British contemporary – which offered a similar, but not identical, perspective on the same subject.[11]

Although the condition of individual areas apparently varied according to whether they were subject or 'settled', Gildas subscribed to a single and universal explanation of the present Saxon domination of all southern Britain barring only the Celtic west. His might be described as a 'big bang' theory of England's origins. Whether or not, he was close enough to this treaty – which certainly occurred within his own lifetime – for his testimony to be accepted as historical, even without the confirmation of its broad outlines by the Gallic Chronicle of 452. Orosius had remarked on the intention of King Athaulf of the Visigoths to replace *Romania* with *Gothia* with himself as if Caesar Augustus.[12] Athaulf's plans proved abortive but this may be what a Saxon leader achieved, in the comparative isolation of the island diocese of Britain.

Gildas sought an end to this Saxon domination of the present. He believed that it resulted from a breakdown in that 'perpetual treaty' between God and His people – indeed, he contended that that *foedus* had even been superseded by the current 'treaty with death and with hell'. His solution was, therefore, couched very largely in moral terms. If the Britons could be persuaded, both *en masse* and as individuals, to renew the appropriate totality of obedience to the Lord, then His aid would enable a British 'David' to evict the Saxon 'Goliath' from the erstwhile paradise of Britain.[13]

To this end did he explore the characters of the five British kings of the west, who were the principal commanders of British soldiers – and the only such free of Saxon rule, at least within his own horizons. To this end did he also abjure the British clergy to withstand the heathen with such closed ranks and steadfastness as

their predecessors had withstood Diocletian – and he offered a
series of Christian martyrs, both continental and insular, as exemplars. Only by 'lighting the lamps of martyrdom' could the
Church hope to regain God's help, such as had vouchsafed them
triumph in the past.[14] Gildas had outlined this solution, just as he
outlined the problem, in his exordium, wherein he elaborated his
theory of salvation through twelve quotations from the New
Testament.[15]

In its appropriate literary context, therefore, the 'War of the
Saxon Federates' must be assumed to have ended in Saxon victory
and the seizure of 'rule' over at least the southern lowlands of
Britain. This necessarily encompassed part of the province of
Britannia Prima and all of Maxima Caesariensis. Saxon penetration
of, and in this context perhaps political control over, the other
two provinces may also be implied by the spread of 'early' Saxon
artefacts into the Trent valley and even Yorkshire by the date at
which Gildas was writing.[16] The extent of tribute collection may,
therefore, have been very broad indeed, with groups of Saxons
established in what may have been quite isolated settlements in
each of the more distant provinces in order to supervise, or receive,
their tribute.

It is, however, only the most careful scrutiny of the full text of
the *DEB* – with appropriate attention to its allegorical content –
which reveals this outcome to the war. More perfunctory reading
of the 'historical' account offers a very different vision of its end,
which resolves any ambiguity by culminating it with a resounding
British victory at mount Badon. Welsh scholars of the central
Middle Ages were the first to make this mistake but it set up an
uncomfortable tension between this victory – for which they apparently had the most impressive authority of St Gildas – and the
obvious fact of ultimate Saxon victory, so the emergence of
England. It is from this tension that there emerges, in chapter fifty-
six of the *HB*, the person of King Arthur, to whom was ascribed
the victory of mount Badon as the twelfth of a great, if entirely
stereotypical, battle list. Subsequent English victory, despite
Arthur, was explained by reference to a continuing flow of
Germanic reinforcements from the continent, and so rendered the
more palatable to a Welsh audience who could thereby comfort
themselves with the notion that they had lost only after a valiant
struggle against the odds. To similar purpose did the *Historia*

Brittonum explain away the loss of the south east to the Saxons, in part as Vortigern's bride-price for Hengist's daughter (in chapter thirty-seven), and in part as his ransom (chapter forty-six).

If the 'War of the Saxon Federates' was won by the Saxons, rather than the Britons, and by small numbers of Saxons, at that, who imposed their will on the mass of a civilian, diocesan population, then no such heroic period of British triumphs existed. There was, therefore, no heroic age fit for the deeds of a King Arthur. In that case, there is, and was, no case for inventing a character to fulfil the role of British commander in this 'mother of battles' – a role which Gildas, of course, left unfilled. In reality, King Arthur was no more than the requisite British hero whose appearance, appropriately armed and horsed on the boards of history, was necessitated by the fundamental misunderstanding of Gildas's text by less erudite Welsh scholars, centuries later, when the context in which Gildas wrote was indeed a 'Dark Age'. As an historical figure, he should be laid to rest once more as an unwarranted and retrospective, if readily intelligible, intrusion on the fifth century by a perplexed but anonymous ninth-century cleric, writing in, and primarily of, far distant Gwynedd, wherein Gildas's 'dragon' had once dwelt. Not only did Arthur himself not exist but the age which led to his invention was no less fictional.

When Gildas came to the end of his own work, he chose to offer a prayer as epilogue:

> May almighty God of all consolation and pity preserve the very few good shepherds from all evil and, conquering the common enemy, make them citizens of the heavenly city of Jerusalem, that is the congregation of all the saints, the Father, the Son and the Holy Ghost, to whom is the honour and glory for ever and ever. Amen.

Some of his best favoured images, and his most compelling imperatives, are enshrined even in this brief prayer: the paucity of truly virtuous Christians, the omnipotence of God and His providential role in history, the image of Jerusalem – that city whose destruction exercised such a fascination for Gildas, but here applied to heaven. The common enemy are, of course, the Saxons – who were 'hated by man and God' and who are otherwise represented in his text by so many metaphors, both biblical and otherwise. It is their ejection which Gildas craved and for which he here prayed to almighty God, but to no avail.

211

Notes

1 *DEB*, XXI.
2 See pp. 125–41.
3 Lamentations, II, 10.
4 As argued most forcefully by E. A. Thompson, 'Gildas and the history of Britain', *Britannia*, X, 1979, pp. 223–6.
5 See above, p. 112.
6 See above, p. 138.
7 *DEB*, XXVI, 2.
8 *DEB*, XXVI, 1.
9 *DEB*, LXVII, 2. See also CVII, 4.
10 See discussion, p. 161.
11 *DEB*, XCII, 3.
12 Orosius, *Histories*, VII, xliii, 5.
13 As so described in *DEB*, III.
14 *DEB*, XII.
15 *DEB*, I, 7–10.
16 E.g. most recently, J. Hines, 'Philology, archaeology and the *adventus*', in *Britain 400–600: Language and History*, eds A. Bammesberger and A. Wollmann, Heidelberg, 1990, p. 34, figure 1.

Index

abbots, 110, 139–40, 159
Abraham's dream, in Genesis, 37,
    138–9.
adventus Saxonum, 3–4, 25, 42,
    91, 122; *see also* Saxons,
    arrival of
Aegidius, 121, 141
Aeneid, 41, 95, 126, 127–9,
    135–6
Aëtius, 121, 141, 204, 206
Age of Arthur, 210–11
'Agitius', 24, 29, 35, 92–4,
    120–37, 156.
agriculture, 102, 111, 166
allegory, in *DEB*, 43, 53–7, 68,
    72, 76, 82–3, 156–7, 160–4,
    176, 188, 203–4, 208, 210
Ambrosius Aurelianus, 45–7, 50,
    57, 77, 108, 126, 134–5,
    148–9, 156–7, 166, 179, 207
Amorites, 138–9
Angles, 139
Anglesey, 180–4
Anglo-Saxon Chronicle, 139
Anglo-Saxons, 3–5, 169–71, 175,
    193, 206; *see also*, Angles,
    England, 'English Settlement',
    Saxons
animal imagery, in *DEB*, 37,
    53–6; *see also under*
    individual species;

annona, 40
anonymity, of Gildas, 54, 97, 150
apostacy, 75, 77, 79, 82
appeals from Britain
    to 'Agitius', 120–39, 141, 206
    to Rome, 24, 36, 101, 120–37
    to Saxons, 25, 39, 96, 121, 131,
    133, 137
archaeological evidence, 3, 98,
    104, 136, 168–70
Arianism, 18–19, 21, 101, 127
Arthur, king, 203, 210–11
Assyrians, 37, 53
augury, 41, 135, 140, 164–5
Aurelius Caninus, 55, 110, 177–8,
    182–3
authorship, of *DEB*, 7, 96

Babylon, 164
Babylonian captivity, 37, 147, 164,
    191, 203
Babylonians, 36, 71–5, 83, 138,
    146, 179
Badon hill, *see mons Badonicus*
Balaam's ass, 203
barbarians, 15, 19, 22–6, 29, 36,
    44, 52–3, 79, 82, 84, 91, 94,
    101, 156–7, 161, 167,
    171–3, 191, 193, 205–11
    as Roman soldiers, 39–41, 43,
    126, 140

213

Index

Bede, 3–4, 38, 124, 139–40
Bible
 Gildas's use of, 11–13, 36–7,
  43–4, 52, 54, 67–76, 78–83,
  150, 177, 180, 185, 187–90
bishops, 158–9, 165, 190, 193
blindness
 of Britons, 27, 36–7, 50, 57, 73,
  147
 of Zedekiah, 73
Boudicca, 17, 55, 152
Britain, 14, 21, 37–8, 55, 74–5,
  82, 90–1, 94–5, 101, 103,
  121, 127, 146, 153, 157,
  166–7, 185–7, 205, 209
 authority over, 15, 23, 28, 36,
  38–40, 43, 77, 78, 97, 110,
  156–7, 161, 167, 171–3,
  191, 193, 205–11
Britanniae, 90, 137, 153; *see also*
 provinces
Britannia Prima, 102, 112, 171,
  175, 210
Britons
 cowardice and military
  incompetence of, 16, 19, 22,
  24, 28–9, 73, 101, 148–9
 inconstancy of, 19
 killing of, 17, 44, 73
 as rebels against God, 19, 20,
  23, 25, 28–9, 36, 58, 73, 104,
  133, 149, 167
 as rebels against Rome, 17, 19,
  20, 24–5, 28, 38, 104, 133,
  148, 152, 167, 176
 resisting barbarians, 26, 36,
  44–7, 49, 170–1
 sins of, 16–17, 20, 23–9, 37,
  80, 85, 146–93, 208
 slavery of, 16–17, 26, 36, 44,
  52, 73, 77, 96, 104, 131, 157,
  161, 167, 190–1
 as unenthusiastic converts, 17,
  19

Brittany, 90
burials, pagan English, 170

Canaanite woman, 79, 82–3
Caerleon, 103–4
Caerwent, 178
Carmarthen, 110, 177
Casey, P. J., 124–5
Celtic Britain, 171, 175, 191, 209
Celtic fields, 102
Chalk downlands, 103
Channel, English, 96, 99, 101,
  108, 123, 176
Chilterns, 170
Christ, 79–81
 passion of, 176
Christianity, 7–9, 12, 14, 16, 19,
  79
Christians, 37, 75–6, 95, 111,
  113, 147, 153, 158, 171, 177,
  186, 188
chronology, of *DEB*, 4–5, 7, 113,
  118–41
Church, 27–8, 52, 75, 77–9, 82,
  84, 97, 103, 147, 153, 158–9,
  162, 170, 176, 179, 184, 203,
  209–10
 bereavement of, 124
Church histories, 7–9, 17, 119,
  146, 148; *see also by author*
Cirencester, 102
cities, *see* towns
civil wars, 27, 38, 52, 147–9, 177,
  179
civitas, 157, 175, 177
clergy, *see* priests
climate, 103
coinage, 42–3, 76, 107, 140, 184
complaints, 57, 73, 75, 81, 108,
  149, 208
 against clergy, 159–64, 190
 against kings, 174–90
conquest of Britain
 by Romans, 16, 20, 166, 171,

214

178, 193
by Saxons, 3–4, 37, 170, 193
Constans, 21
Constantine I, 7
Constantine III, 21, 39, 46, 156
Constantine of Dumnonia, 110,
176–8, 180–1, 183
Constantius, the author, 119, 153,
159
Constantius, the general, 27, 155
conversion, of Britain, 17
Cornovii, 171
council, British, 38; *see also*
'Vortigern'
Cuneglasus, 110, 127, 179–80,
182, 187
cyules, 164

damages and afflictions, of Britons,
10–12, 15–16, 20, 29, 36,
47, 56–8, 67–77, 79, 83,
146, 153–4, 173, 189
DEB, *see De Excidio Britanniae*
Deceangli, 180
De Excidio Britanniae
as allegory, *see* allegory
audience of, 9–11, 14–15, 35,
44, 50, 54, 58, 67, 72, 74,
97–100, 118, 120, 146, 185
biblical dependence of, 36–7,
43–4, 52, 54, 67–76, 78–
83, 150, 177, 180, 185,
187–90
as a call to arms, 139, 163
causation in, 19–20, 35, 45, 53,
56, 119–20, 204
contemporaneity of, 13–29, 35,
52, 68, 71–2, 81, 204
entertainment value of, 10–11
geographical introduction of,
99–103, fig. 1
historical fabrication in, 22, 24,
28
historicity of, 22–7, 35, 42, 123,

135, 204
language of, 16–17, 37–8, 43,
52, 67, 75, 82, 127–8, 160,
211
literary context of, 7–9, 21,
126–9, 146
literary sources of, 14, 21,
130–3, 136, 152
locality of, 7, 90–113
political context of, 56–8, 67–
85, 107–13, 146, 203–11
prefaces of, 51, 150–1
purpose of, 4–5, 9–14, 19–20,
26–7, 35, 52–8, 67–85,
163, 191, 204
retrospection in, 22, 24, 27, 35,
40, 50
rhetorical content of, 9, 13,
21–2, 24, 27–8, 36–8, 42,
45–6, 49, 57, 103, 106, 120,
133–6, 138, 141, 146,
148–9, 159, 167, 191, 205
selectivity of, 20–1
structure of, 14–21, 35, 54, 204
style of, 9, 14, 16, 67, 72, 82,
118, 129, 131, 150–1,
160–1, 179, 190–1, 204,
208
universality of, 38–9, 93, 95–7,
118, 121, 140, 166, 207, 209
Demetae, 110, 169, 177
demonic possession, 79, 82; *see
also* devils, *diabolus*
desert places, 26, 44–5
devils, 27, 52, 57, 77, 82, 128,
160–3, 177, 185–6, 191,
204, 209; *see also* demonic
possession, *diabolus*
diabolus, 160–3; *see also* devils,
pater diabolus
dicio, 173–4, 206
Dinarth, *see Dineirth*
Dineirth, 179–80
diocese, of Britain, 38, 93, 107,

152, 173, 205; *see also*
    parochia
Diocletian, 17–20, 26–7, 44, 107,
    152, 155, 162, 176, 210
divortium barbarorum, 103–4
dogs, 37, 53–5, 60, 83, 181, 183
dragons, 180, 211
Dumnonia, 55, 111, 175–6, 183
Dumville, D. N., 91, 130, 137
Durotriges, 112
dux, 21, 147, 152, 155, 157–8,
    182–3, 189
dykes, British, 23, 109, 152, 171

East Anglia, 98, 121
ecclesia, see Church
education, of Gildas, 15, 97–9,
    122, 141, 158
emigrants, British, 44, 101, 122,
    157, 172
emperors, *see* kings
England, 1–5, 47, 77, 170–1,
    175, 182, 191, 206, 209–10
'English Settlement', 7, 123
epistola, 9, 27, 96, 146
estates, 169–70
Eusebius, 7
Ezekiel, 56, 147, 191

famine, 24, 26, 73, 92–3
'father-devil', *see pater diabolus*
father figures in *DEB*, 36, 78,
    160–4, 175, 177, 184, 191,
    204, 209
fatherland, *see patria*
foederati, 1, 40–1, 140, 203
foedus
    with Gibeonites, 68–70
    with God, 11–12, 189, 191, 209
    with Saxons, 40–2, 51, 70,
        77–8, 98, 110, 164–6,
        173–4, 176, 191, 193, 209
frontier, between Saxon and British
    kings, 175–7

Gallic Chronicle of 452, 91, 121,
    136–9, 153, 172–5, 206,
    209
Gallic Chronicle of 551, 172
Garden of Eden, 14–15, 127
Gaul, 8, 18, 20–1, 39, 94, 101,
    121–2, 131, 137–8, 153,
    158, 172, 205–6
gemitus, 120–1, 124–5, 127–8
gentiles, 9, 12, 27, 41, 79, 162
geography, of Britain, 5, 104,
    152–5, 170, 175–6, 191–2
    in *DEB*, 4–5, 14, 35, 93–6,
        99–106, 146, 164, 166
Germans, 3, 178–9
Gerontius, 21
Gibeonites, 68–72
Gildas
    as historian, 13, 20–2, 35, 45,
        49–50, 91, 93, 187, 204
    the man, 7, 90, 97
God
    aid of, 16, 18, 20, 25–9, 51–2,
        58, 68, 151, 185, 207–9
    anger of, 12, 14, 16–18, 190–1,
        208
    of battles, 29, 52, 148, 185
    charity of, 17–19, 36–7, 44
    contract of Britons with, 189–
        91, *and see foedus*
    correction administered by, 13,
        27, 55, 68, 205
    disobediance to, 19, 25, 28,
        36–7, 49, 73, 128, 188, 190
    as doctor, 36, 178
    as father, 36, 161, *and see* father
        figures
    laws of, 13, 190
    obedience to, 15–16, 28, 46, 52,
        177, 191, 209
    role in providential history, 7–
        11, 18, 46, 68–9
    tests His people, 19, 50, 147–8,
        157, 208

use of Saxons, 37, 56, 134, 165, 177–80, 191
gold, 76, *see also* precious goods
Gomorrah, 44
governor, *see rector*
Gratian, 21
groans, *see gemitus*
Gwynedd, 98, 181, 211

Hadrian's Wall, 24, 106, *see* walls, Roman
HB, see Historia Brittonum
heathenism, *see* paganism
hell, 43, 56–7, 77, 160, 166–7, 177, 179–81, 191, 204, 209
Hengist, 193, 211
heresy, 18–25
hides, 170
Historia Brittonum, 139–40, 210
'Honorian Rescript', 23, 120
Honorius, 21
hospitalitas, 40
Humber, 102

imports, to Roman Britain, 101–2, 140
invitation to Saxons, *see* appeals
Isaiah, 27, 36–7, 55, 138, 189, 191
Israelites, 13, 15, 37, 68, 79, 129, 148, 158, 162, 179, 186–7, 203–4

Jeremiah, 15, 55, 70–6, 79, 83, 164, 187, 189, 191, 205–6
Jerusalem, 36–7, 43, 71–5, 187, 211
  sack of, 43, 72–5, 83–5, 138, 146, 164, 179, 203, 205
Jones, M. E., 124–5
Judas, 84
judges, 154–5, 188–9
justice, 79

Kerlouégan, F., 4
kings, 9, 52, 153, 155, 157, 191, 205–6, 209
  British, 38–9, 52, 55, 73, 78, 94, 97, 108–11, 146, 149, 150–61, 167, 175–6, 204, 206, 208–9, *see also by name and* tyrants
  Saxon, 161, 175, 182, 191, *see also* Saxons, king of

lamentation, 9, 28, 52, 67, 70–1, 79, 121, 127, 161, 204
landscape, of fifth century Britain, 102, 111, 166
letter, *see epistola*
Letter to Coroticus, 96
lions, 17, 37, 53, 55–6, 176–83
Llandaff, 178
Loire valley, 122
London, 96

Maelgwyn, *see* Maglocunus
Maglocunus, 27, 55, 76, 78, 110, 119, 127, 132, 180–7, 193
  court of, 182–4, 186
  education of, 110, 182, 186
  status of, 182–7
Magnus Maximus, 19, 21, 38, 45, 101, 120, 135, 137, 155–7, 182, 205
marriage, as allegory, 103–4; *see also* wives
martyrdom, 17–18, 55, 103, 163–4, 167, 176, 190, 210
martyrs, British, 103–7
Maxima Caesariensis, 210
Miller, Molly, 91
miracles, 49, 102
monks, 44, 97, 110, 113, 159, 176, 183, 185–6, 189–90
mons Badonicus, 47–52, 57, 77, 113, 118, 120, 134–5, 137, 148, 151, 154, 207–8, 210

morality
of British community, 146–55
of British kings, 146–7, 176–90
of British priests, 147–8, 159–
64
mount Badon, *see mons Badonicus*

Nebuchadnezzar, 43, 72–5, 164,
203
nefandus, 53
nobility, British, 71, 75, 170
'northern Gildas', 91–3, 96–7,
108, 206

oral sources of *DEB*, 22, 35, 130,
136, 140–1, 165
Orosius, 7, 11, 14, 21, 75, 90,
95–6, 99, 101, 111, 119,
155–6, 164, 209
'overkings'
of Britons, 182–6, 193
of Saxons, 182, 193

paganism, 176, 185
of Britons, 15, 79
of Diocletian, 18
of the enemeies of Israel, 37, 70,
186
of Saxons, 53, 70, 77, 79, 160,
163, 165, 170, 191–2, 204
of Scots, 141
parental relationship, as metaphor
in *DEB*, 24, 28, 36, 78, 104
parochia, 159
pater diabolus, 160–1, 177, 191,
204, 209
patria, 10, 20, 38, 46, 51, 58, 67,
72, 95, 106, 146, 154, 156,
165–6, 187
peace, of Gildas's adult life, 5,
50–2, 57, 77, 98, 107, 151,
168, 203, 206–7
Pelagianism, 21
Pharaoh, 38, 156

pharisees, 80–1
Picts, 20, 22, 24, 36–7, 39–44,
91–6, 101, 127, 133, 169,
178, 204, 206
locality of, 107–8
pilgrims, British, 104
plagues, 36, 55
polygamy
of British kings, 149
of Saxons, 168
population, 166–9, 171
postrema, 51, 207
Powys, 180
precious goods, 55, 71–2, 76, 182,
184
priests, British, 9, 26–7, 55, 74,
123, 146–7, 149, 151–4,
159–66, 186, 190, 209–11
shortcomings of, 159–64,
208–9
princeps, 27–8, 38, 163
privati, 151, 157
prodigal son, parable of, 177
prophecy, *see* augury
prophets, 13, 15, 70, 73, 146, 149,
185, 187, 192
'proud tyrant', *see superbus
tyrannus*
providential history, 11–13, 16,
20, 25, 52, 58, 71, 84, 134,
167, 187, 204–5, 208, 211
provinces, 28, 93–6, 112–13,
137, 141, 146, 152–3,
157–8, 170–5

rector, 75, 95, 108, 141, 151–9,
164, 173, 193
regio, 92–6, 156
region, *see regio*
rhetoricians, 110, 186
Rhos, 110, 180
Roman advice to Britons, 23, 25,
29, 52, 147
Roman Britain, 4–5, 10, 15, 17,

19, 22, 38, 77, 90–4, 106,
140–1, 152–4, 156, 169,
171–2, 204–6
fall of, 19, 22, 25, 133, 205
Roman expeditions to Britain, 22,
39
Roman garrison in Britain, 39, 41
Roman government, 151–55
as precedent, 39–41
Roman imports, 101–2, 140
Romanisation, 152, 170–1, 192–
3
Roman law, 79, 98, 154, 158–9,
192
Roman protection, of Britain,
16, 20, 22–5, 28, 42, 103,
148
Roman rule, of Britain, 3, 5, 16,
19, 90, 138, 155
legitimacy of, 7–8, 15, 19, 22,
46, 155
Romans, virtues of, 16, 19, 22, 46,
148
Rome, 75, 165
British disobedience towards, 17,
19, 148, *see also* appeals to;
Britons, rebellions of
ruin of Britain, 37, 70, 75, 84, 138,
208

Saint Aaron, 103, 106, 111, 178
Saint Alban, 18, 102, 106, 111,
128, 155, 160, 163
Saint Augustine, 8
Saint Germanus, 119, 132, 137,
159
Saint Gildas de Rhus, 90
Saint Gregory, 151
Saint Ignatius, 55–6, 164, 176
Saint Jerome, 95, 152
Saint Julius, 103, 106, 111, 178
Saint Patrick, 96
Saint Paul, 9, 27, 80, 83, 160
Saint Peter, 84

Saint Stephen, 84, 163, 190
Salvian, 8–9, 20, 122, 173
Salway, P., 48
Satan, 27, 161, *see also*, demonic
possession, devil, *pater
diabolus*
Saul, 69, 187
Saxons, 11, 16–17, 20–1, 24–9,
36–58, 77, 83, 98, 103, 118,
128, 148–9, 153, 157–9,
162, 173, 175–8, 186, 203,
208, 211
arrival of, 25, 36–42, 73, 91,
93, 96, 131, 136–9, 155, 164,
173, 205, *see also adventus
Saxonum*
characteristics of, 37, 40
conquest of, 1–2, 37, 136–7,
170–1, 190
domination of, 56–8, 74, 77,
79, 83–5, 97, 111, 121,
136–7, 148, 161, 164–8,
173, 175, 183, 186, 191–3,
204, 208–11
king of, 161, 166, 171, 175–6,
184–5, 191, 193, 204, 209
as mercenaries, 39–41, 204–5
numbers of, 41, 167–9
protection of, 97, 167, 176, 191
raid of, 43–5, 76, 93, 151, 156,
165, 193, 208
rebellion of, 42–53, 76–7, 93,
101, 137, 151, 157, 168–9,
172, 205, 207
settlement of, 2, 92, 95, 98, 104
Saxon Shore, forts of, 106
Scots, 20, 22, 24, 36–7, 39–40,
43–4, 91–2, 95–6, 101, 127,
133, 141, 169, 178, 204, 206
seas around Britain, 101, fig. 1.
Severn, 101
sexual morality, 81, 104, 176–7,
179, 190
shrines, Christian, 18, 103

Shropshire, 170
sieges, 47–52, 57, 73, 77, 118, 165–6, 208
Silures, 177
simony, 159–60
Sims-Williams, P., 91
slavery, 73, 76, *see also* Britons, slavery of
Slebhine, abbot, 139–40
Sodom, 44, 163, 204
Solomon, 36, 181, 187–8
speculator, 75, 108, 154, 158, 164
Stenton, Sir F. M., 48
Strathclyde, 90
sub-Roman Britain, 206
superbus tyrannus, 38–9, 45, 73, 134, 156, 205, see also, tyrants, 'Vortigern'
superlatives, use of in *DEB*, 182

taxation, 76, 152, 159
temple of Solomon, Jerusalem, 44, 73, 75–6
Thames, estuary, 99
  river, 101–3, 106, 112, 128, 176
  valley, 98, 104, 111, 121, figure 2
Thompson, E. A., 91–2, 96
Tiberius, 17
trade, 101–2, 140
transhumance, 102, 166
treaties, *see foedus*
tribes, British, 175–7, 180
tribute, British, 54–5, 75–8, 83, 154, 161, 164–5, 167–8, 170–1, 184, 191, 203–4, 210
Troy, sack of, 43, 126, 136

tyrants, 9, 19, 21, 27, 38, 73, 97, 104, 109–11, 147–9, 150, 154–7, 161–2, 164, 166, 174–89, 191, 205–6, 209, *see also* kings
  geography of, 108–11, fig. 3

Verulamium, 18, 103–4, 111
villas, 113
Virgil, 41, 95–6, 126–7
Visigoths, 122, 209
'Vortigern', 36, 38–42, 73, 135, 147, 155–7, 192, 205, 211, *see also superbus tyrannus*
Vortipor, 110, 177, 179–80

Wales, 90, 99, 106, 171, 176–80, 183–4, 193, 208
walls, Roman, 22–4, 41, 91, 93–4, 106–7, 111, 133, 151, 171
'War of the Saxon federates', 5, 42–53, 58, 67, 72, 77, 84, 92, 134, 137, 139, 149, 157, 173, 175–6, 179, 186, 191, 203, 205–7, 210–11
wilderness, *see* desert places
Winterbottom, M., 4
wives, of British kings, 178–9, 186
women
  British, 178–9
  Saxon, 168
Wroxeter, 169, 171

Yorkshire, 92, 96, 210

Zedekiah, king, 73–4, 146